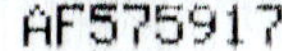

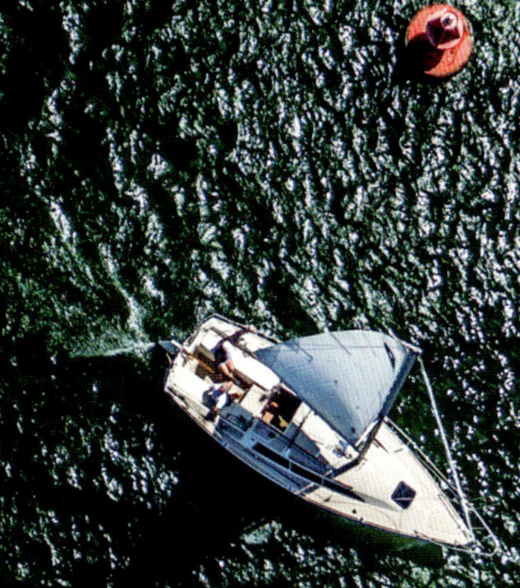

ART FROM ABOVE

CAPE COD

Christopher S. Gibbs

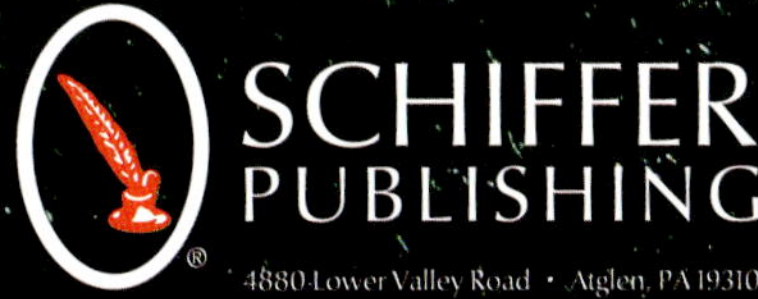

SCHIFFER PUBLISHING®

4880 Lower Valley Road • Atglen, PA 19310

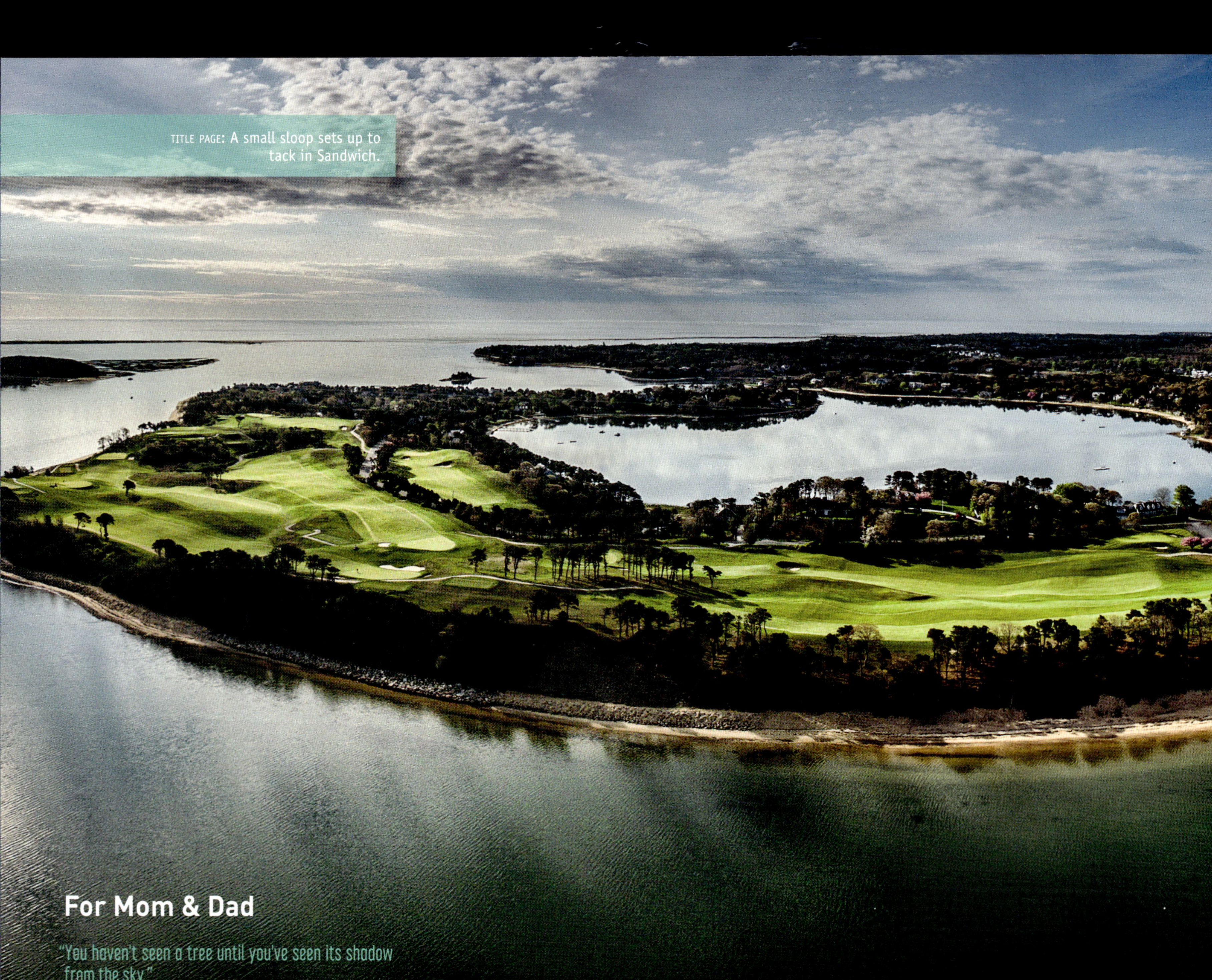

TITLE PAGE: A small sloop sets up to tack in Sandwich.

For Mom & Dad

"You haven't seen a tree until you've seen its shadow from the sky."

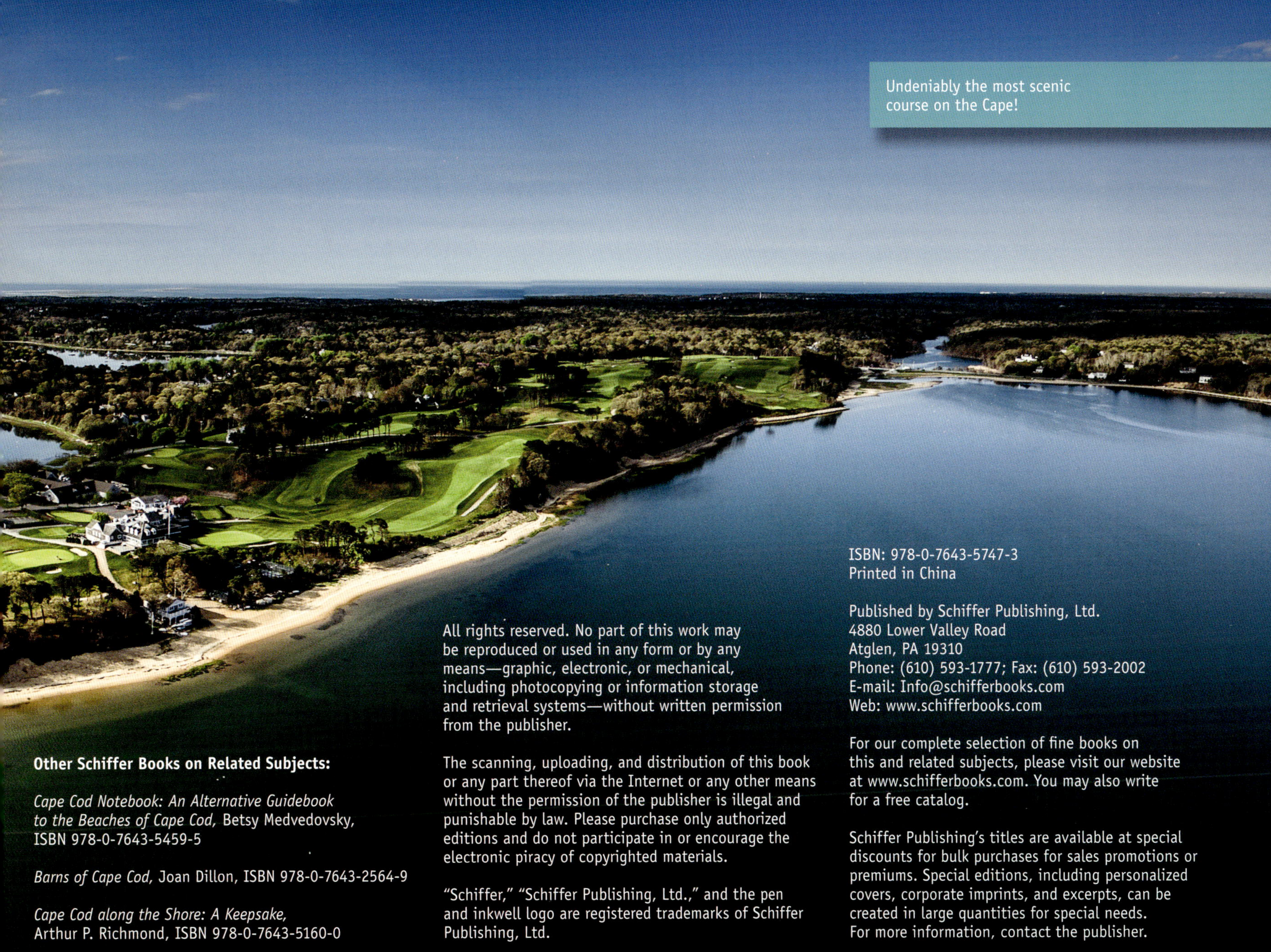

Undeniably the most scenic course on the Cape!

Other Schiffer Books on Related Subjects:

Cape Cod Notebook: An Alternative Guidebook to the Beaches of Cape Cod, Betsy Medvedovsky, ISBN 978-0-7643-5459-5

Barns of Cape Cod, Joan Dillon, ISBN 978-0-7643-2564-9

Cape Cod along the Shore: A Keepsake, Arthur P. Richmond, ISBN 978-0-7643-5160-0

Library of Congress Control Number: 2018957910

Designed by Justin Watkinson
Cover design by Brenda McCallum
Type set in Maribel Suit/DIN/ITC Officina Sans

ISBN: 978-0-7643-5747-3
Printed in China

Published by Schiffer Publishing, Ltd.
4880 Lower Valley Road
Atglen, PA 19310
Phone: (610) 593-1777; Fax: (610) 593-2002
E-mail: Info@schifferbooks.com
Web: www.schifferbooks.com

For our complete selection of fine books on this and related subjects, please visit our website at www.schifferbooks.com. You may also write for a free catalog.

Schiffer Publishing's titles are available at special discounts for bulk purchases for sales promotions or premiums. Special editions, including personalized covers, corporate imprints, and excerpts, can be created in large quantities for special needs. For more information, contact the publisher.

We are always looking for people to write books on new and related subjects. If you have an idea for a book, please contact us at proposals@schifferbooks.com.

ACKNOWLEDGMENTS

I'd like to thank the good people of Cape Cod and the many others I've met along the way while shooting for this book and the others in this series. I've come to depend on the fact that every road I run the old Jeep down—no matter how long, narrow, dusty, or desolate—always seems to end with a story I can take home after the last light and that last flight. Your kindness and generosity, your genuine curiosity about what I do, and your willingness to share your story, or even the best spot to catch a sunset, won't be forgotten. My travels would be exponentially less interesting without the cast of characters I've met along the way and think of often. For you I am profoundly thankful. Hopefully I left something worthwhile behind for you too.

I'd like to thank my friends and family for being my biggest fans during this wild journey as a drone pilot and photographer. You've helped me push my creative boundaries time after time with your extraordinarily "renegade" ideas on what and where to shoot, technically with your individual expertise and incredibly diverse skill sets, and of course you've kept Renegade Airlines on the road by being the best cheerleaders around. You are a remarkable lot, you know who you are, and it's humbling to have you in my life.

I have been extremely blessed to be a firsthand witness to the endless beauty of the ever-changing landscape of Cape Cod. I am obviously very grateful for that. Twenty thousand or so years ago, something truly remarkable happened there when that big old Laurentide ice sheet decided to retreat North and leave the world a much different place. Without that miraculous series of events we wouldn't have much of a book. It has been an honor to be just one of the many to attempt to capture Cape Cod in the way she deserves to be captured. I hope I have done her justice.

More than anyone though I'd like to thank my mother, Elaine. There are simply not enough words to express what your encouragement and belief in me has meant. Love you all! —Chris

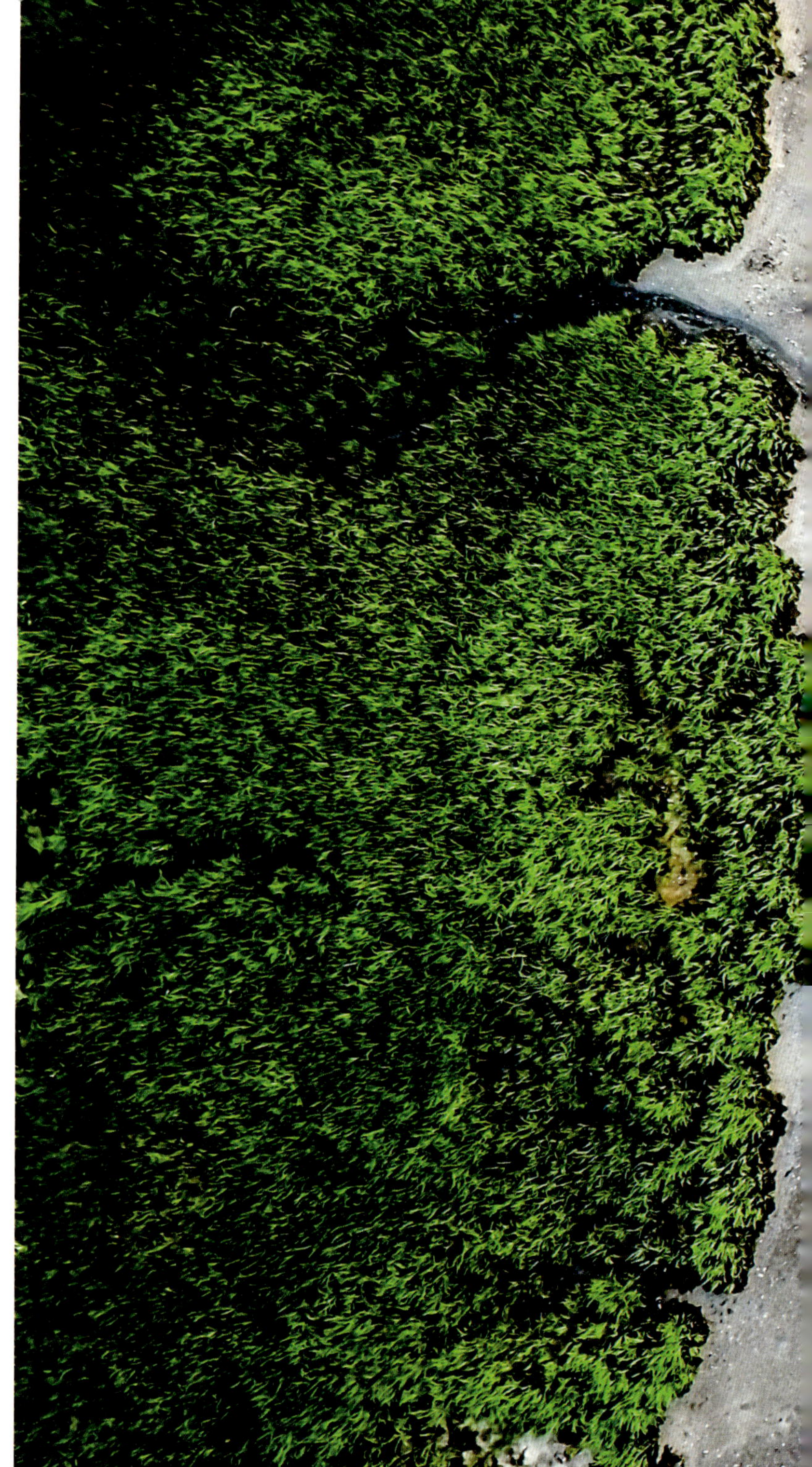

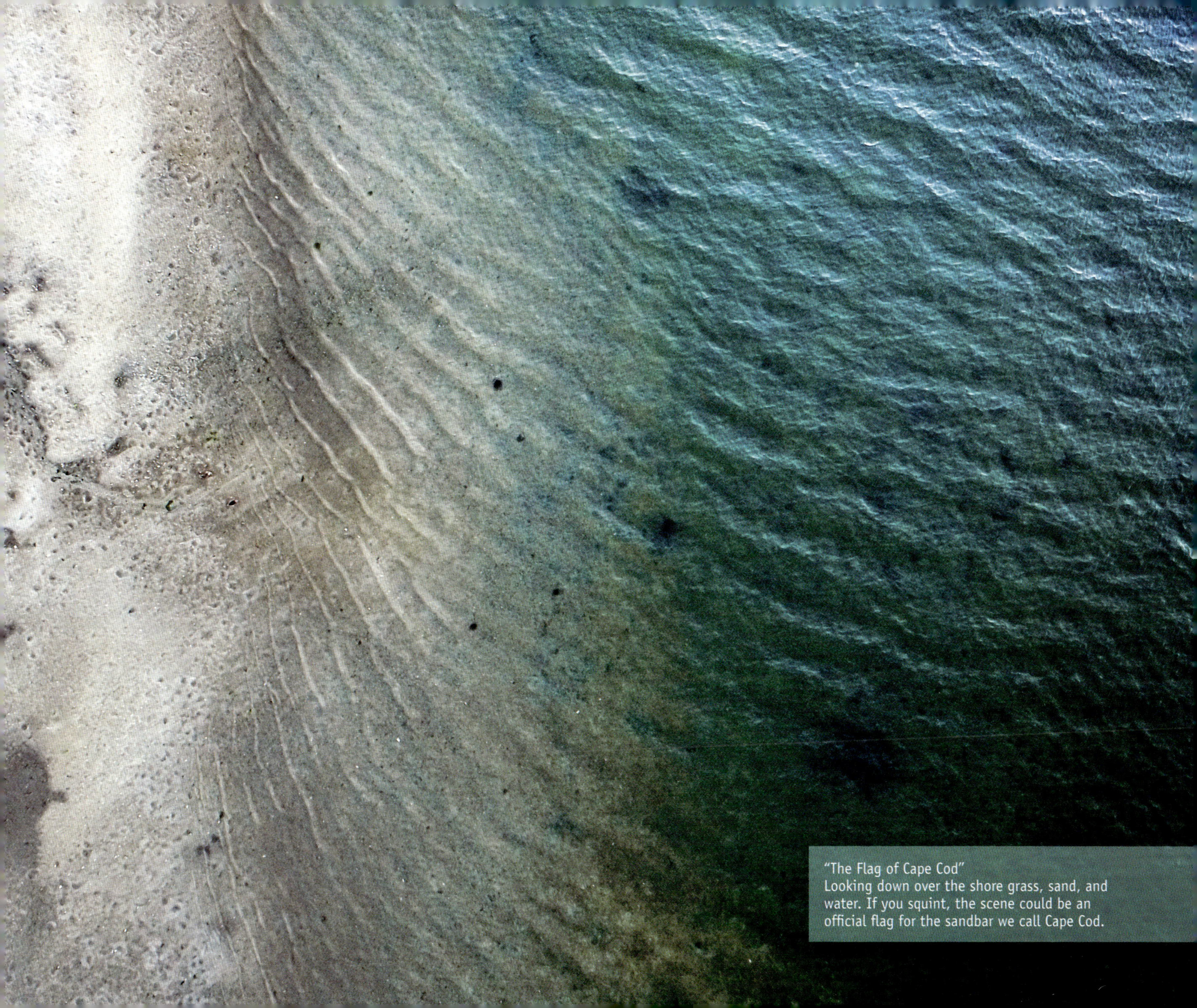

"The Flag of Cape Cod"
Looking down over the shore grass, sand, and water. If you squint, the scene could be an official flag for the sandbar we call Cape Cod.

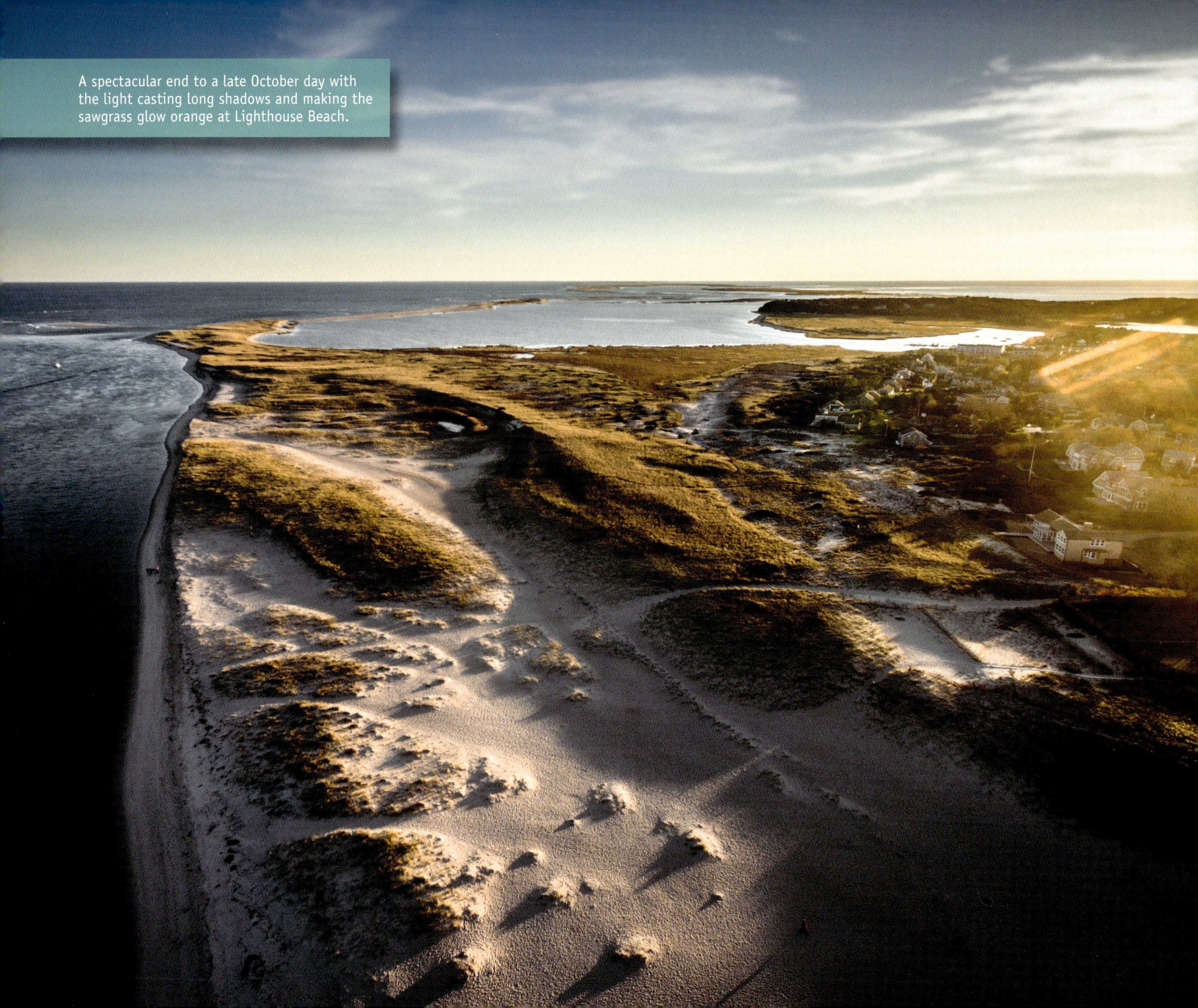

A spectacular end to a late October day with the light casting long shadows and making the sawgrass glow orange at Lighthouse Beach.

INTRODUCTION

Most of the indelible summer memories from my childhood all started off in almost the exact same way. On a Friday afternoon, Mom and Dad would load us kids into the minivan with the beach chairs and blankets, suitcases and beach bags, a deck of cards, and my dad's eclectic music collection for the three-hour family sing-along that meant we were on our way to Cape Cod.

Getting to the highway always felt like the longest part of the trip, but let me tell you, when we hit the highway and Dad let all 90 of those horses fly on that 2.0-liter 1984 Toyota minivan, man that was living! The McDonald's off 495 in Milford precisely marked the halfway point to the little sandbar dangling out in the Atlantic just waiting for our arrival. For three antsy kids, there was nothing like rolling up to that drive-thru, opening the van's sliding windows, feeling the hot summer air hit you like a blow dryer, and getting our hands on the burgers and ice-cold sodas that made the traffic just a little more bearable.

Almost like clockwork, just as we finished stuffing our faces, the towering expanse of the Bourne Bridge would come into view. We'd pass the old New York #16 tugboat and head northeast along the roller coaster of Rt. 6 that parallels the Cape Cod Canal as we spotted ships that slipped along its wild currents like they were on rails. And then there it was, the massive Sagamore Bridge spanning the 1,400 feet between "vacation land" and the rest of the world—you're not on Cape Cod until you cross the bridge, after all. As it always did, the anticipation reached its peak on that last stretch of Rt. 6 to the CQX because we were just mere moments away from settling in, opening the windows, and letting that first sunset fly silently across the living room floor.

From the first breath of that sea air, every moment after was nothing short of a postcard. Taking the dory out and exploring some small, uncharted tidal island and fishing from its shore until the tide inevitably came back in and the sea reclaimed it forever, washing away any trace of us ever being there. Watching Cape League baseball games under the lights in the stillness of a foggy evening as the crack of the bat and the cheers of the crowd seemed to travel for miles. Band concerts and balloons in the park, and making what would become lifelong friends over marathon games of whiffle ball. Lazy days on the beach where the smell of sunscreen permeated the air from every direction and we competed with throngs of tourists for a little space to lay out our blankets to devour our warm, sandy, ham-and-cheese sandwiches and potato chips before seagulls had a chance to steal them away.

I've been fortunate to call Cape Cod my home on more than one occasion since those days in the minivan some 35 years ago. A lot has changed, but infinitely more has remained the same. It's as wondrous a place to me today as it was when I was a kid, and the scene of so many "firsts" in my life. My first swim, my first sail, my first dive, my first date, my first kiss, and now my first book.

—Christopher S. Gibbs

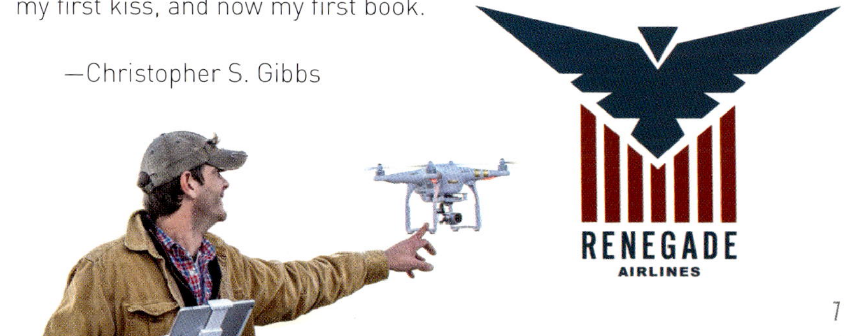

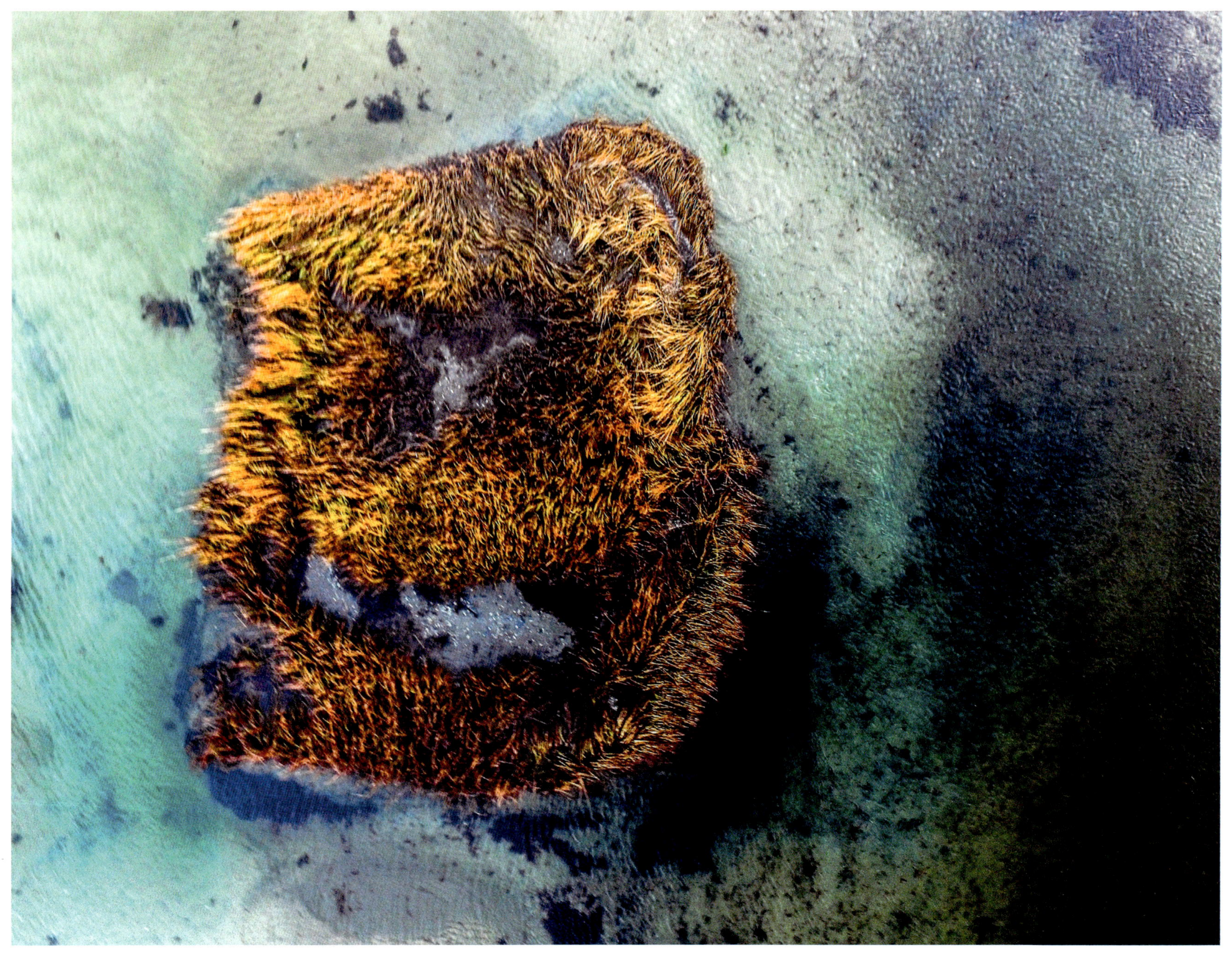

“B is For Betsy” - Flying out over the salt marshes of Ridgevale Beach on a hot July day, I found this little island and claimed it for my late grandmother, Betsy.

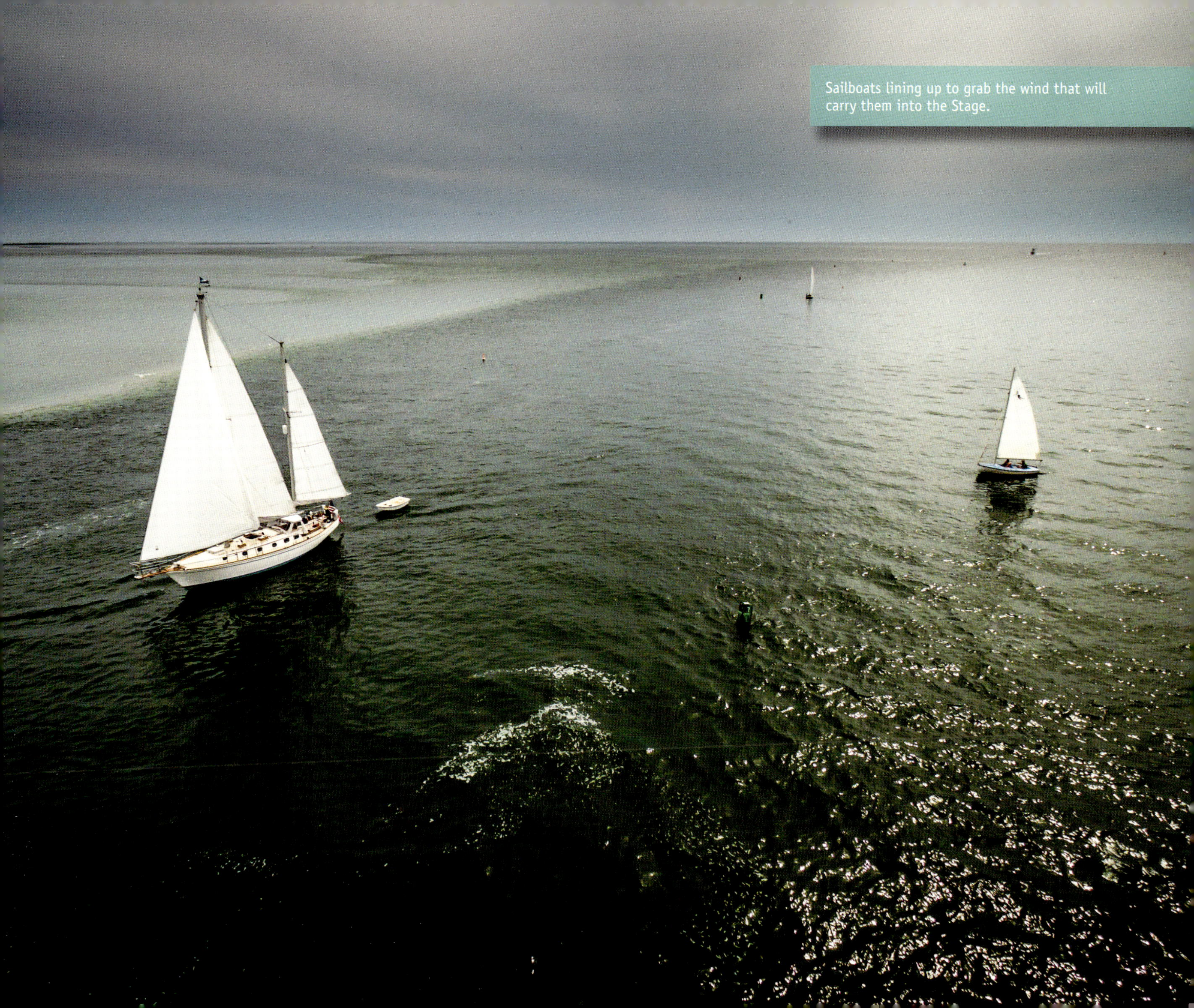

Sailboats lining up to grab the wind that will carry them into the Stage.

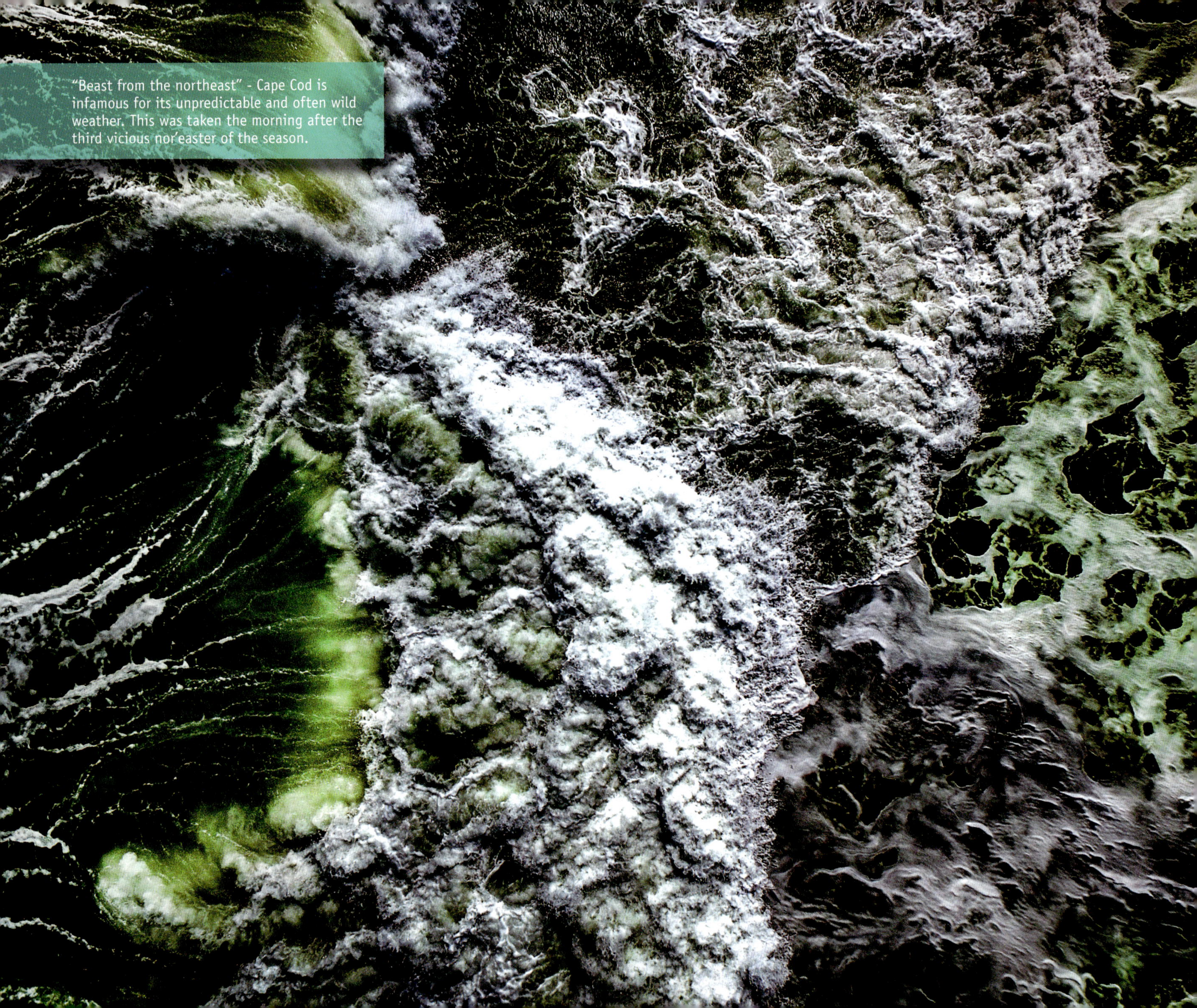

"Beast from the northeast" - Cape Cod is infamous for its unpredictable and often wild weather. This was taken the morning after the third vicious nor'easter of the season.

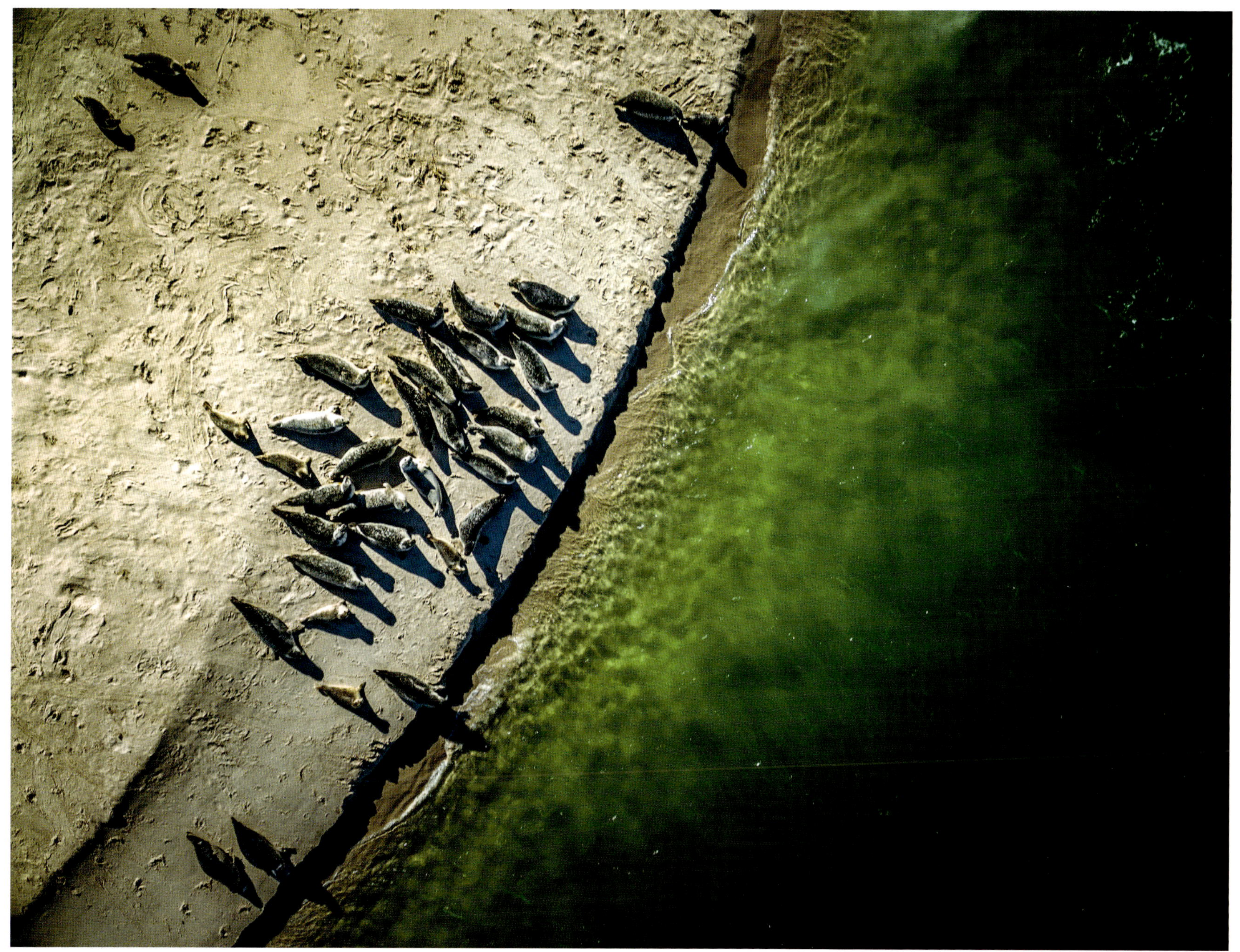

Sea lions cast long shadows in February.

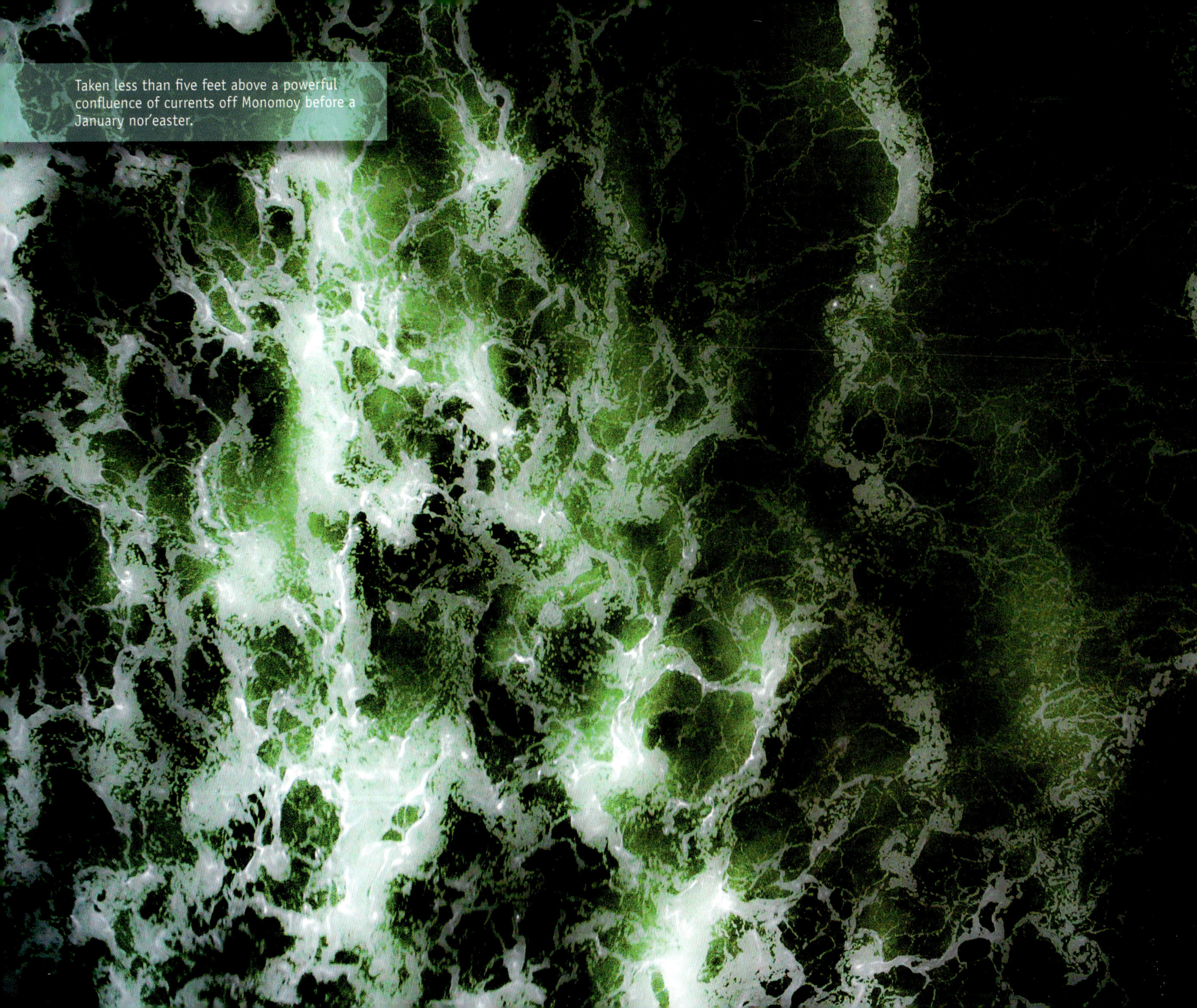

Taken less than five feet above a powerful confluence of currents off Monomoy before a January nor'easter.

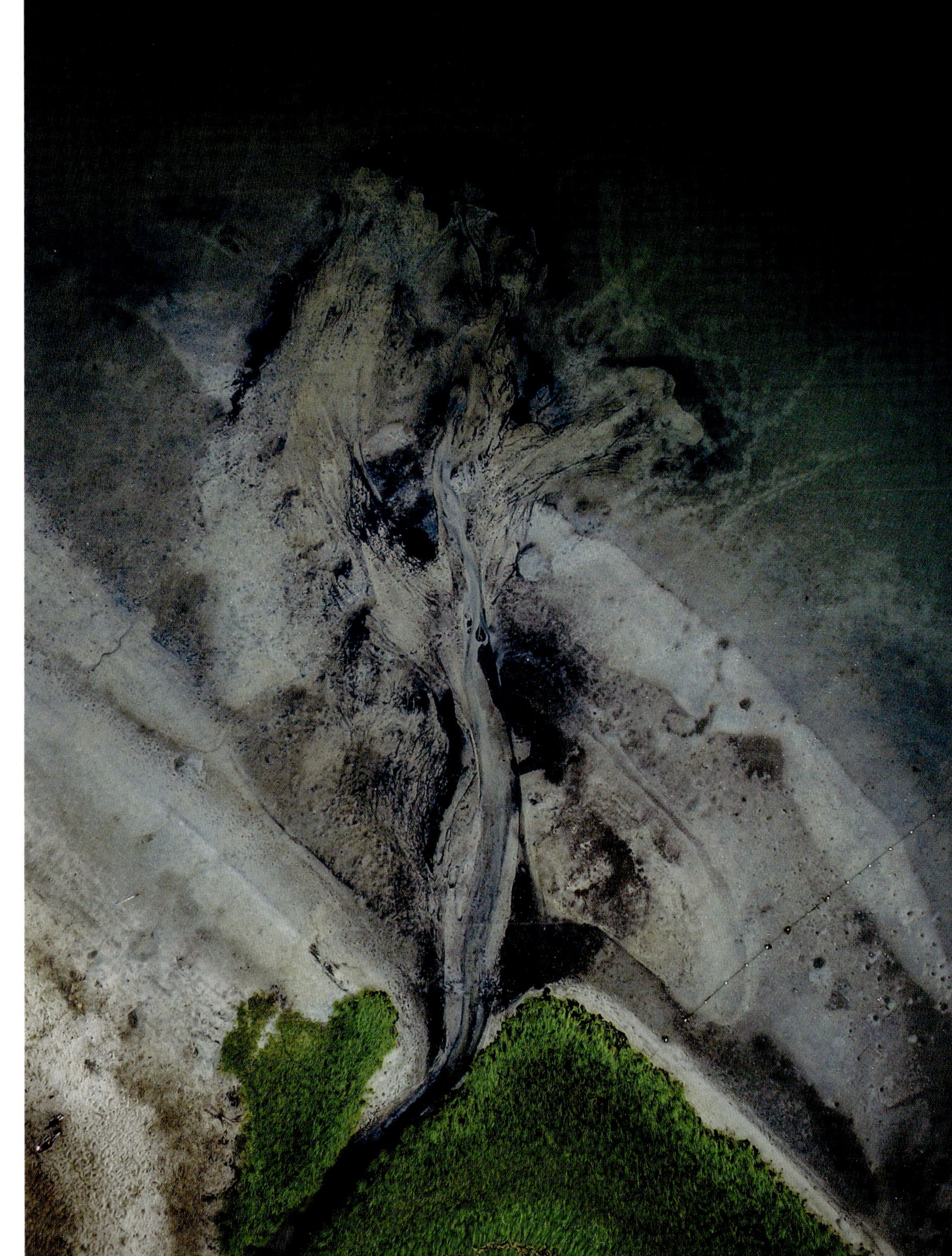

"Big tree on a little hill" - The pattern made when rainwater was released into the Oyster Pond after a storm. If you look closely you can also see the footprints of beachgoers through the dropping tide.

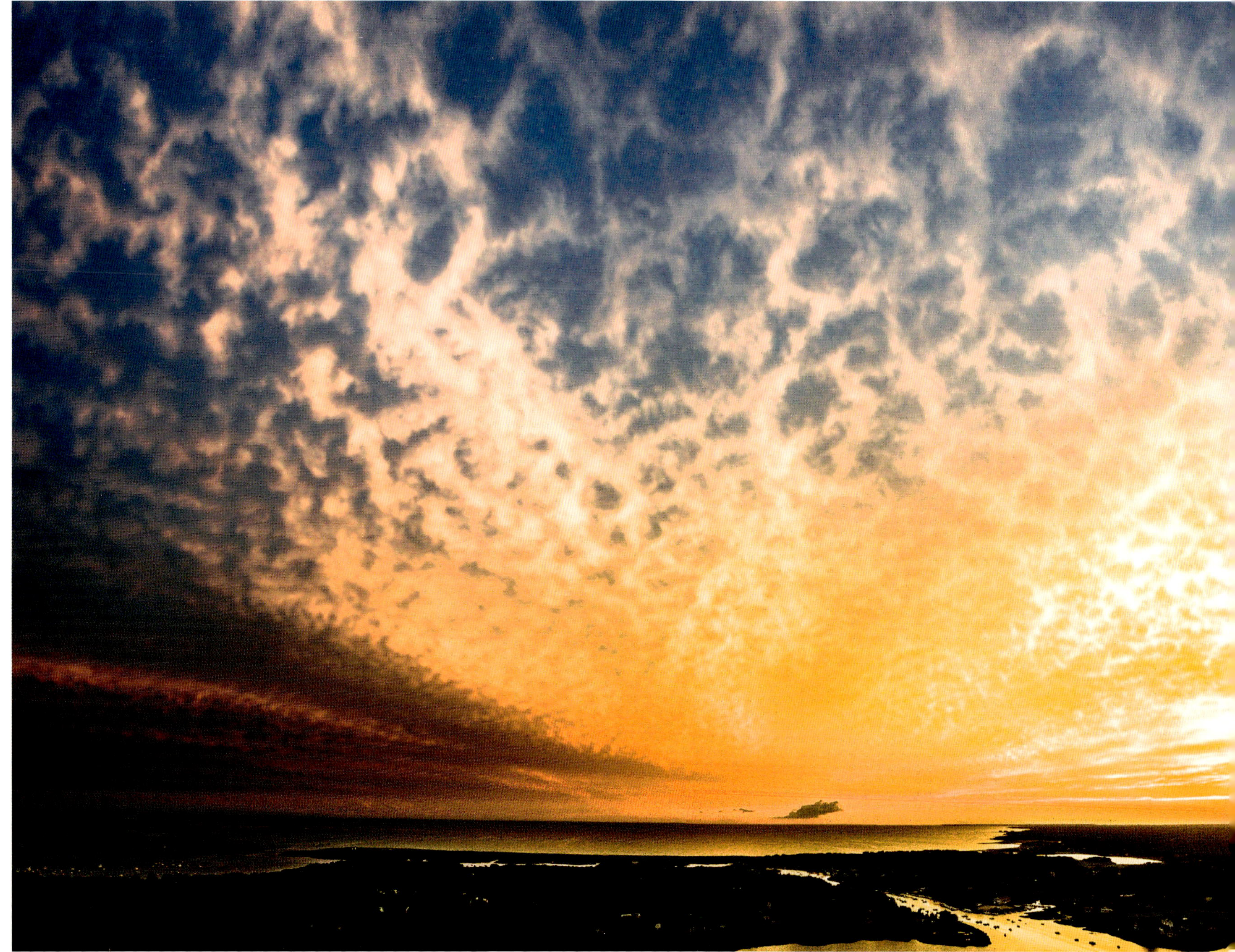

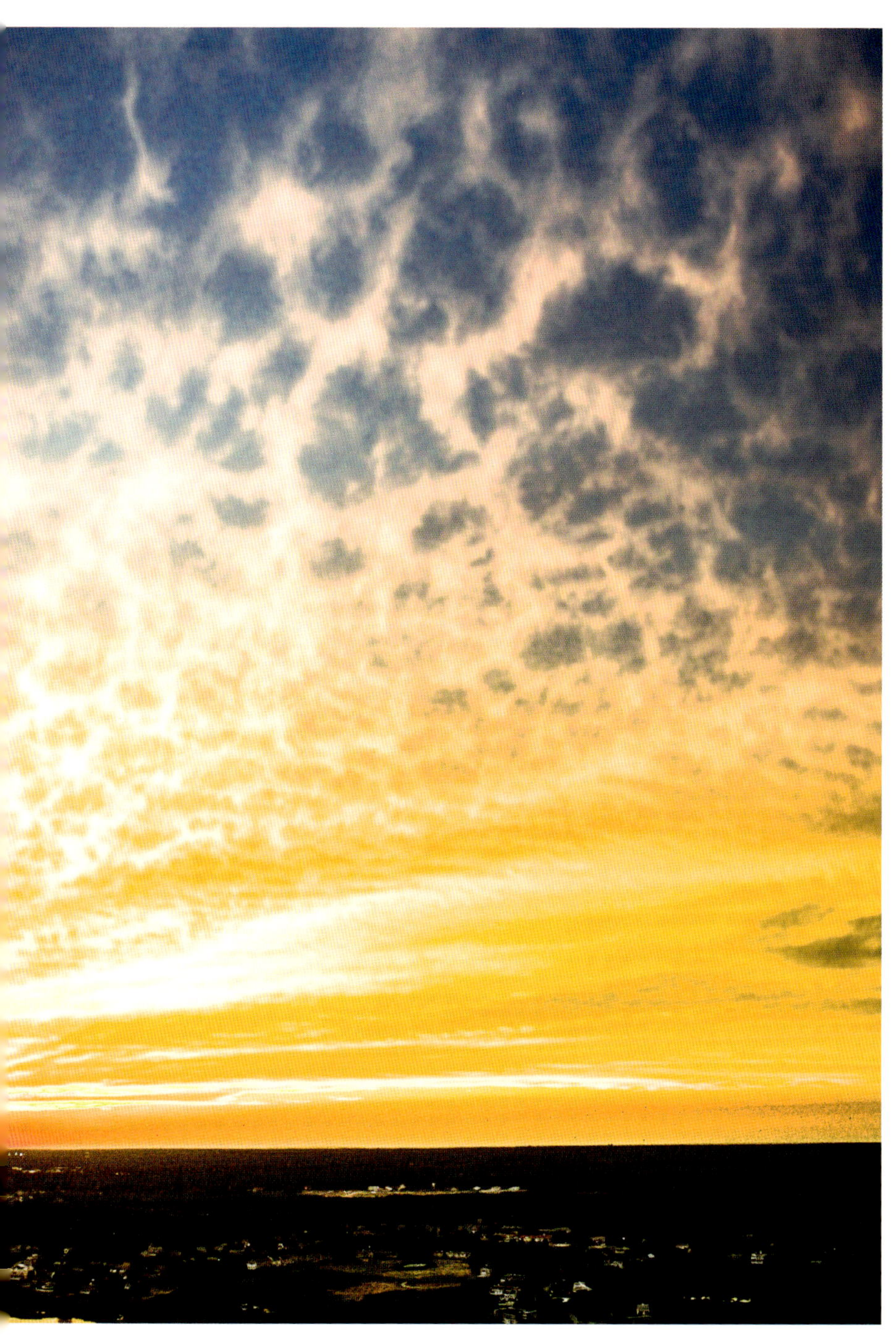

Cirrocumulus or "mackerel sky" clouds frequently appear ahead of a frontal system—in this case, the day before Hurricane Hermine rolled into town on September 3, 2016.

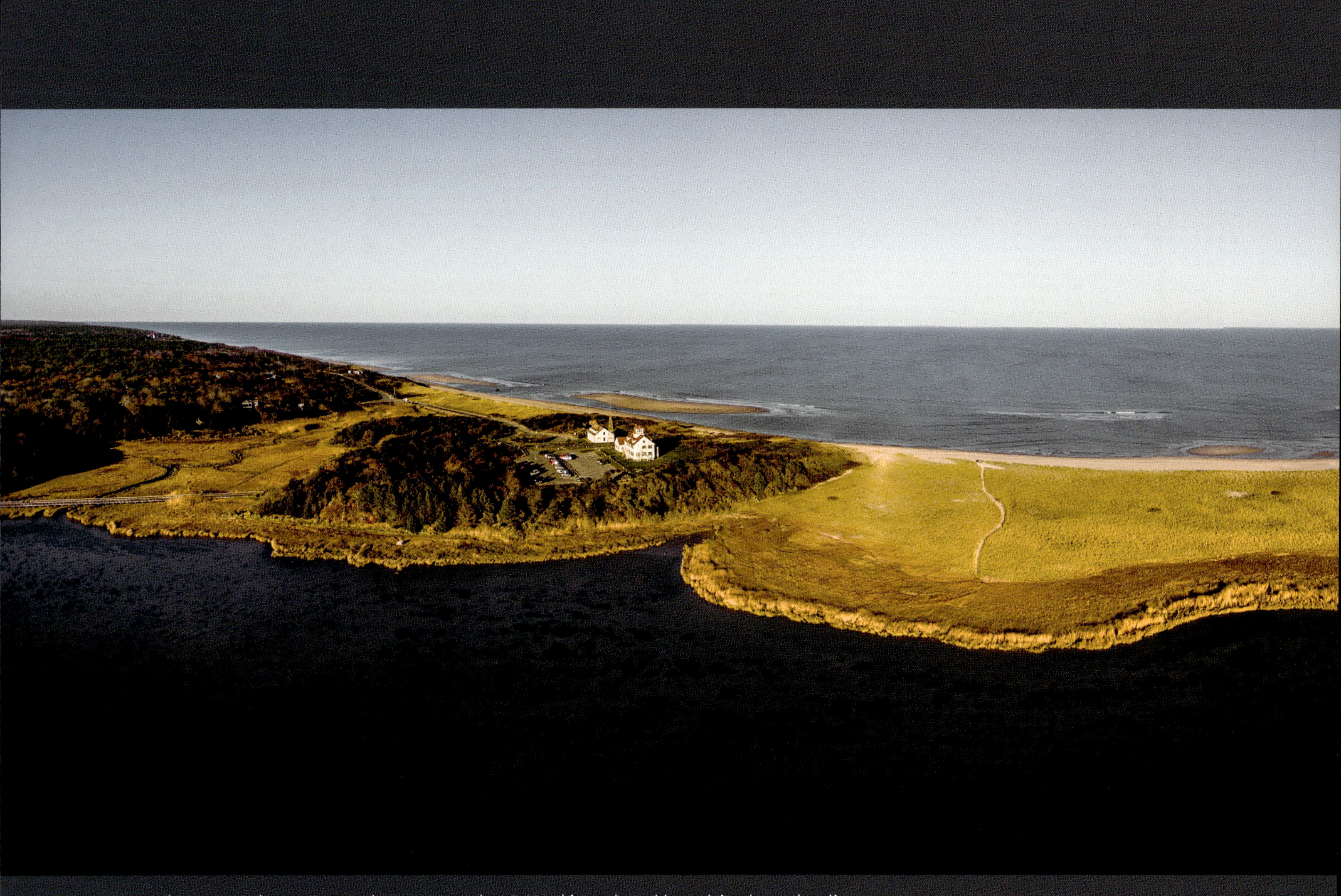

As serene as they appear, these waters are home to more than 3,000 shipwrecks and have claimed countless lives.

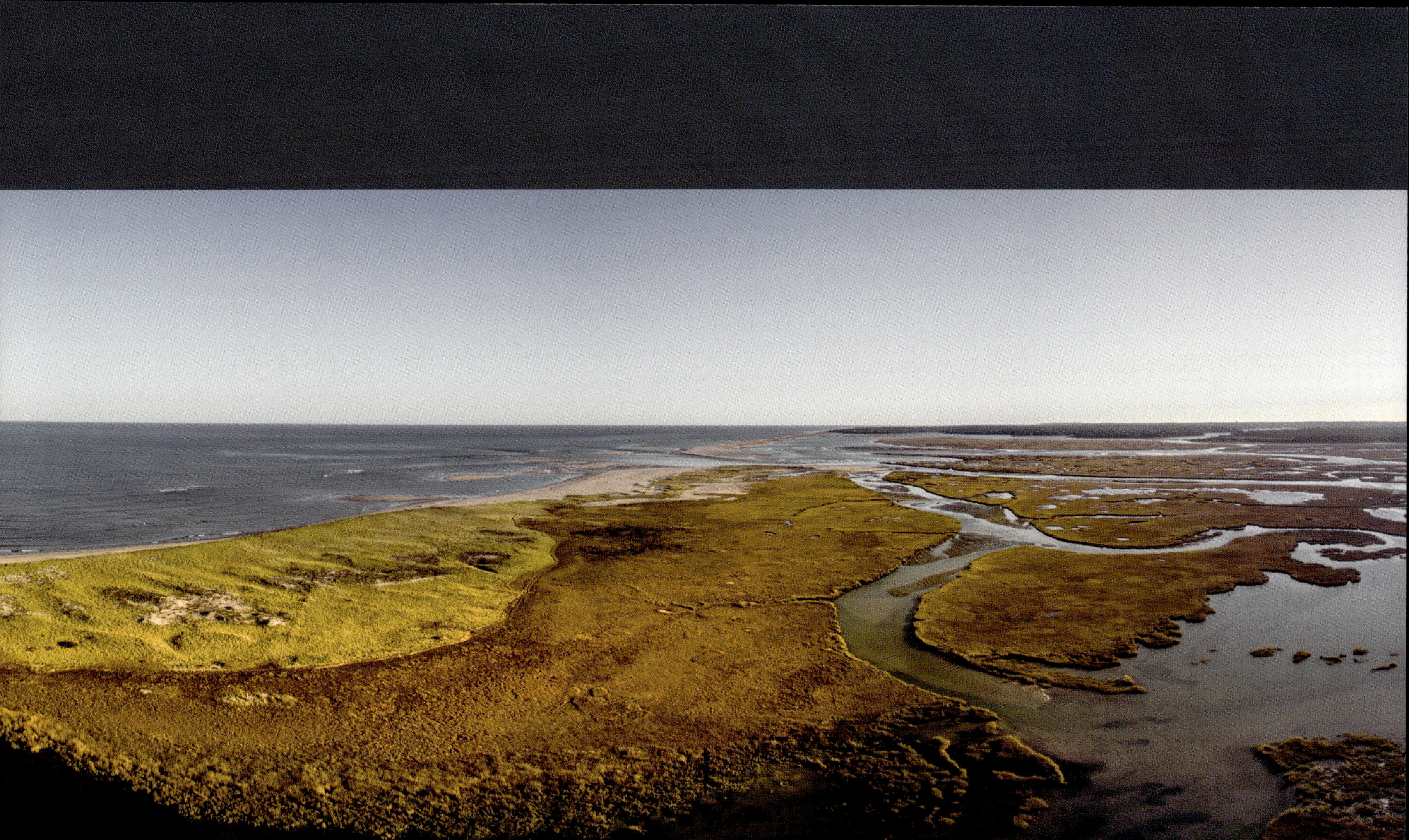

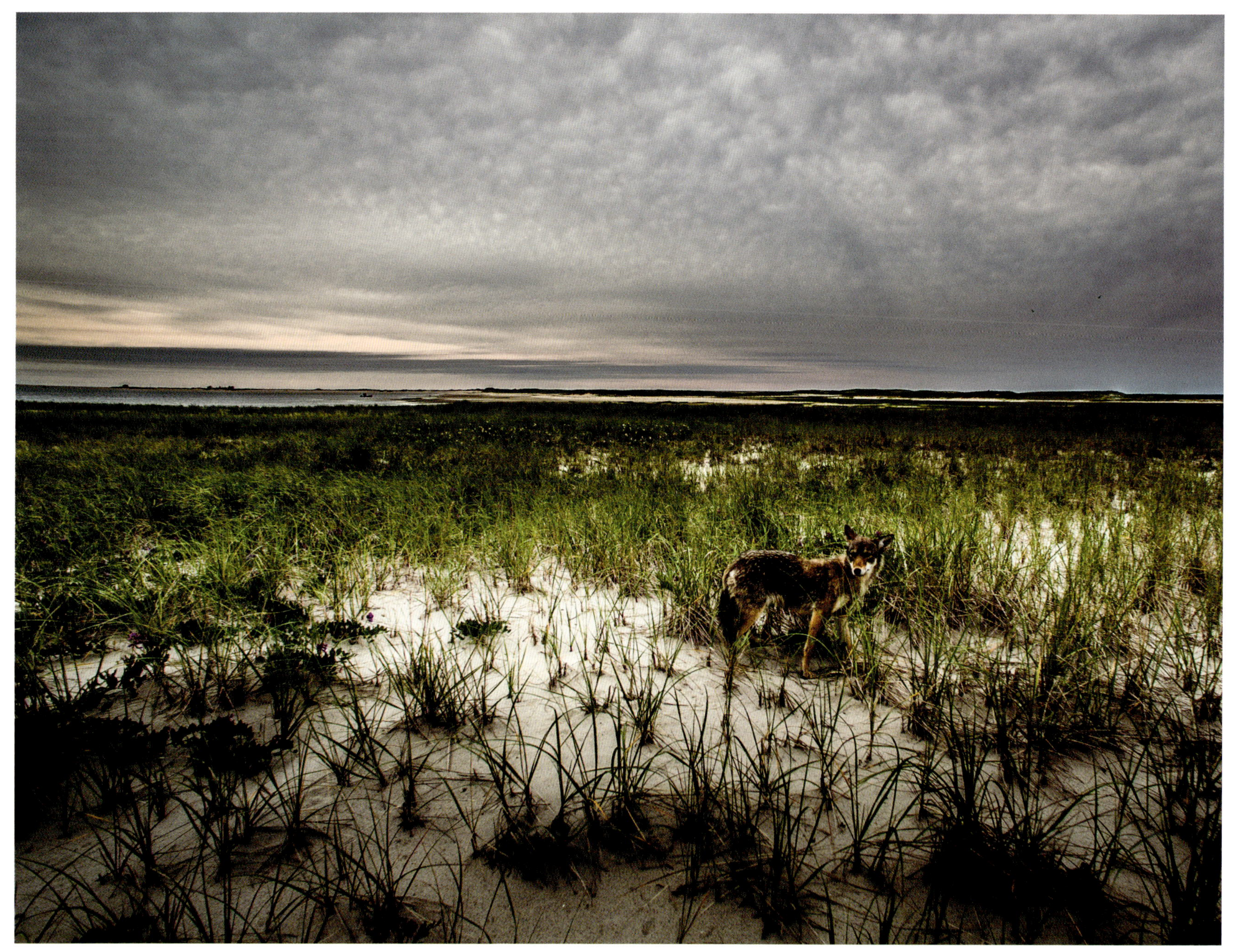

Coyotes are nothing new on Cape Cod, but this little guy swam at least 2,000 feet through shark-infested waters to get to this spot.

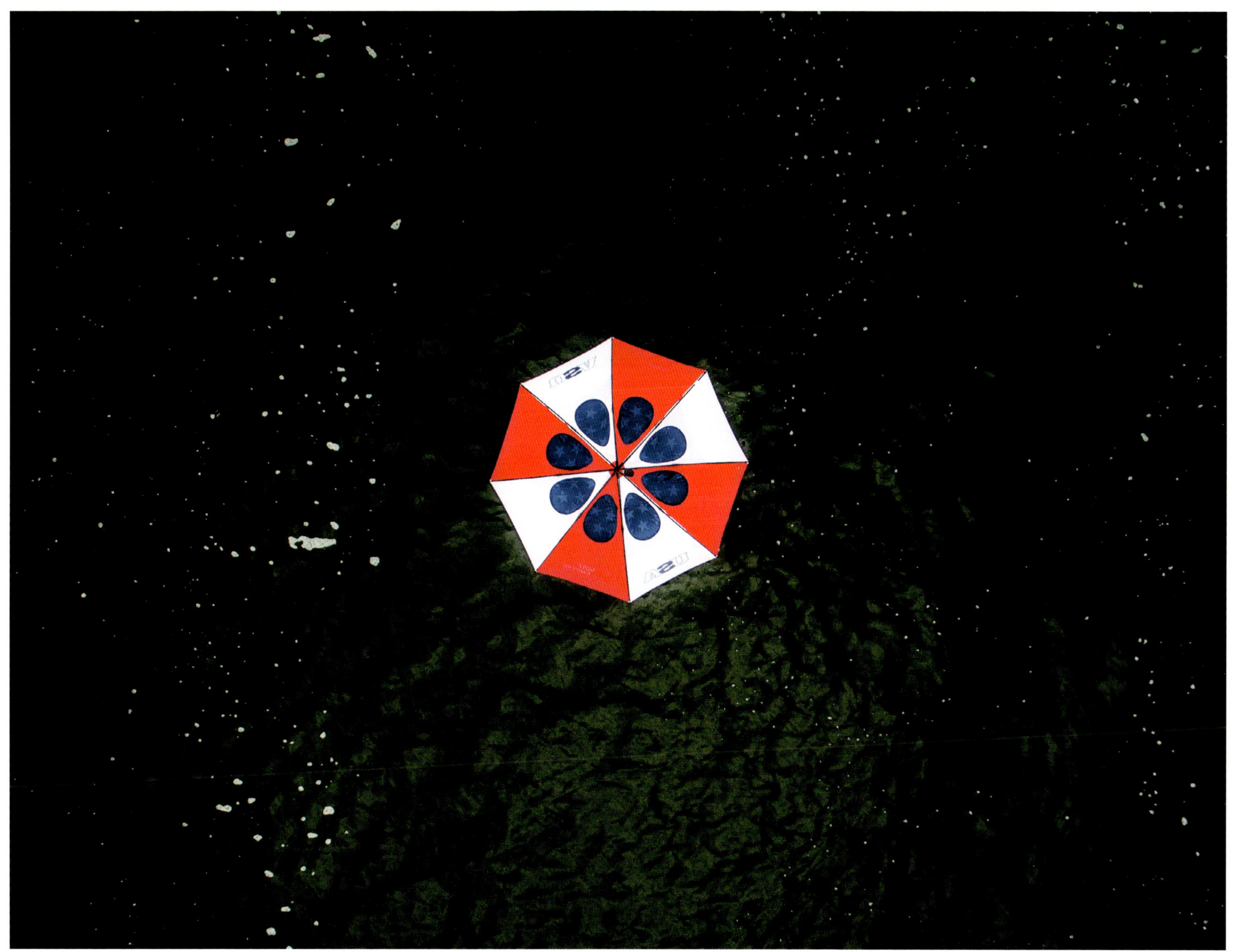

A wayward umbrella that flew off a deck during the annual Chatham Boat Race floating gently down the stream.

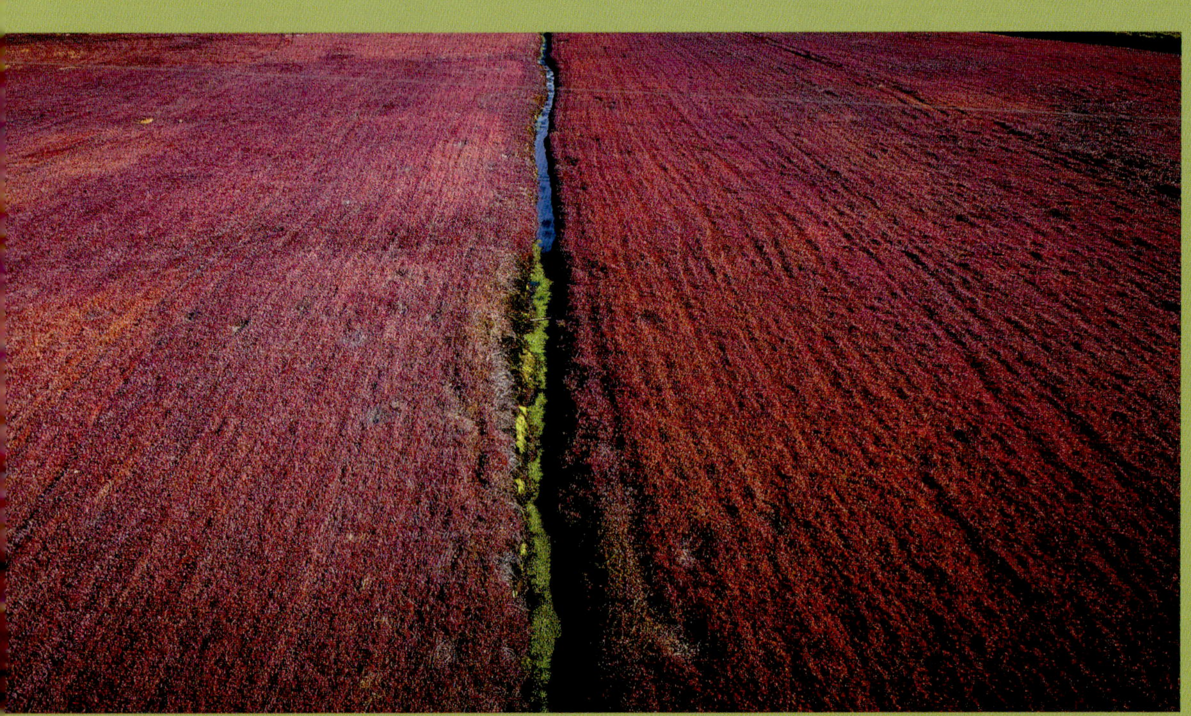

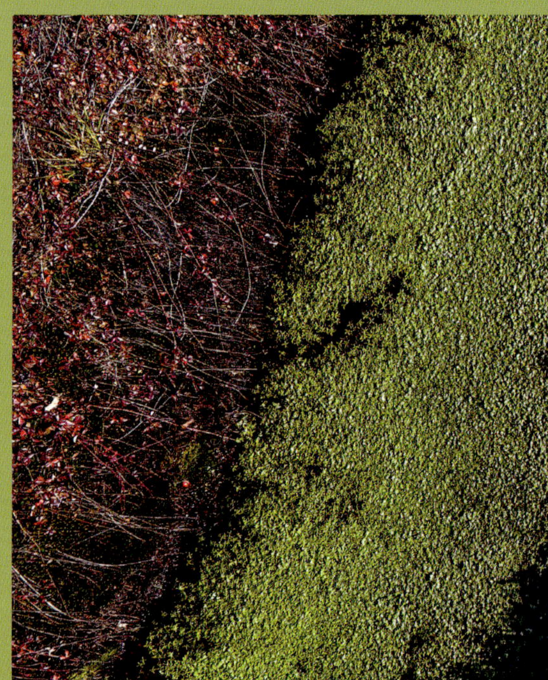

Cape Cod's most important fruit grows on low vines and shrubs in bogs like this one, which will be flooded for the harvest.

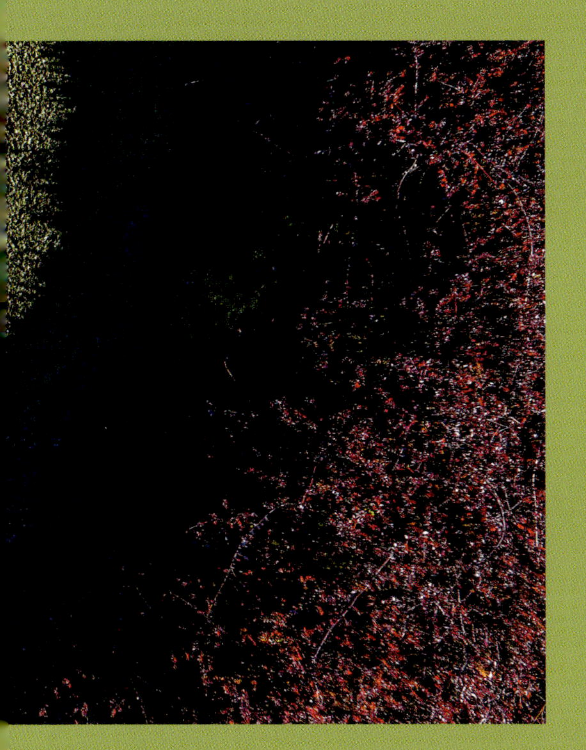

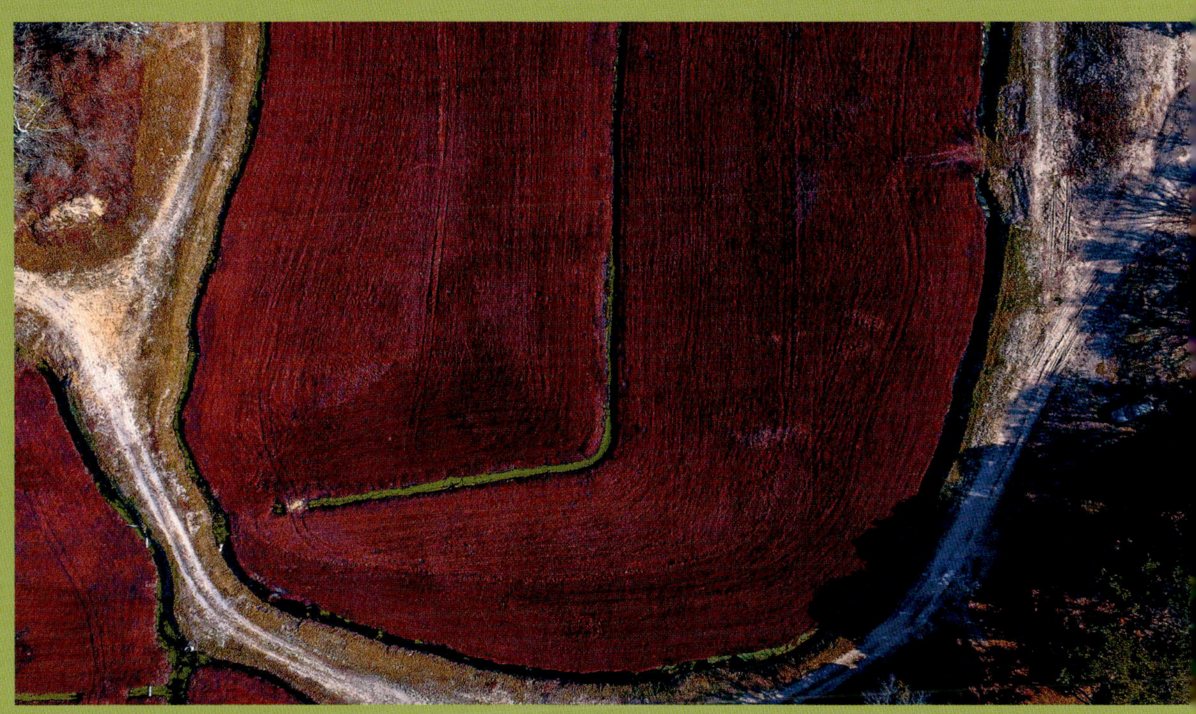

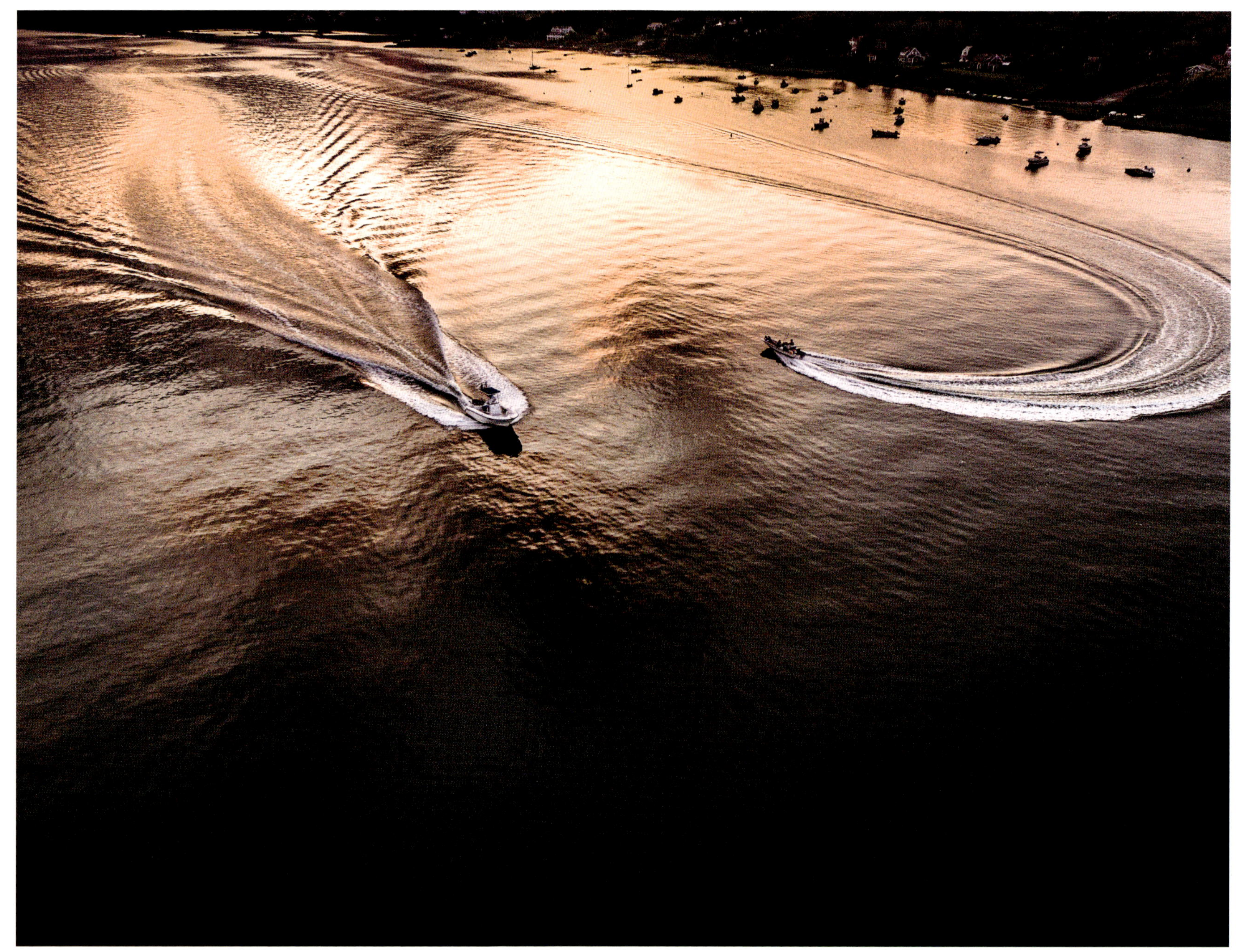

Boaters rip around the pond at sunset on Memorial Day.

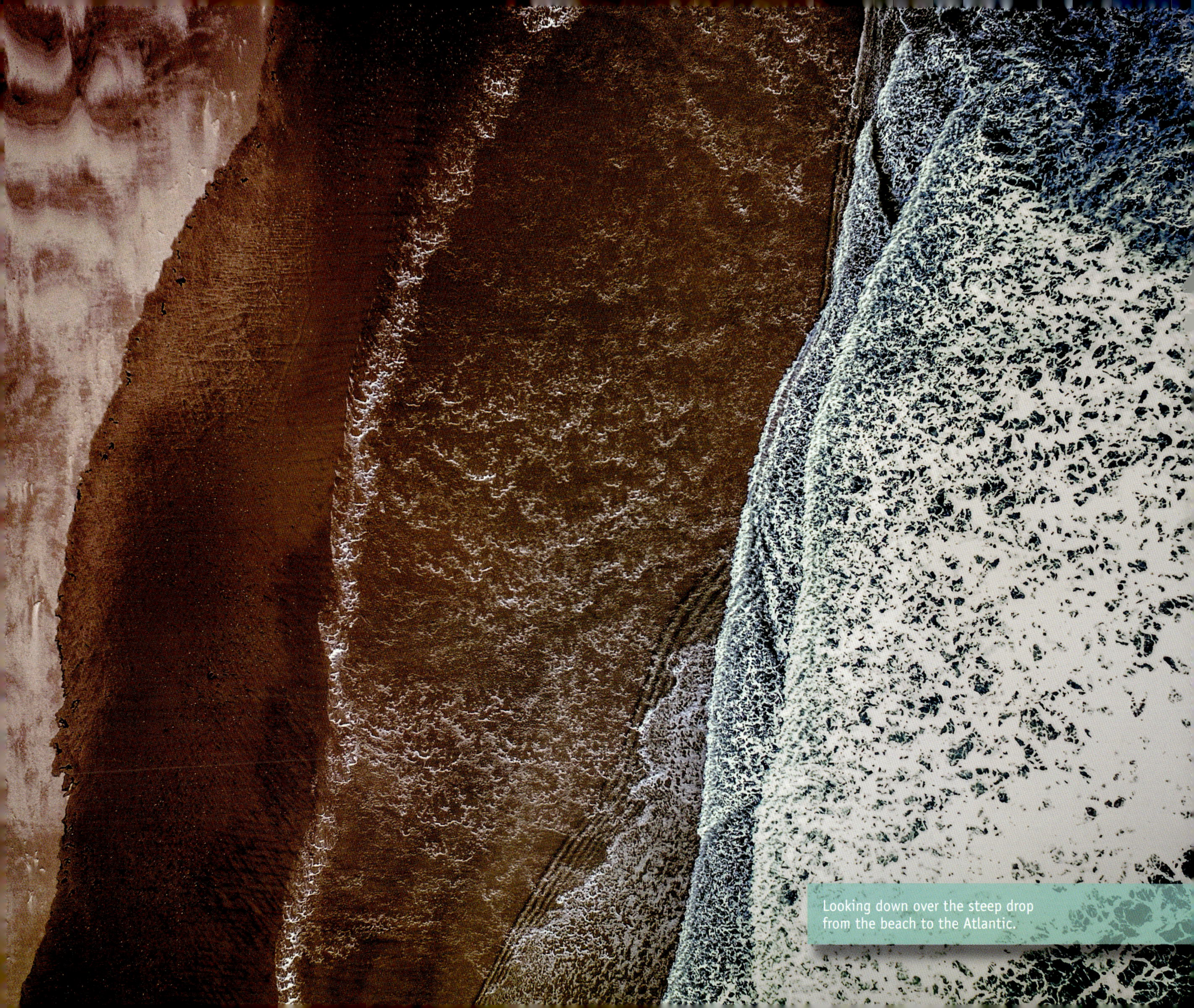

Looking down over the steep drop from the beach to the Atlantic.

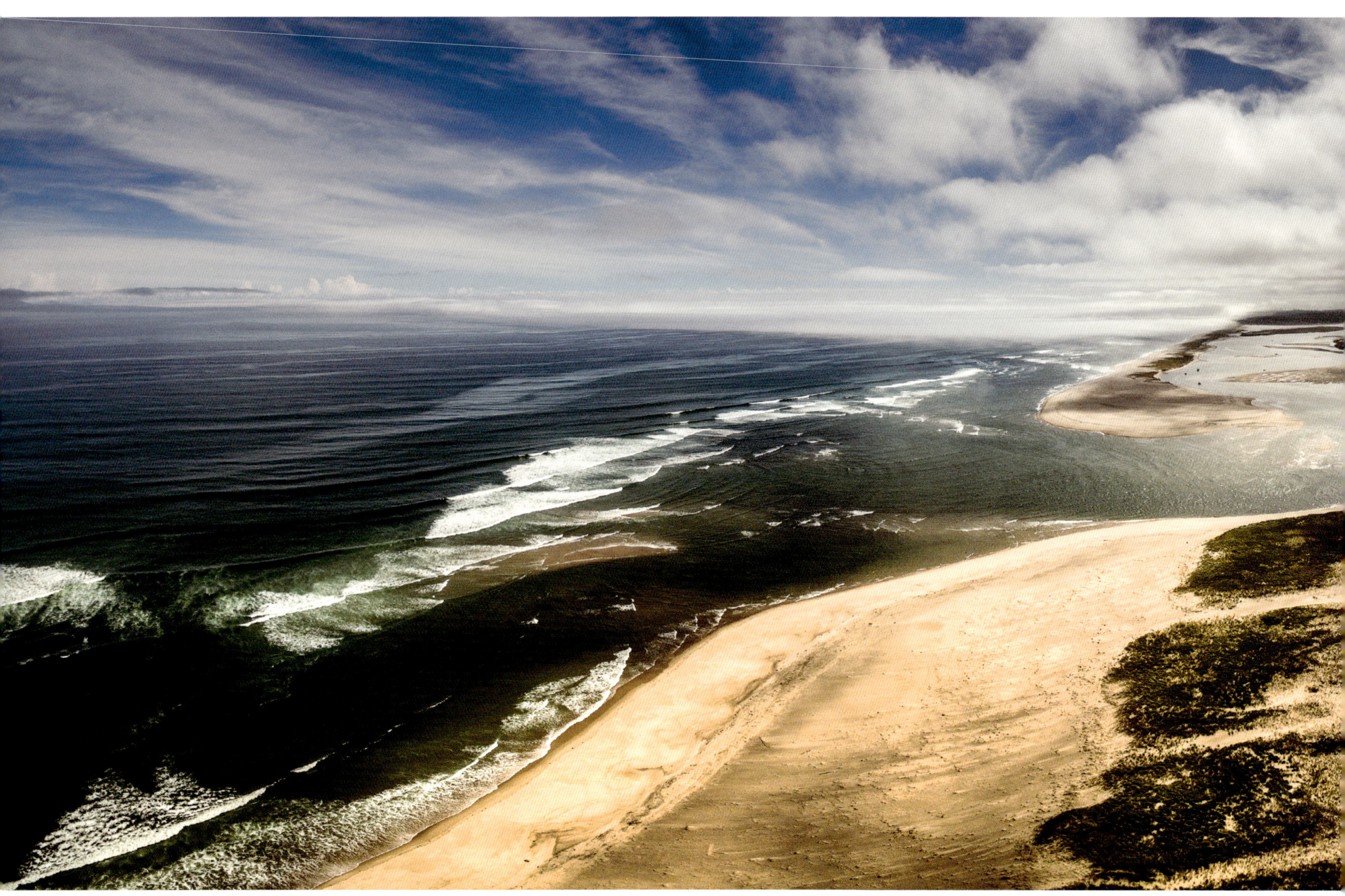

Looking south with Nauset Beach in the distance.

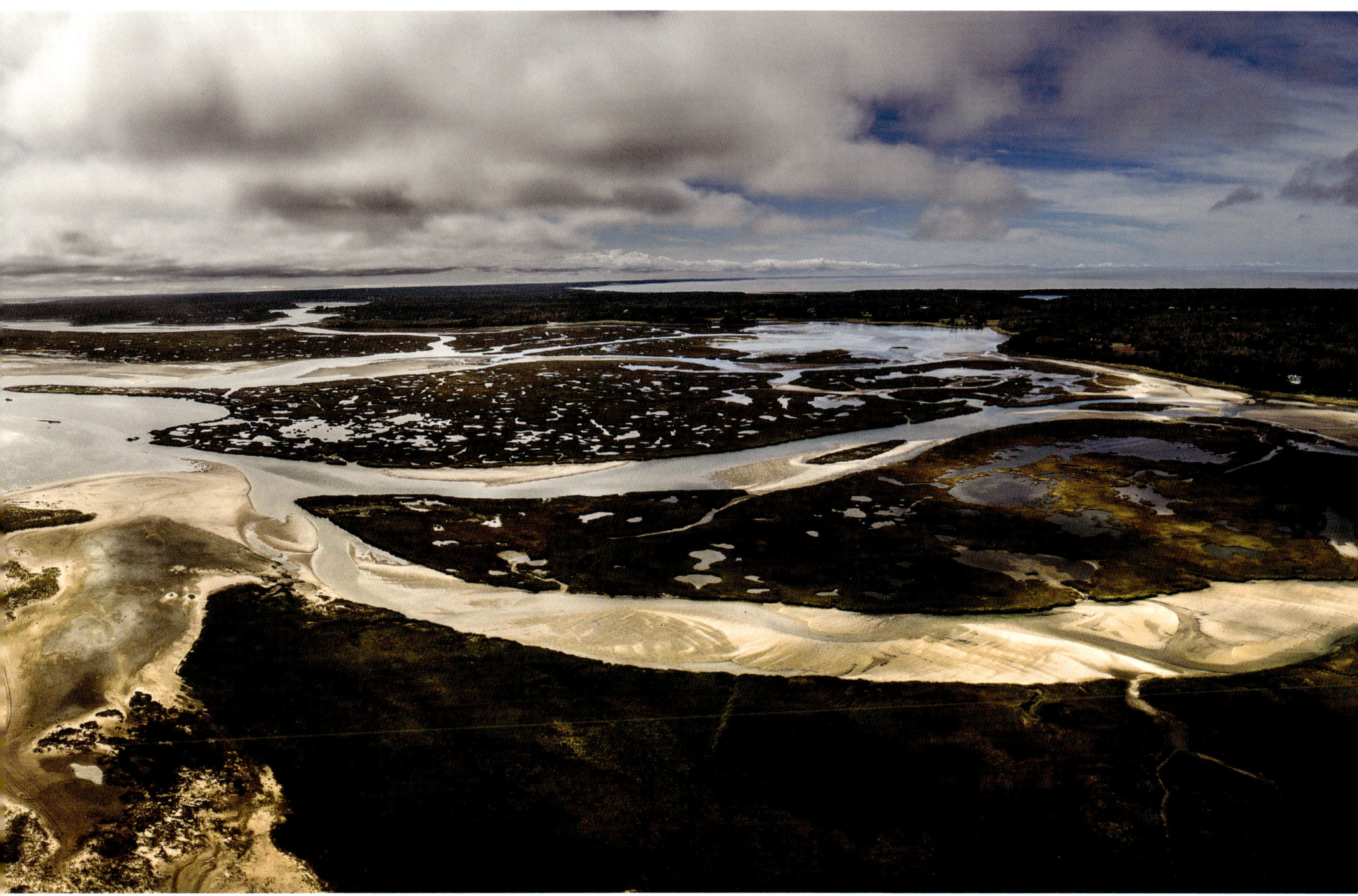

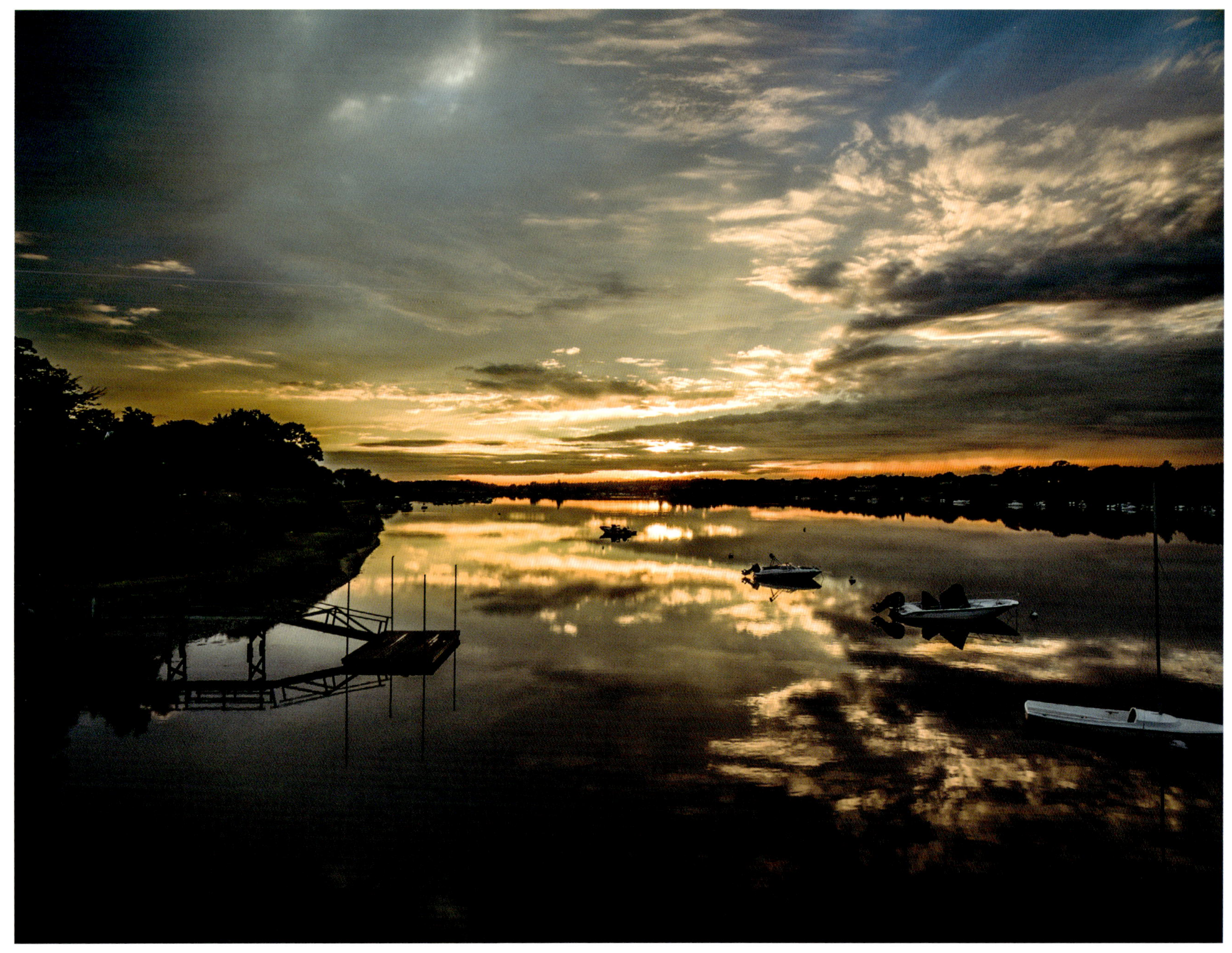

"Dockside" - Sunset comes every day, but not all sunsets are created equal.

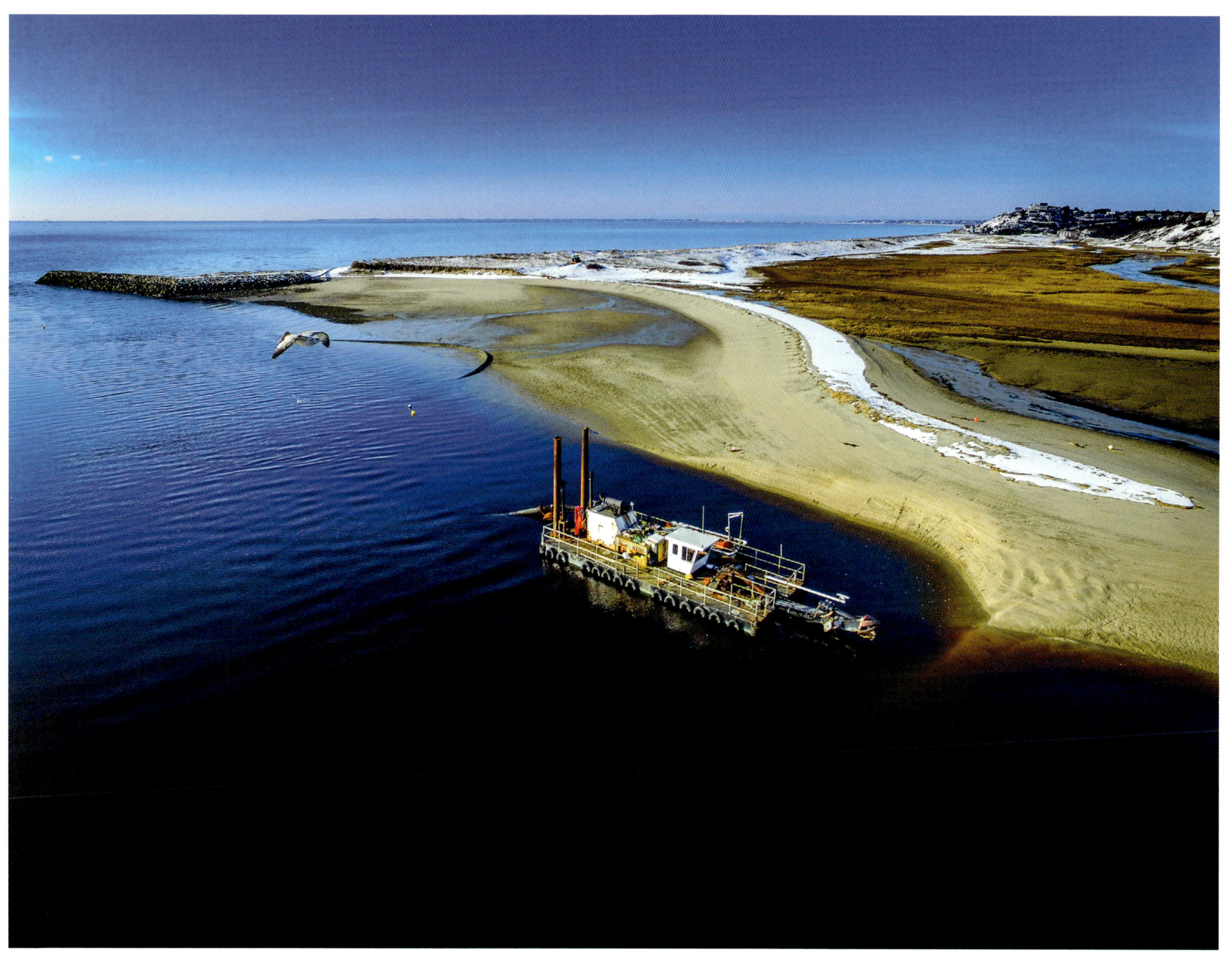

Dredging the constantly shifting sands in the channel at Pamet Harbor.

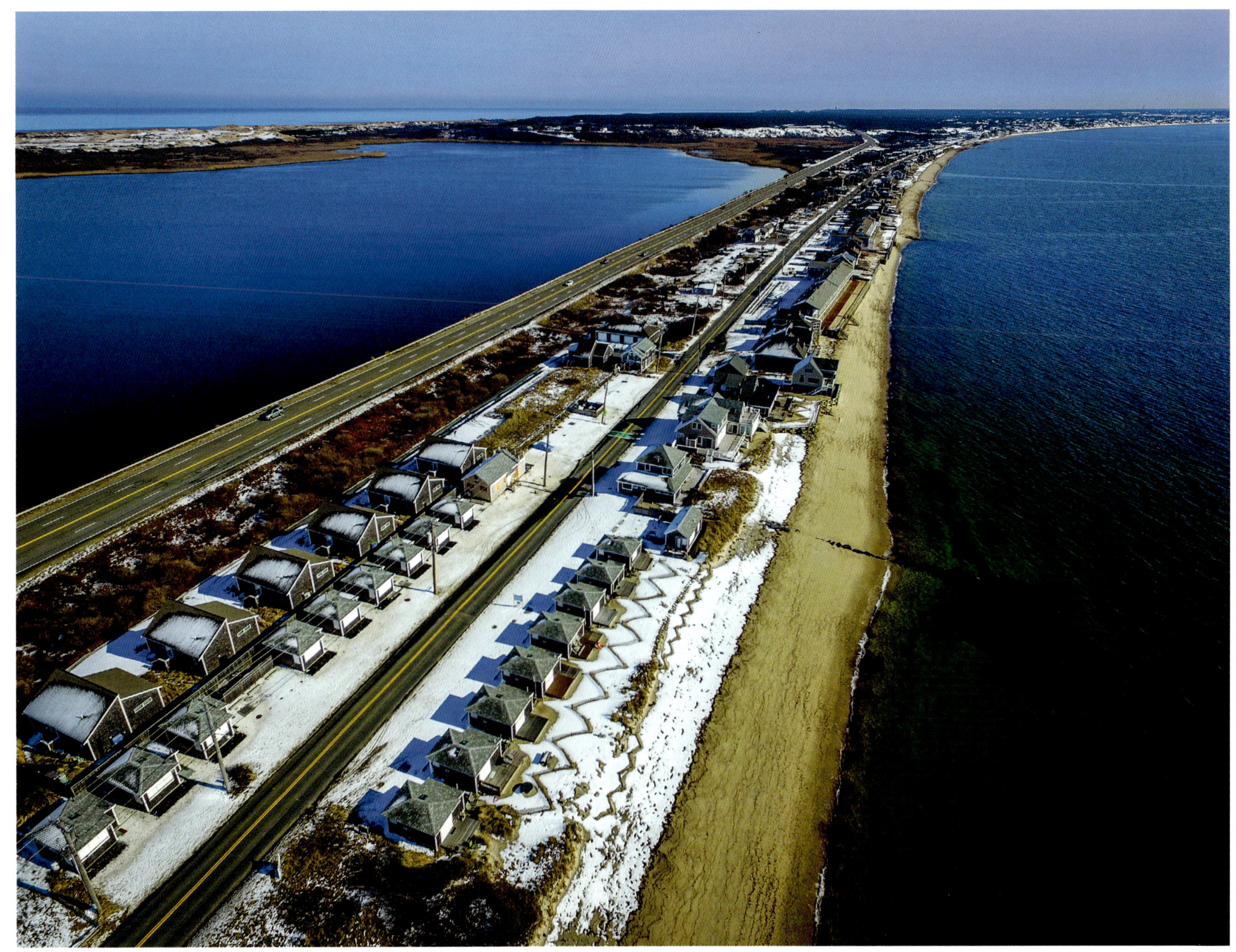

Over the bay side of Cape Cod looking toward East Harbor and the coast of North Truro.

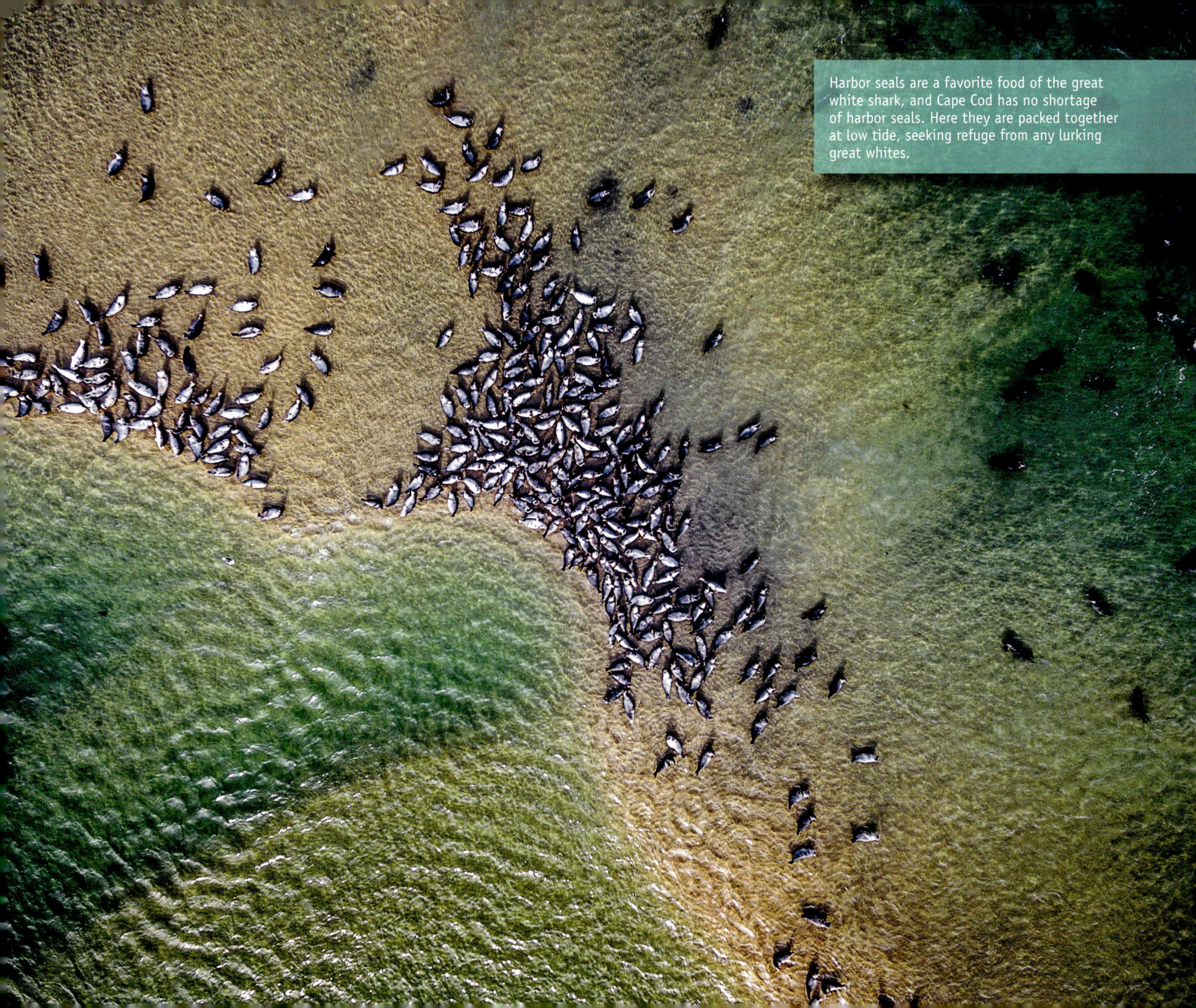

Harbor seals are a favorite food of the great white shark, and Cape Cod has no shortage of harbor seals. Here they are packed together at low tide, seeking refuge from any lurking great whites.

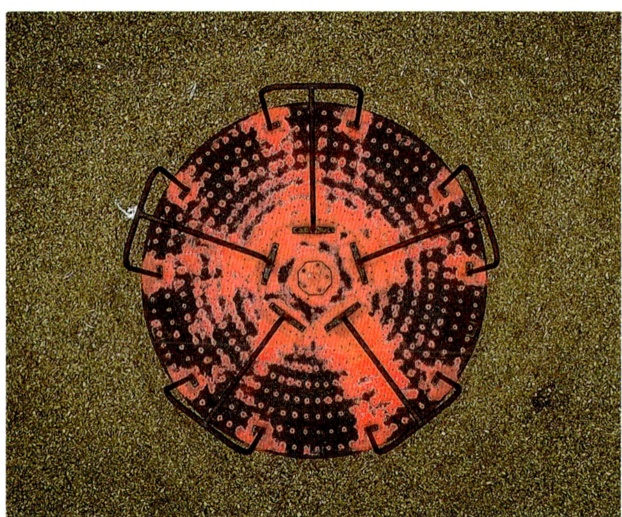

The merry-go-round at the Wellfleet Drive-In Theater—a vomit-inducing death machine and a favorite of countless kids since 1957.

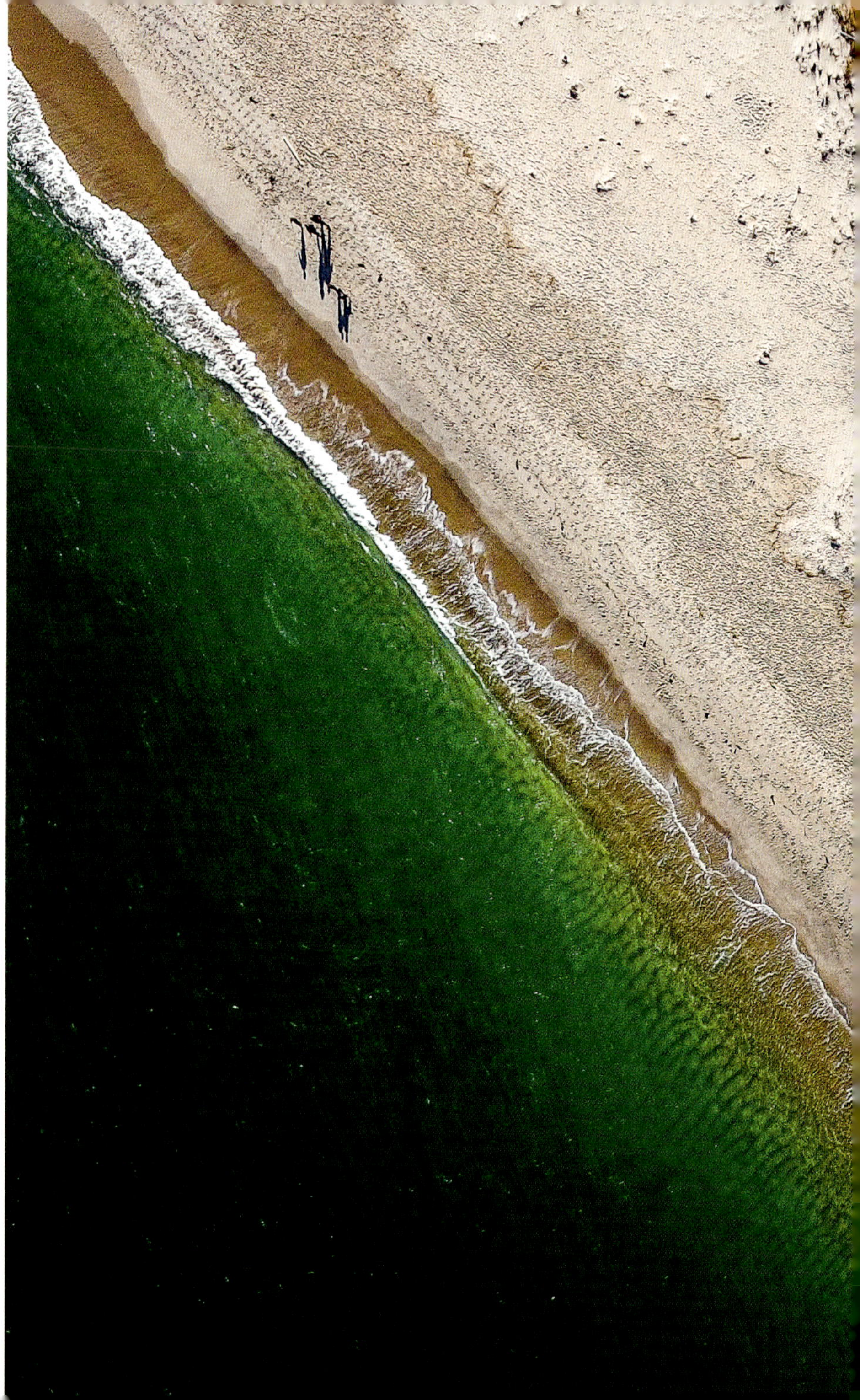

A family strolls down the beach on their last day of vacation.

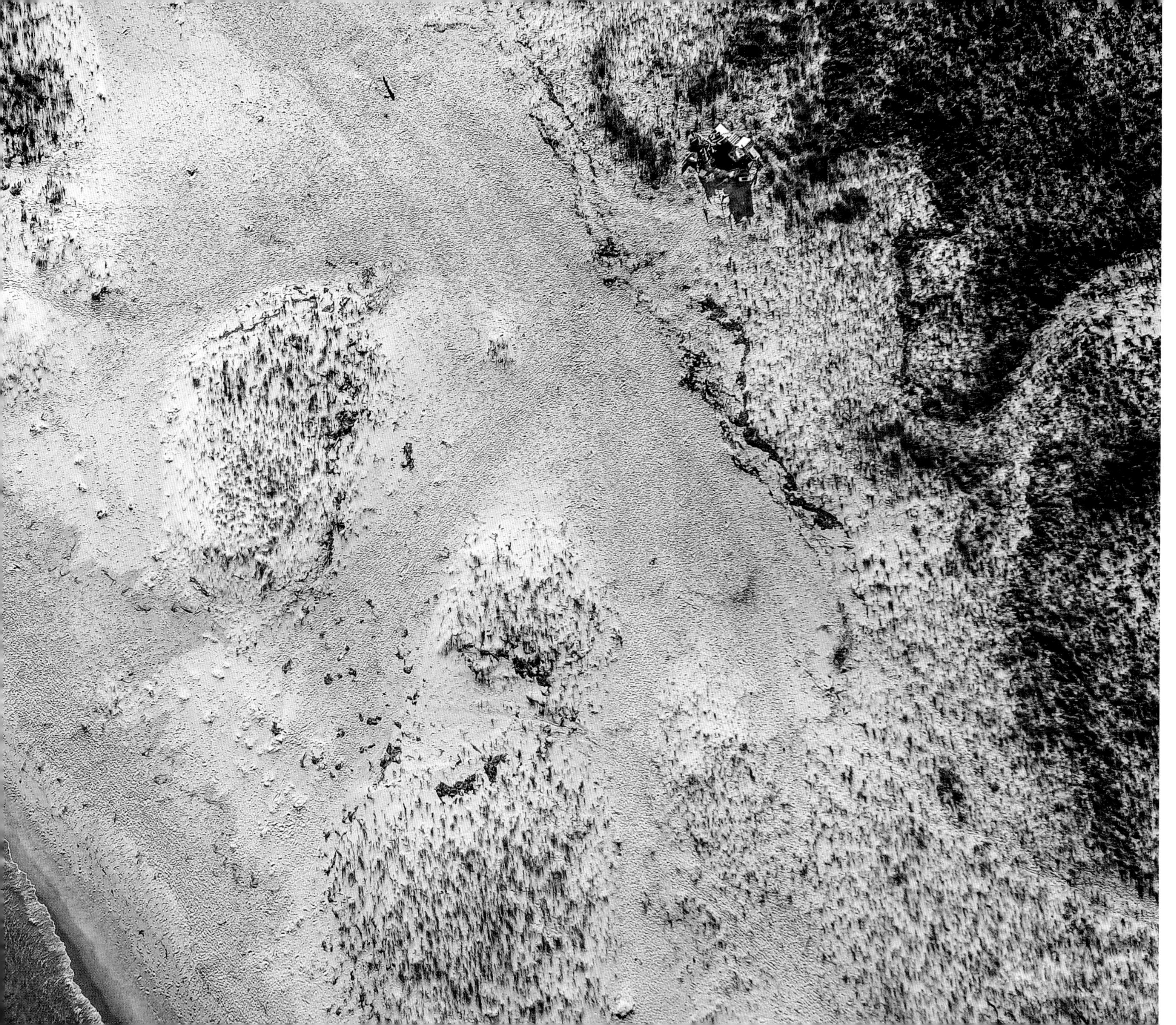

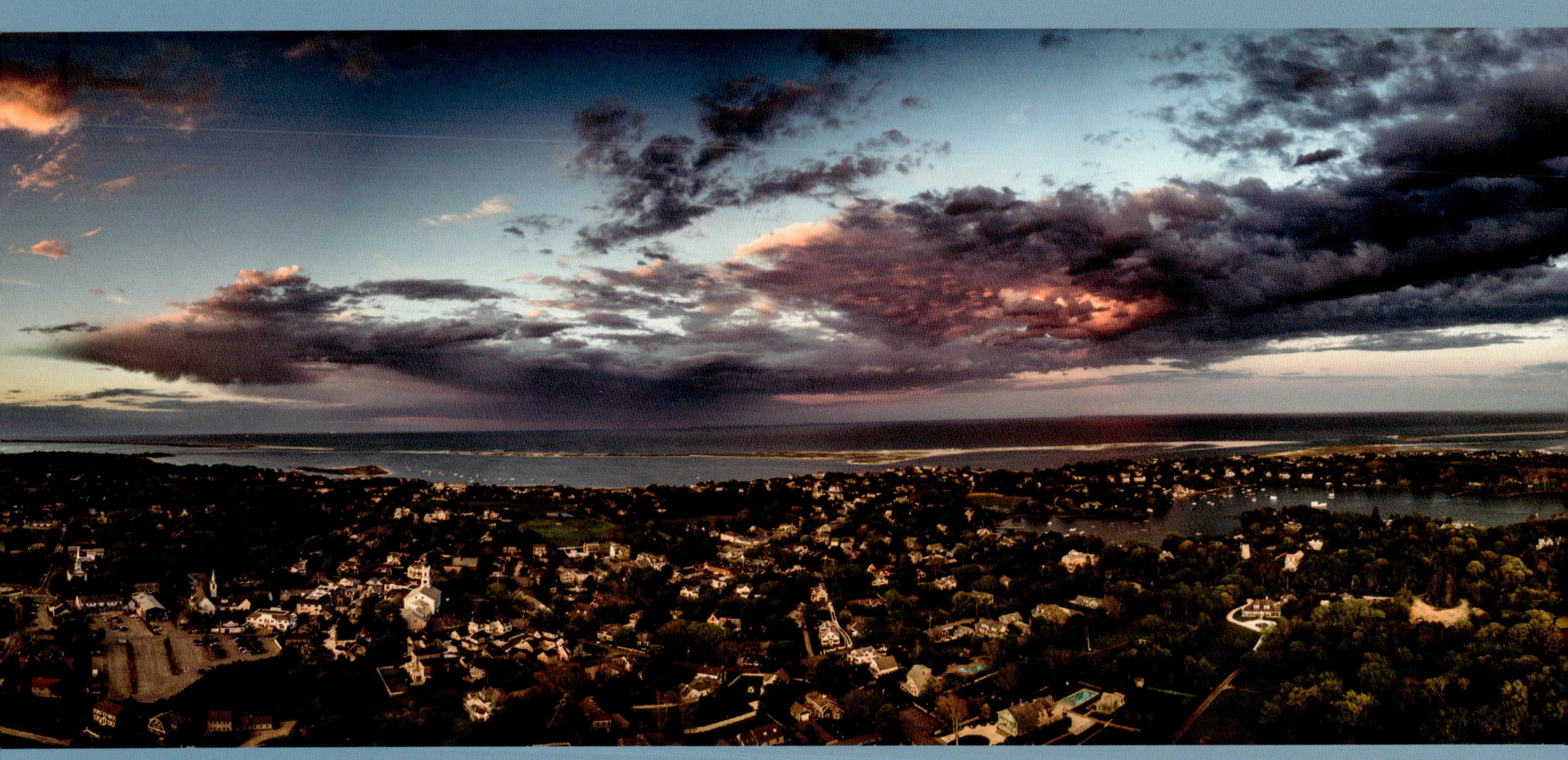

"Fight Night" - Two squalls duke it out like boxers in the ring on their way out to the Atlantic at sunset. Eventually one will consume the other, but no one will ever know who won.

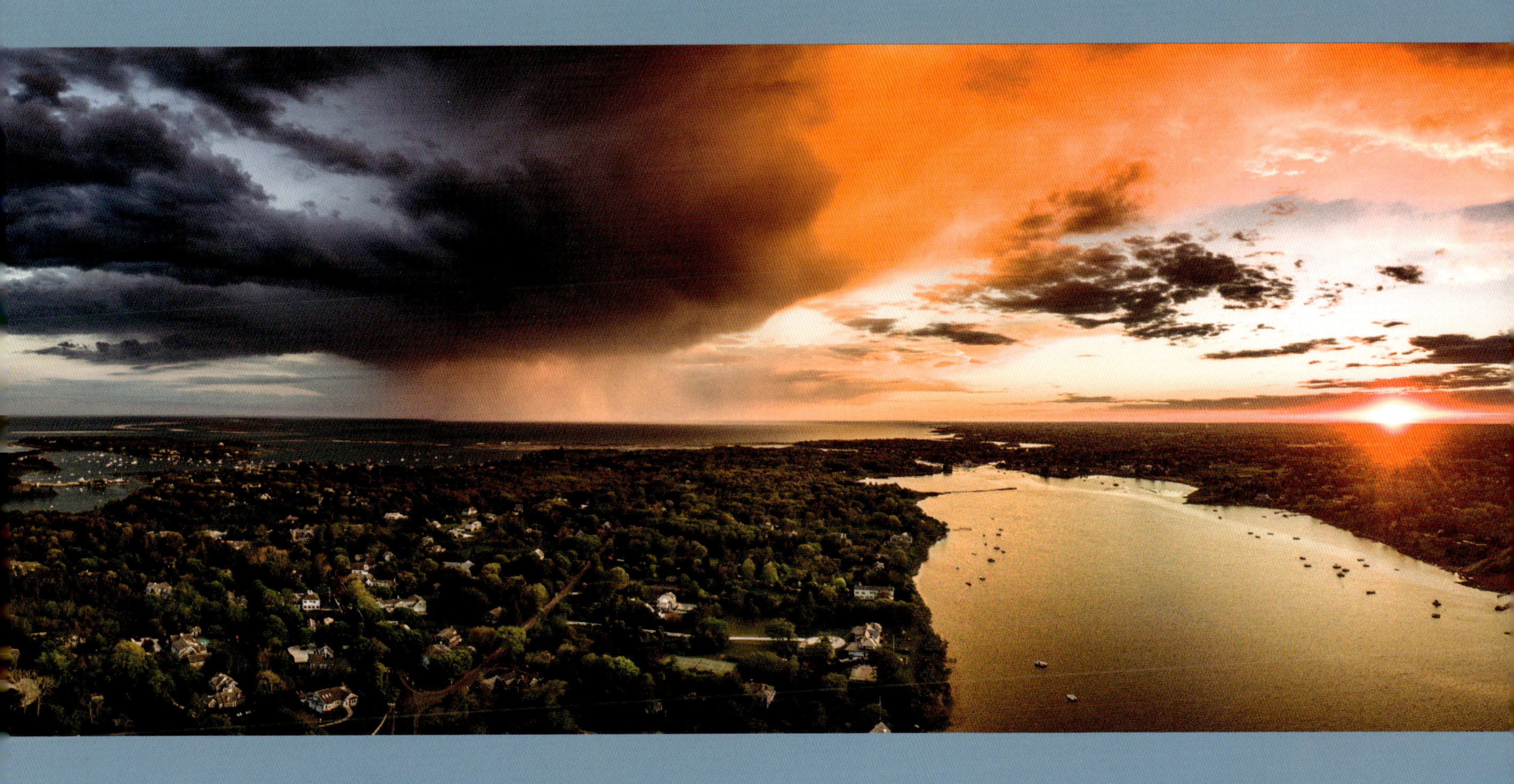

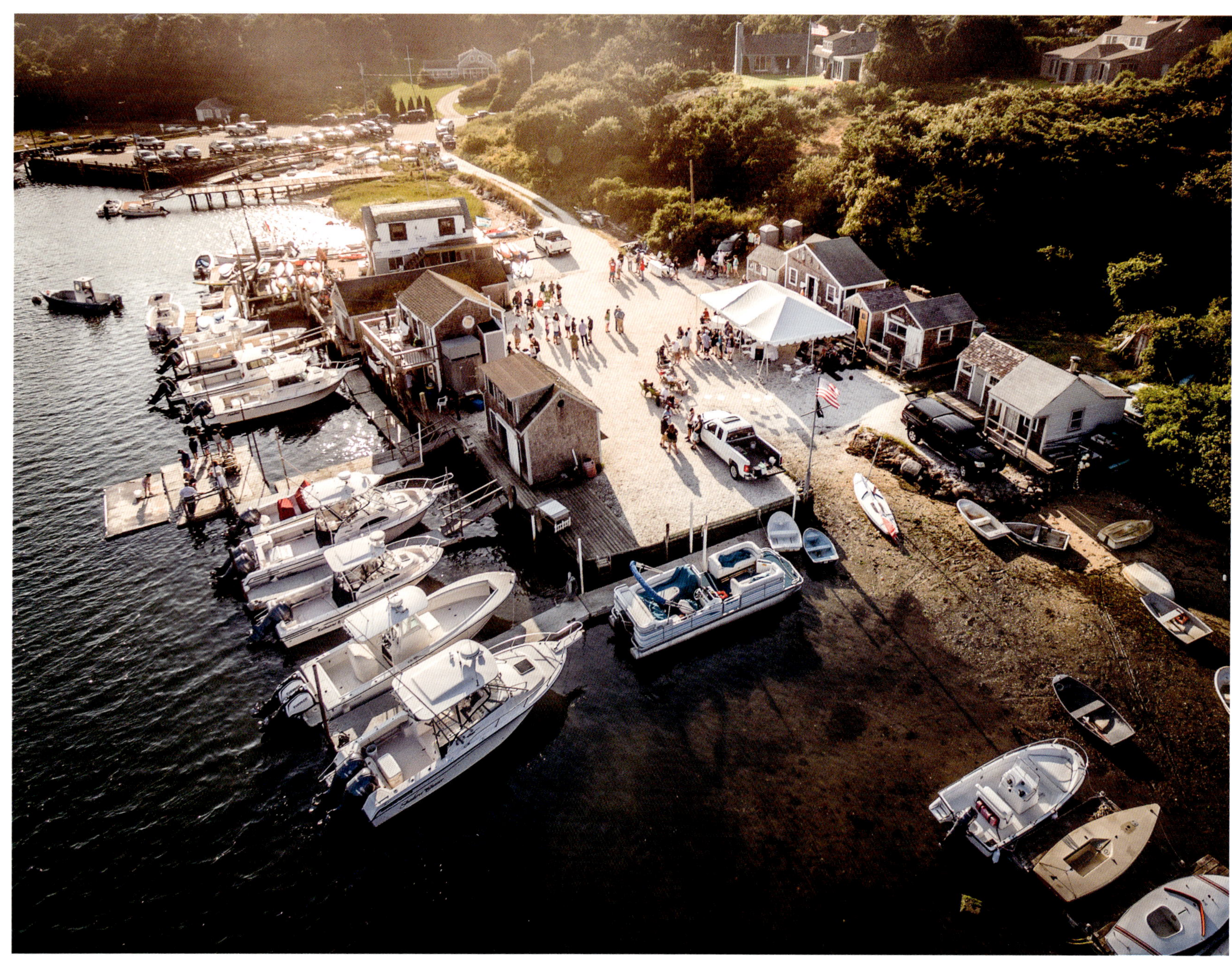

The annual Labor Day party at the oyster shanties.

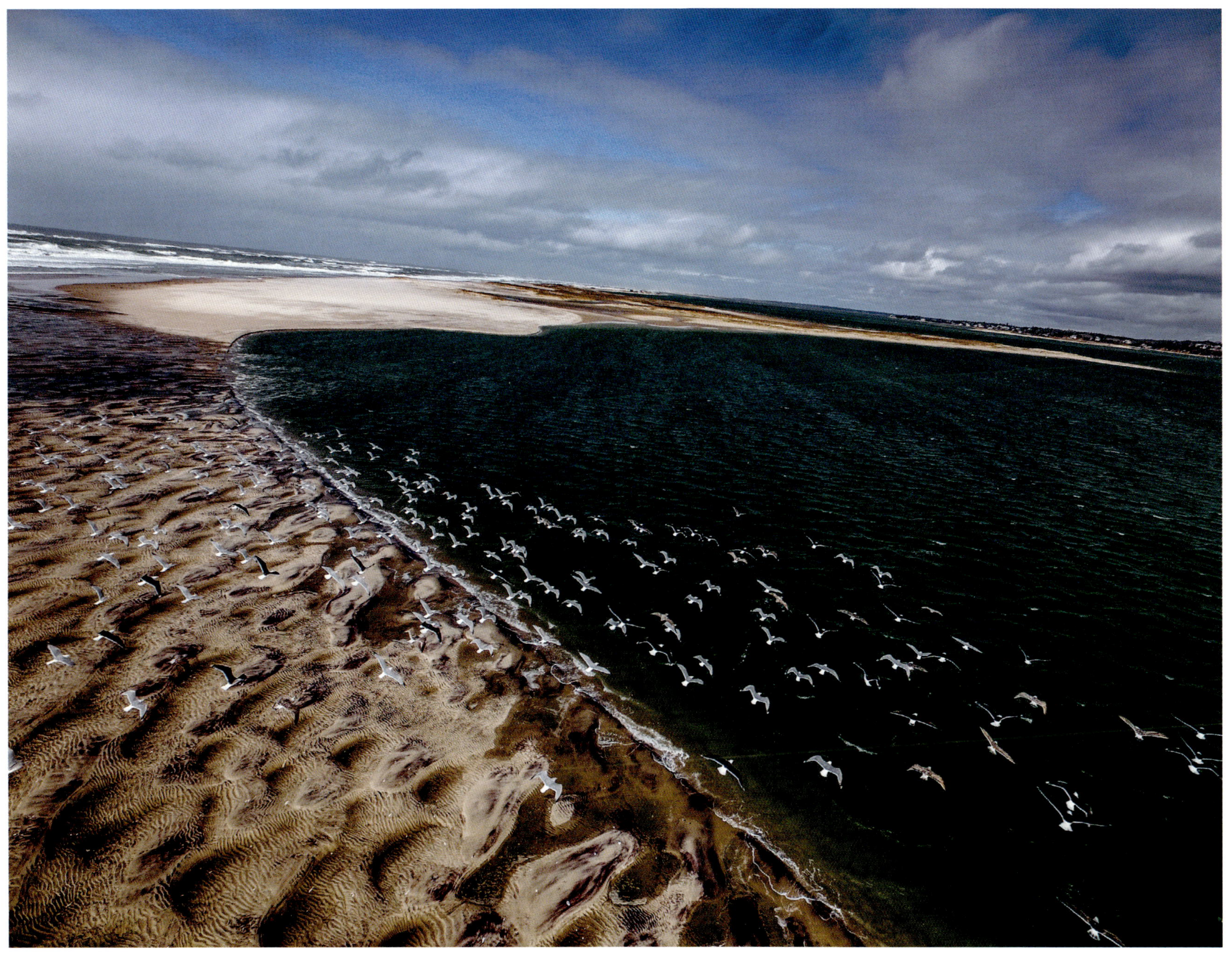

Gulls take off in unison.

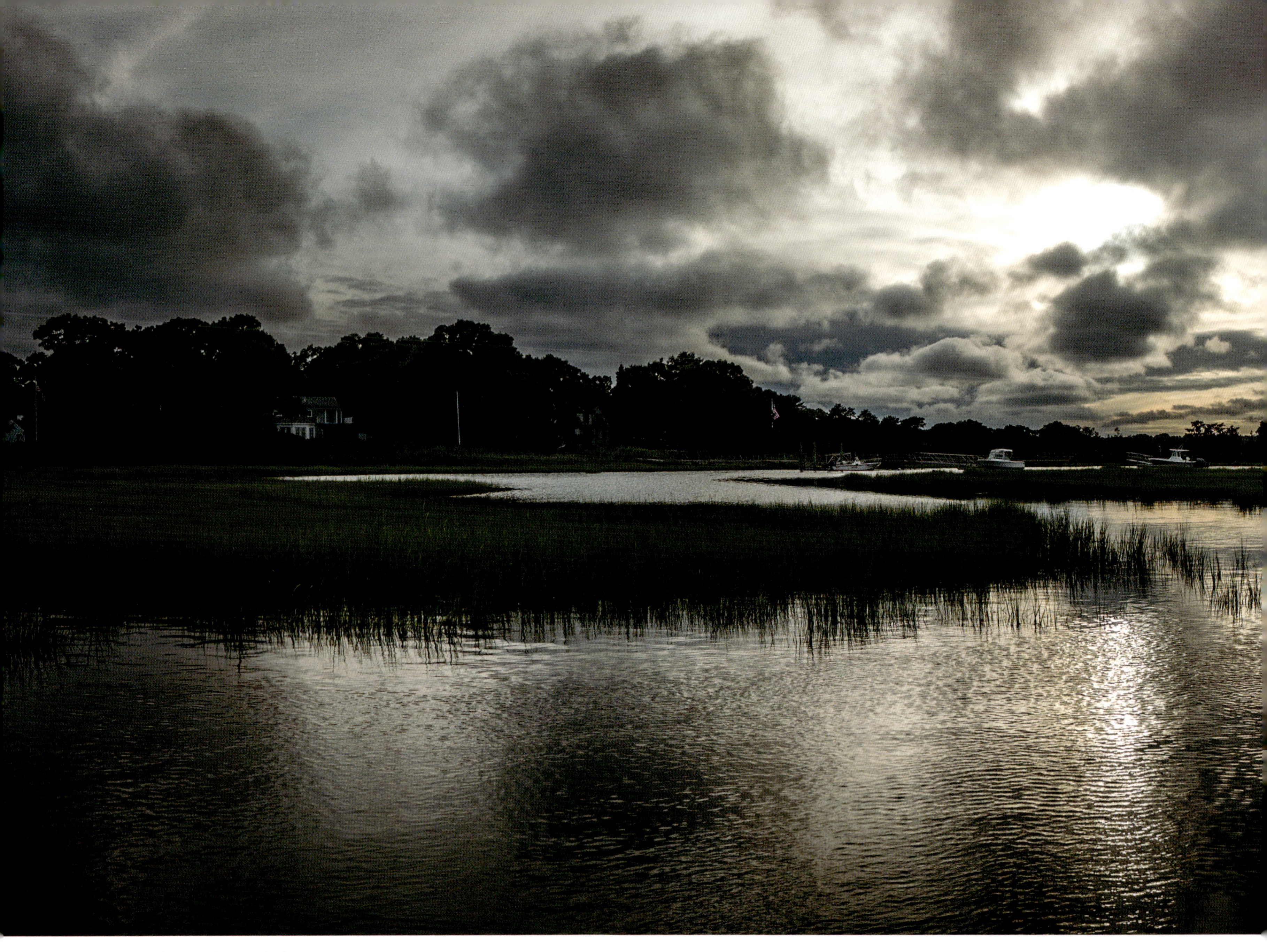

The marshes of Osterville just before sunset.

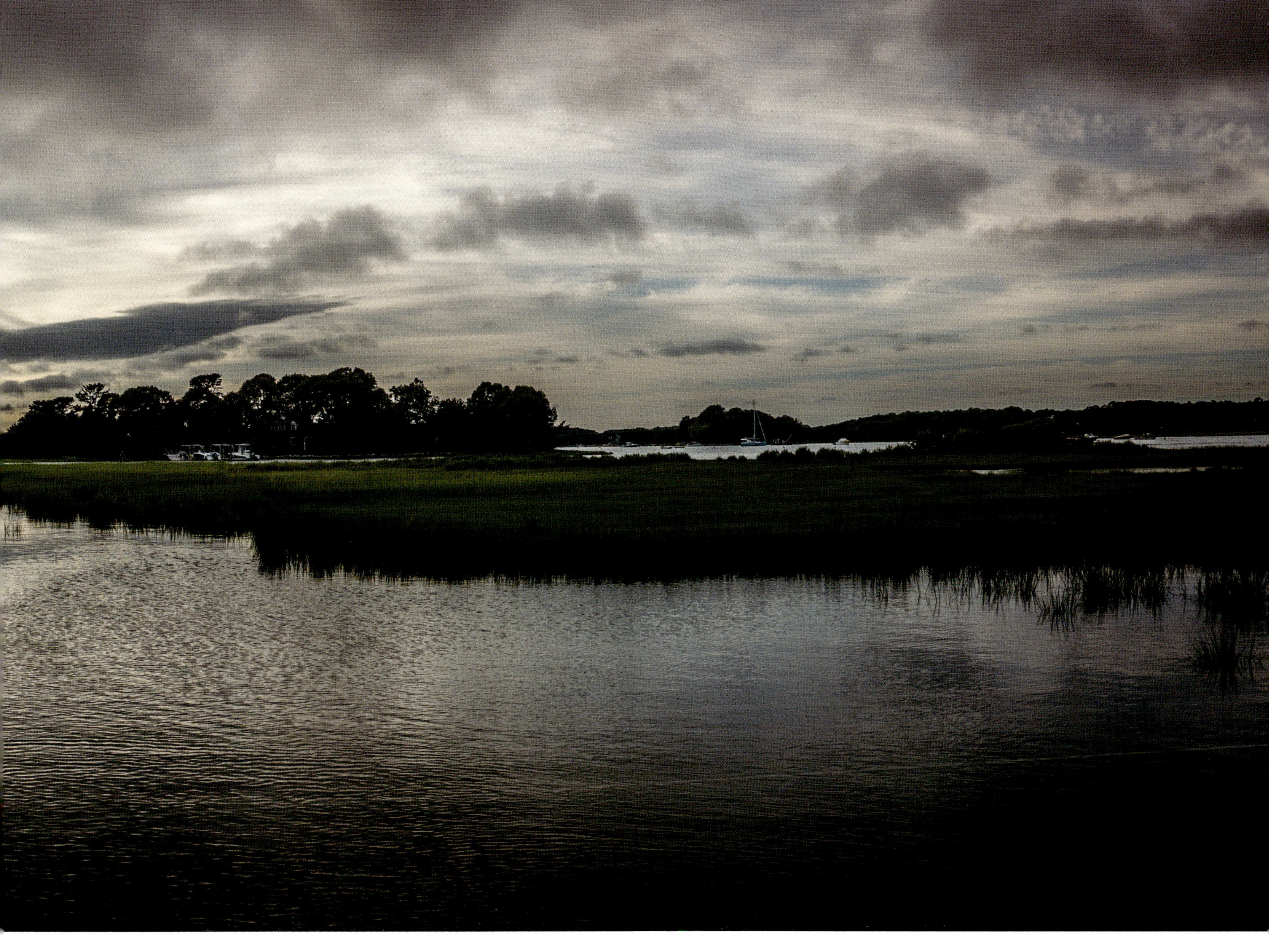

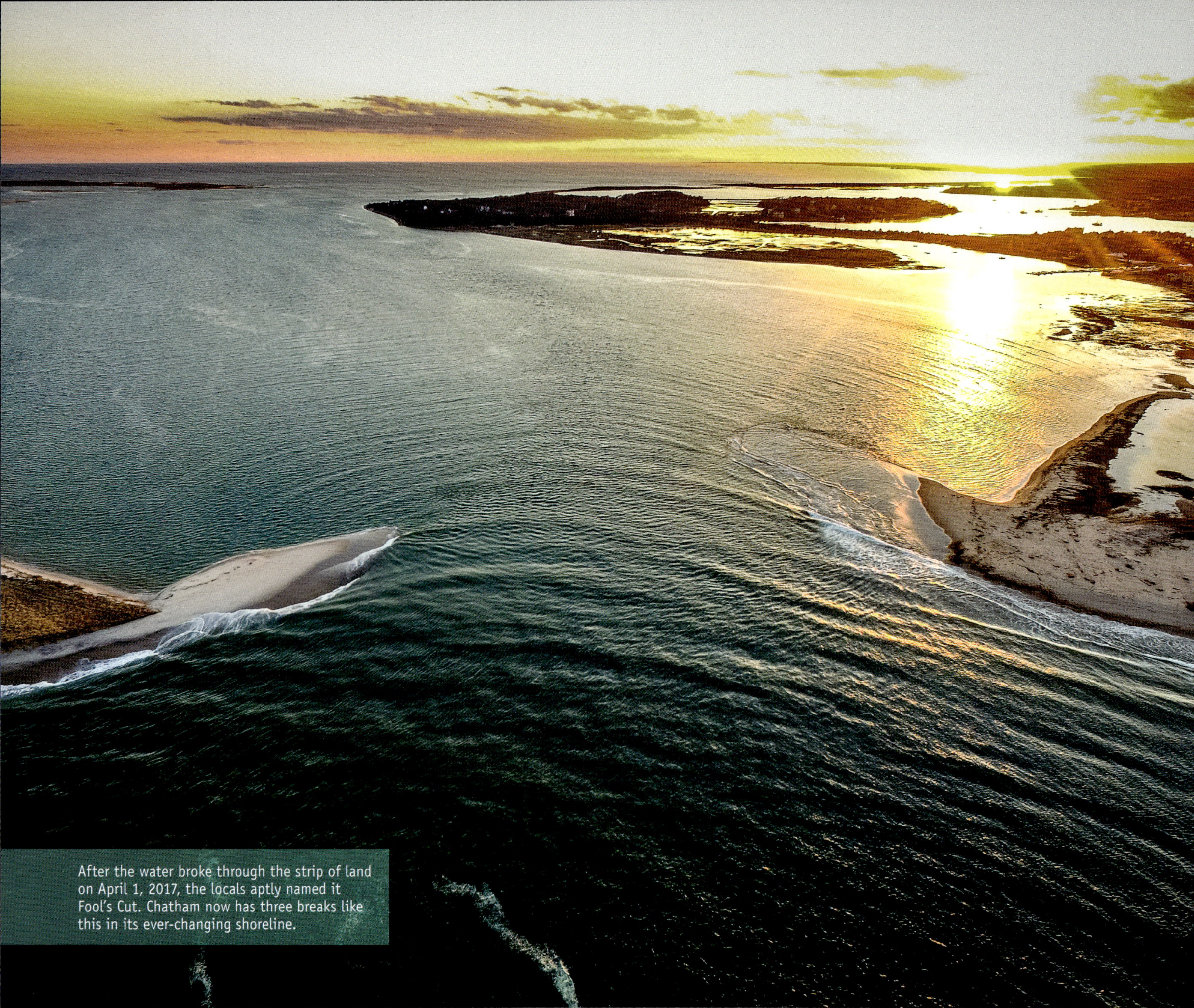

After the water broke through the strip of land on April 1, 2017, the locals aptly named it Fool's Cut. Chatham now has three breaks like this in its ever-changing shoreline.

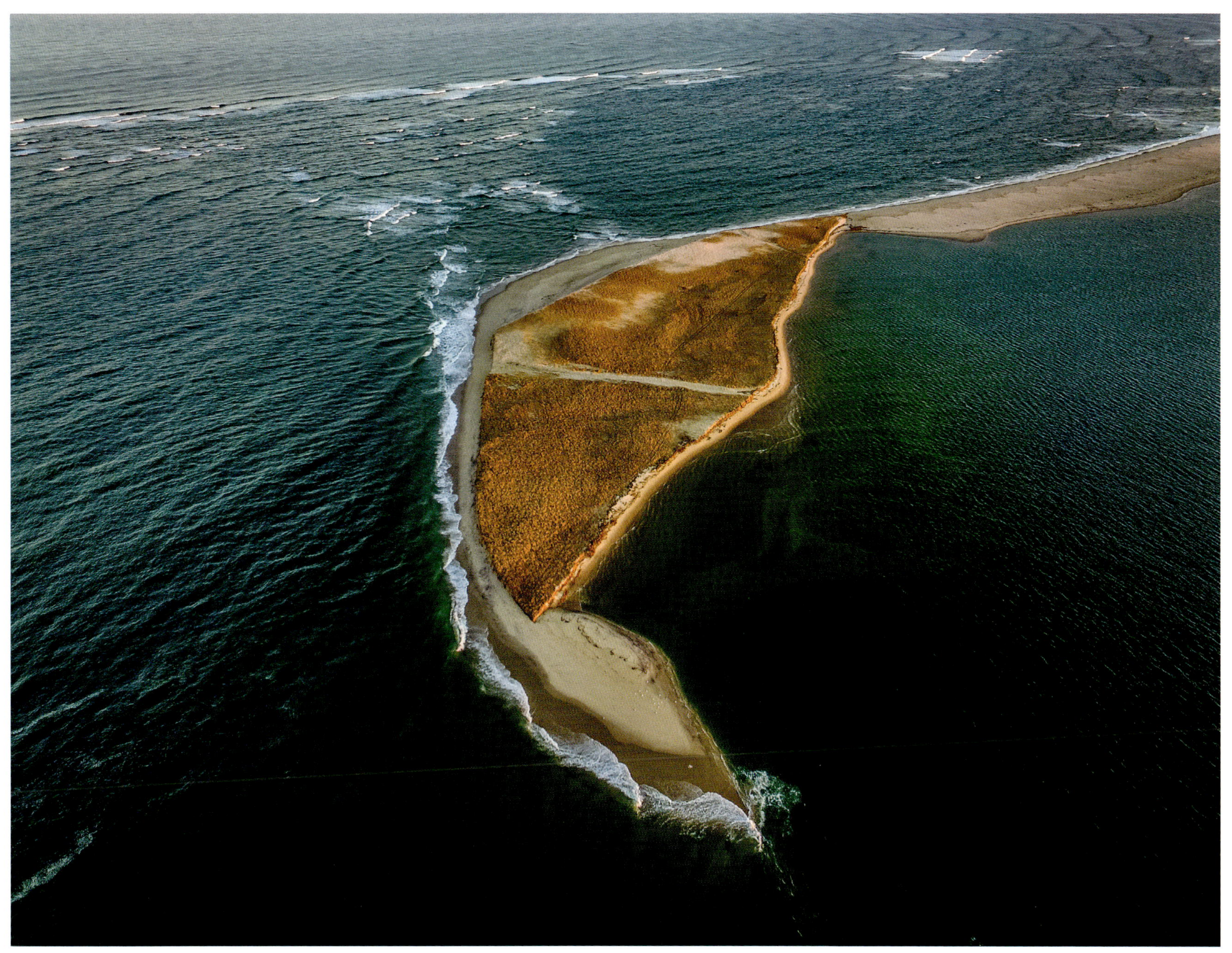

The southern portion of Fool's Cut was attached to the mainland until recently.

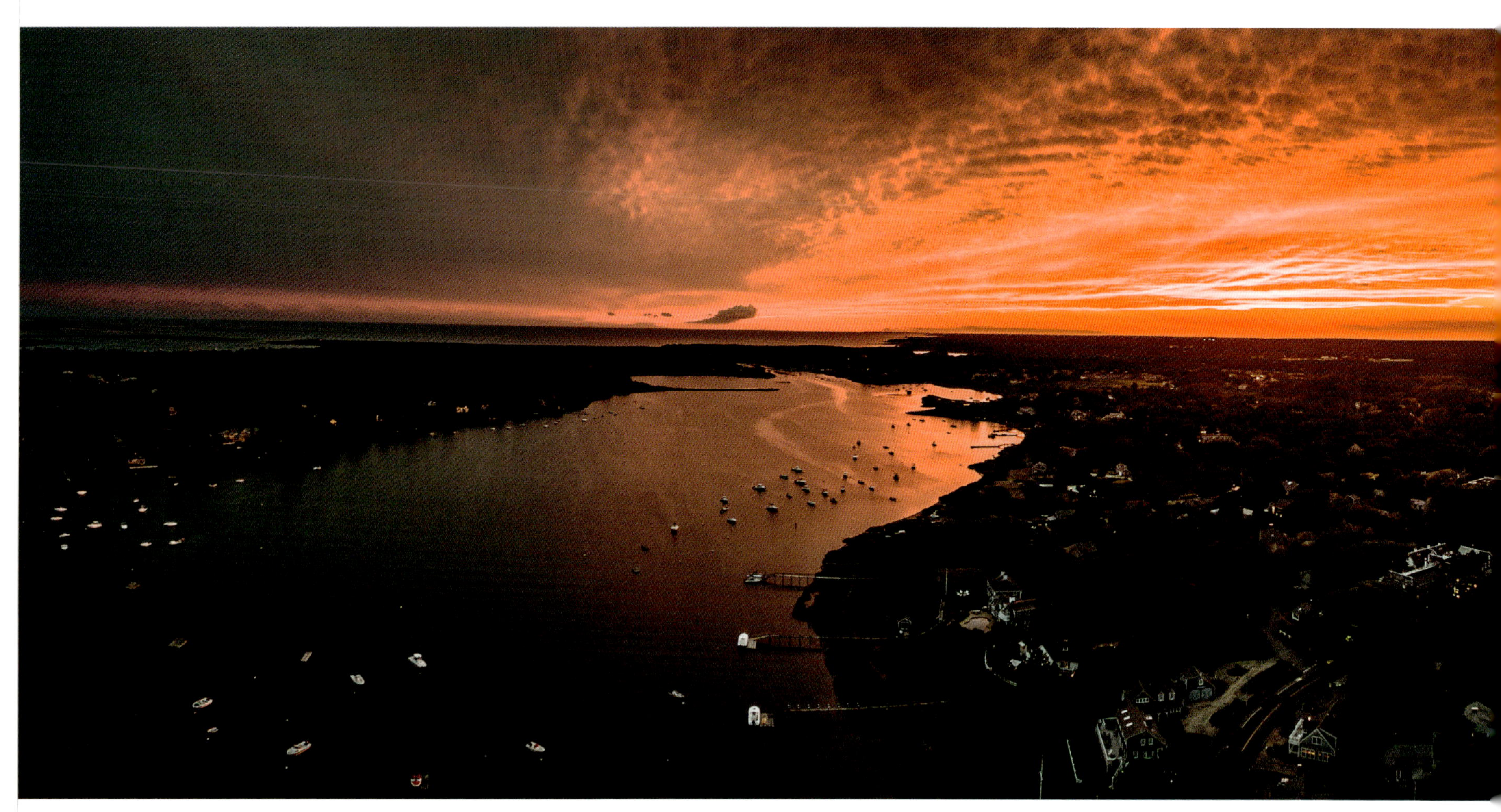

“Goodnight Chatham” - The Chatham Anglers play Cape League ball at Veteran’s Field in July at sunset.

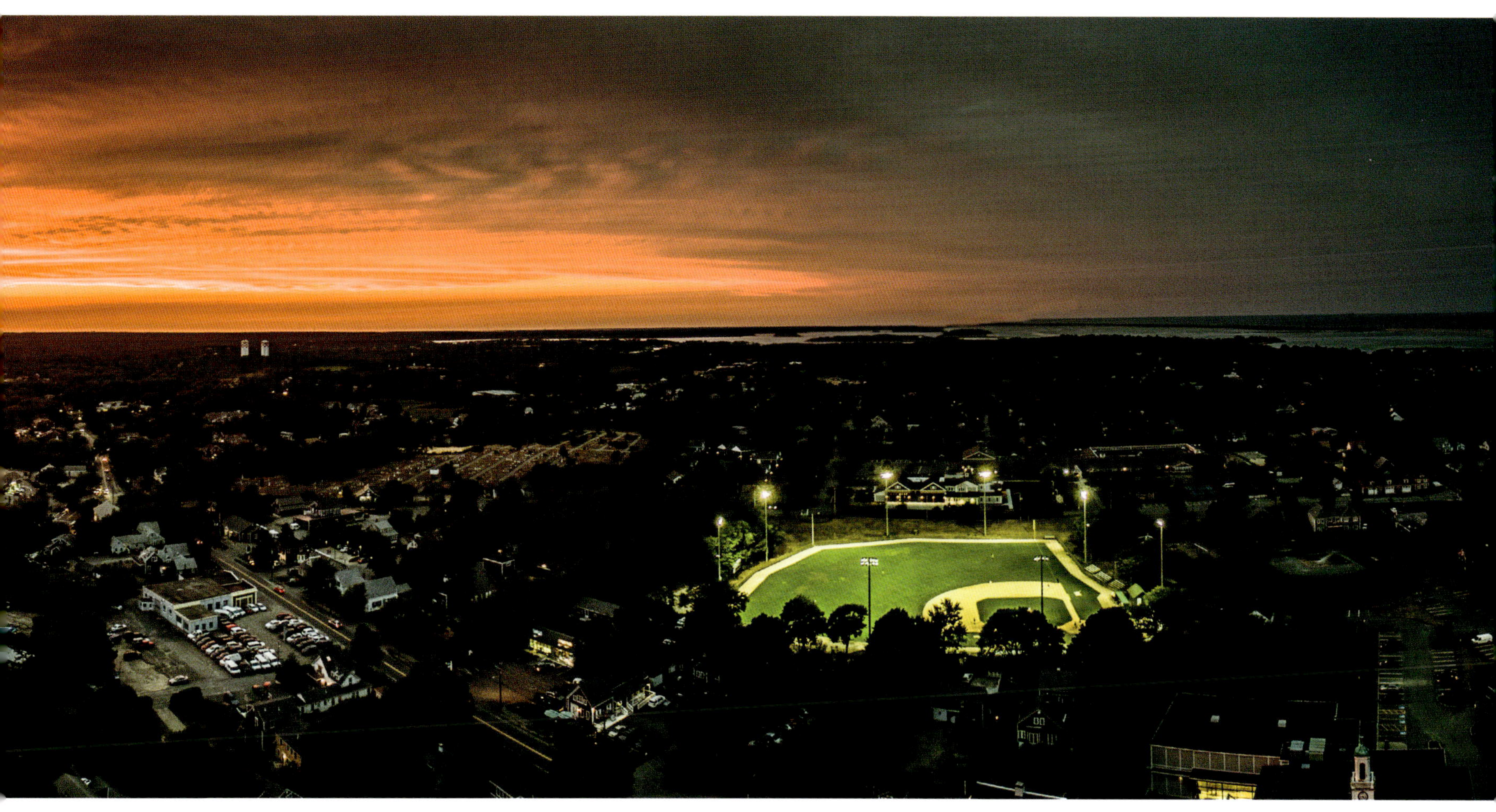

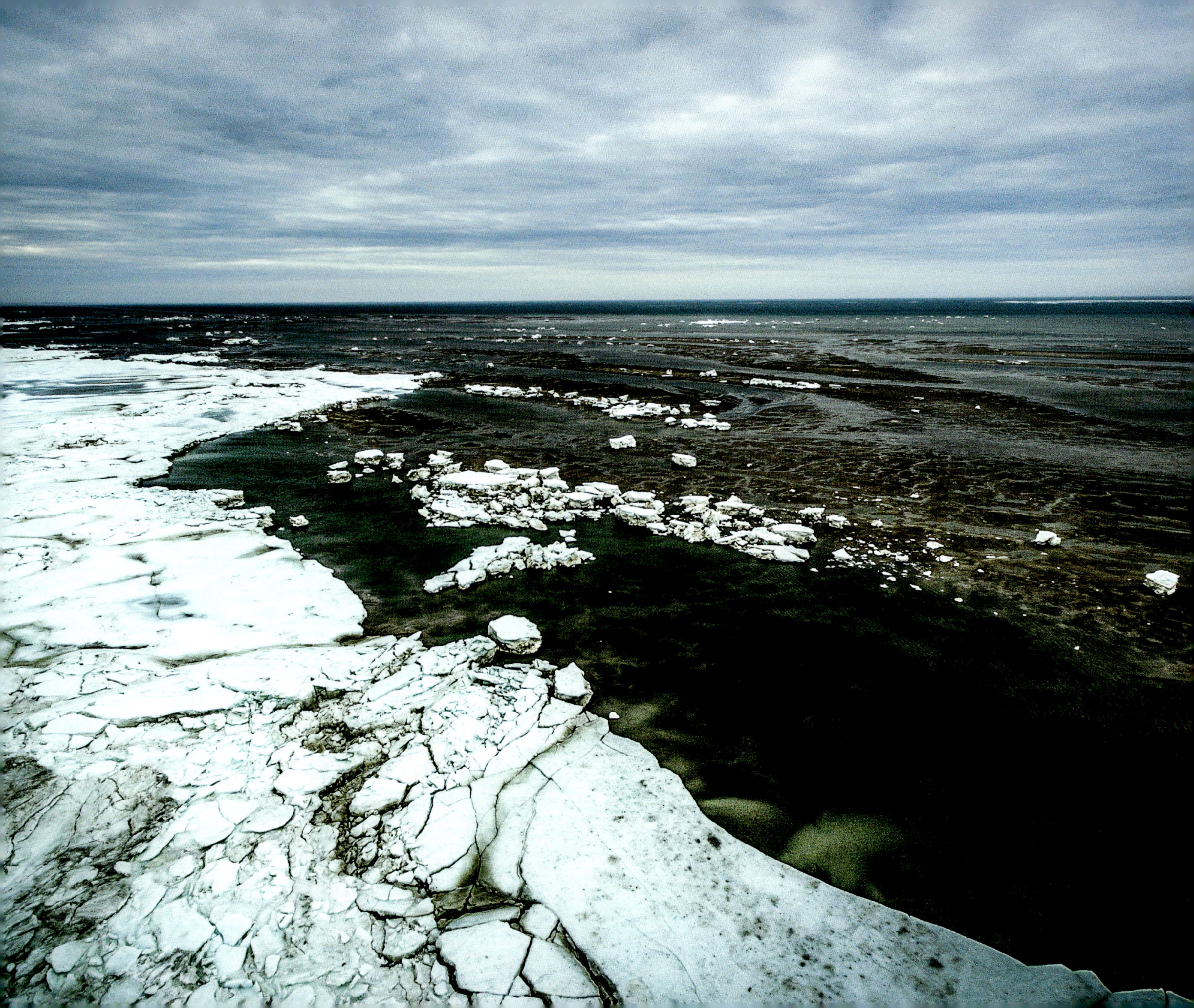

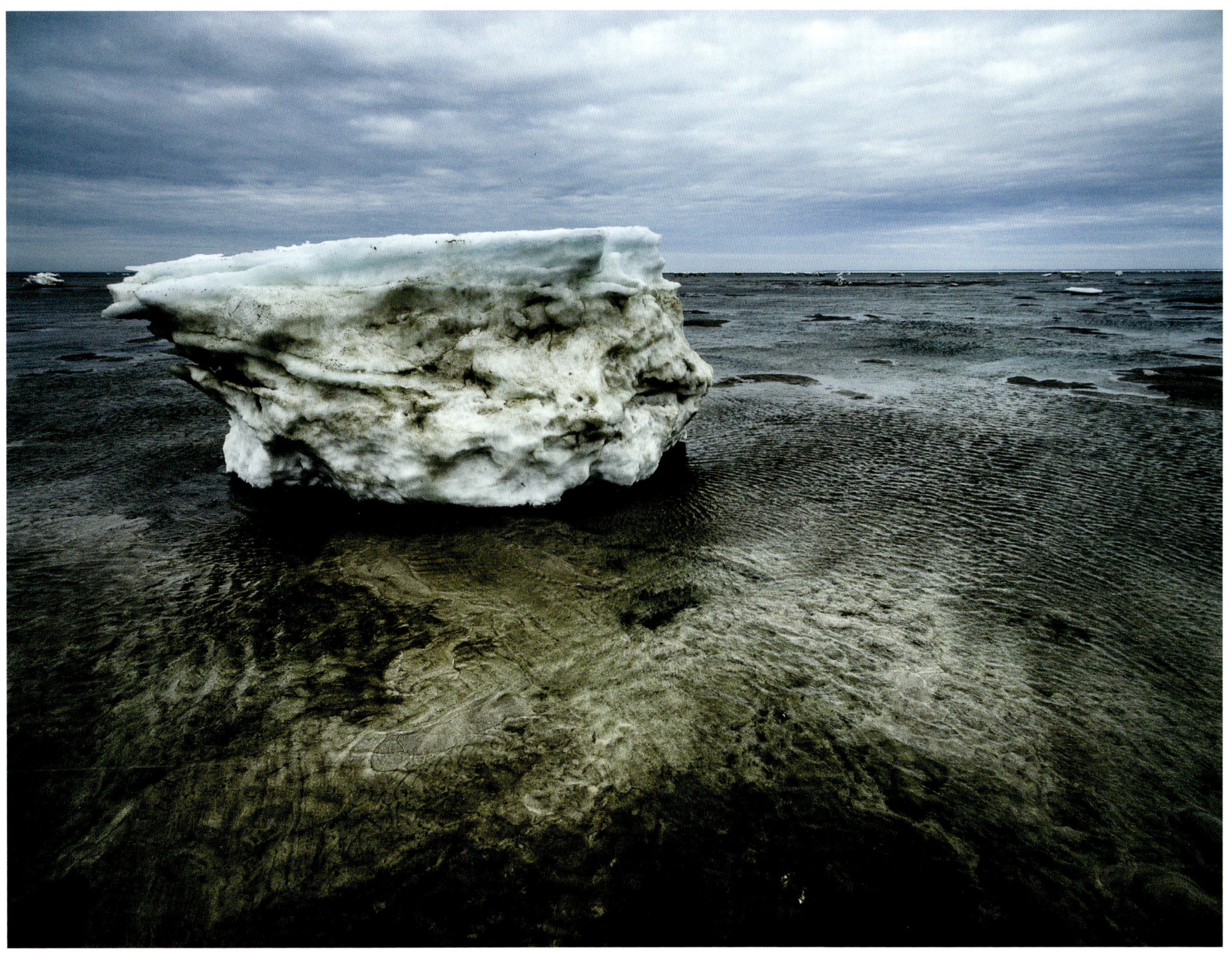

Icebergs break apart in Cape Cod Bay after a deep freeze.

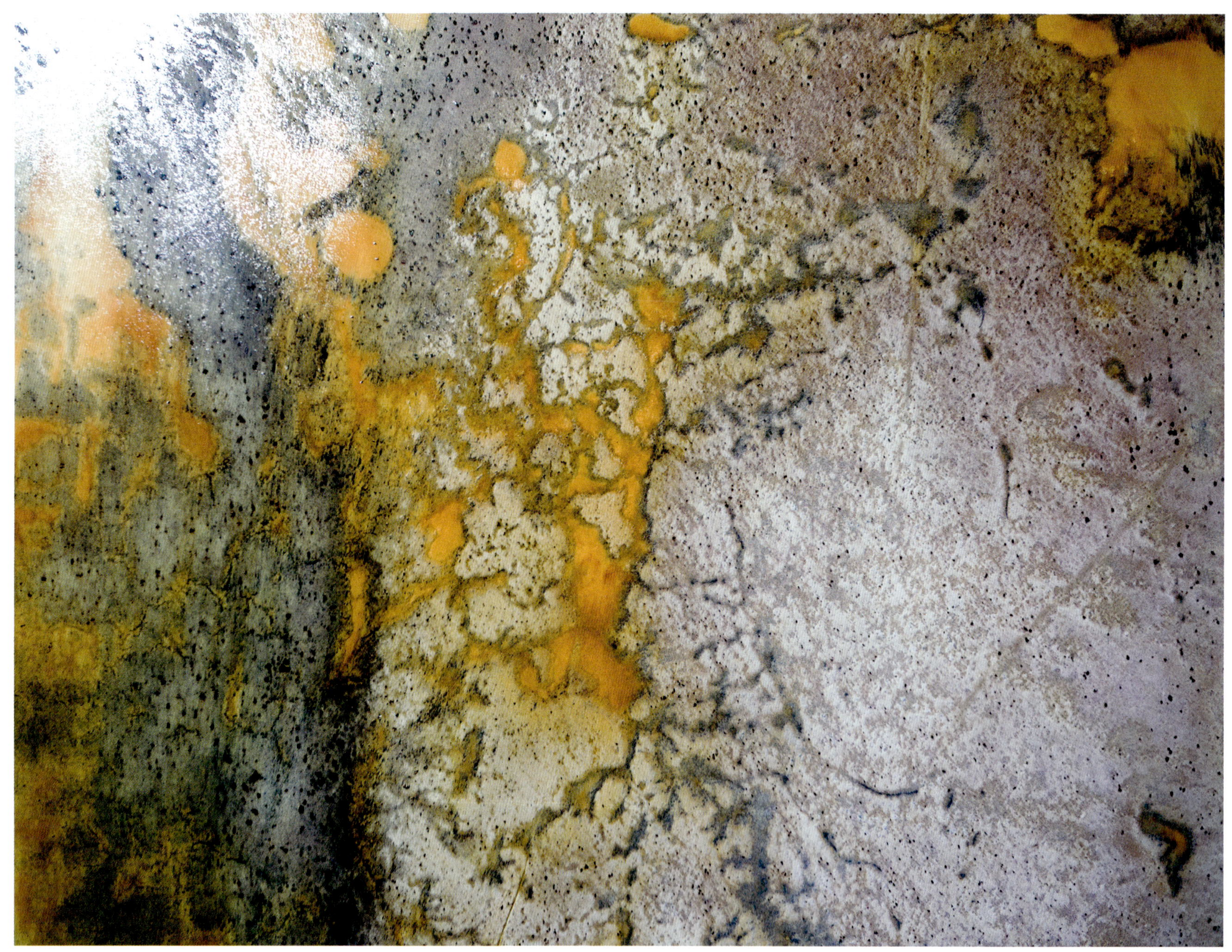

Looking down on the combination of plant life, muck, and laminated layers of silt that makes up a tidal plain at low tide.

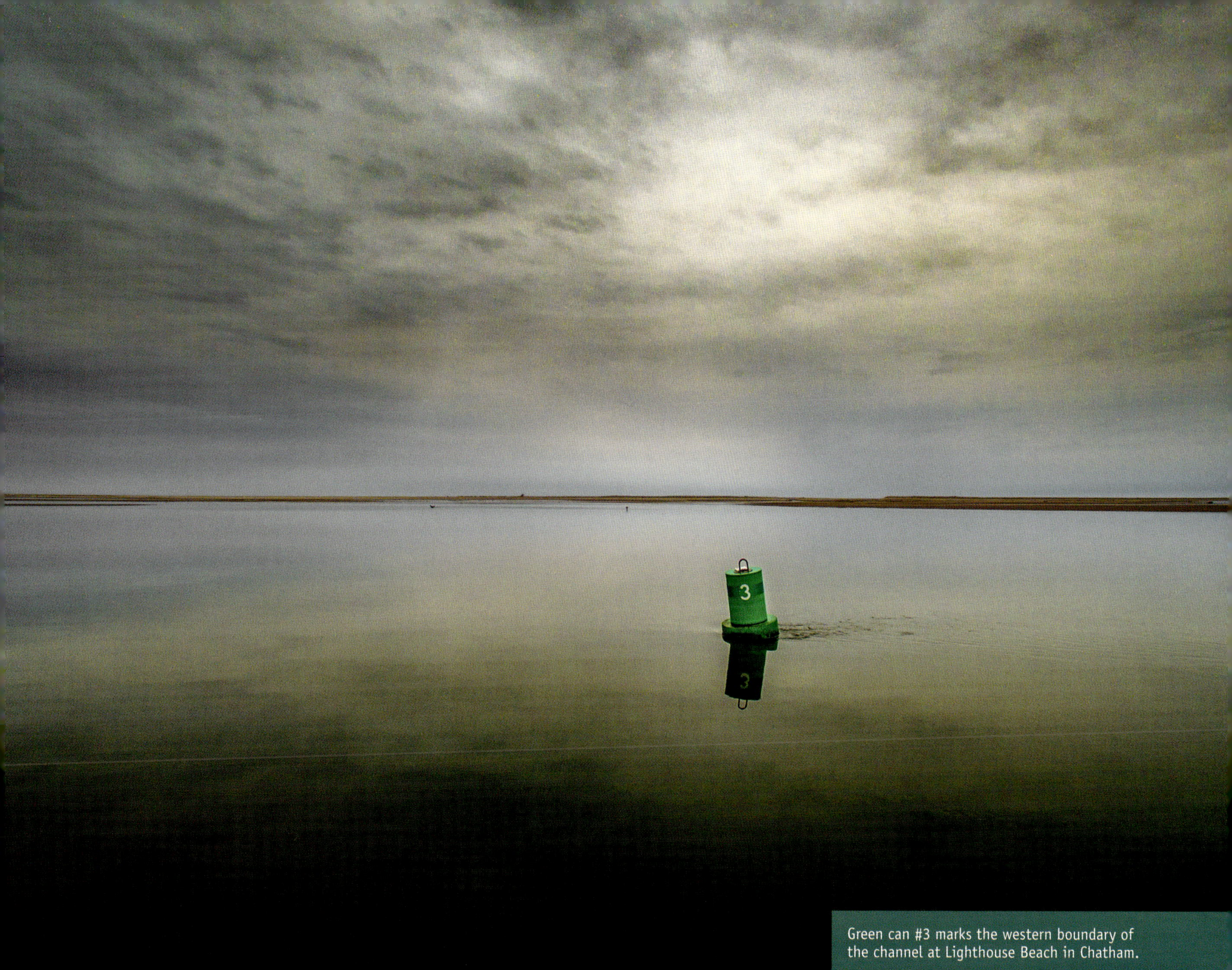

Green can #3 marks the western boundary of the channel at Lighthouse Beach in Chatham.

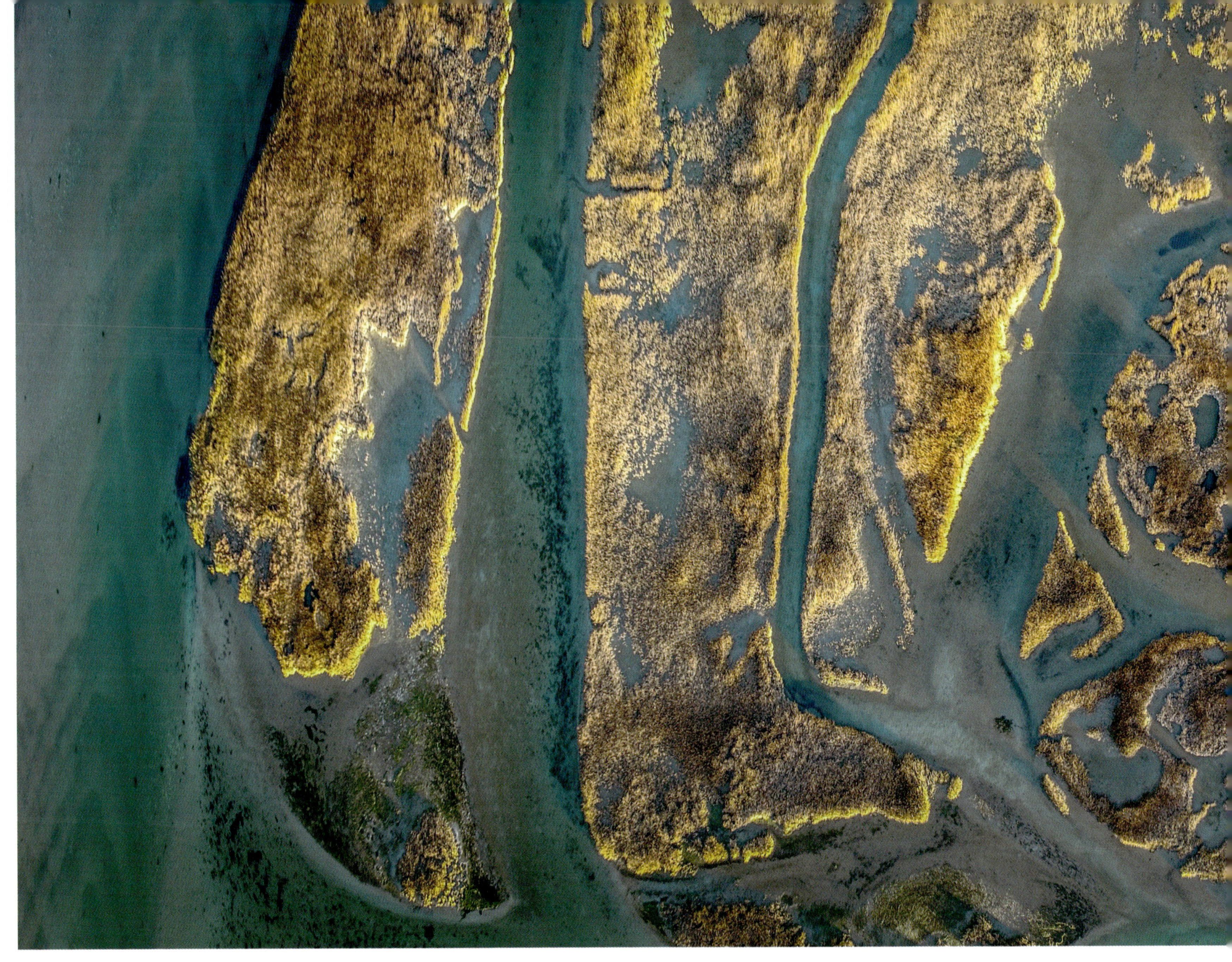

A twelve-shot panorama of Great Marsh in the national seashore.

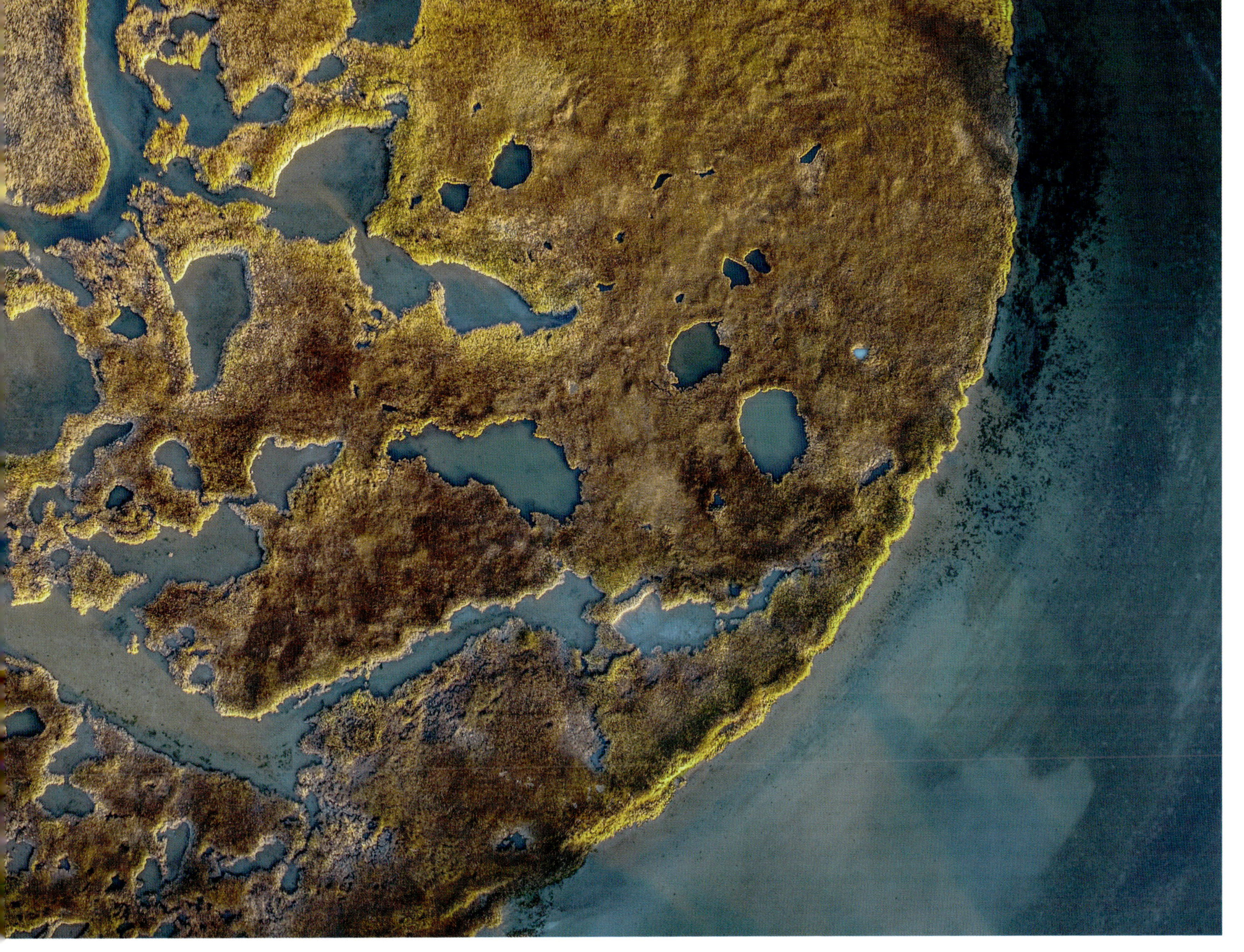

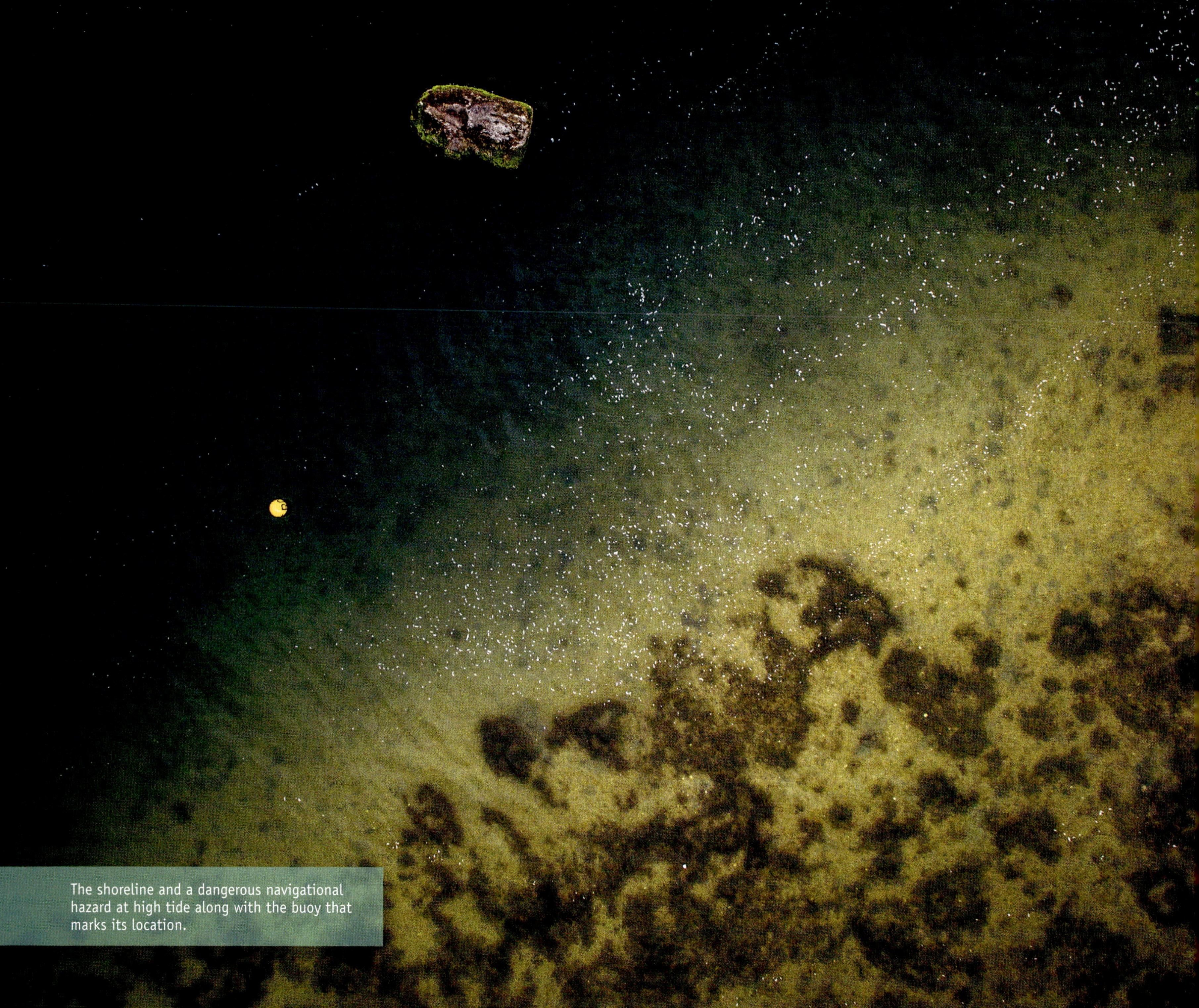

The shoreline and a dangerous navigational hazard at high tide along with the buoy that marks its location.

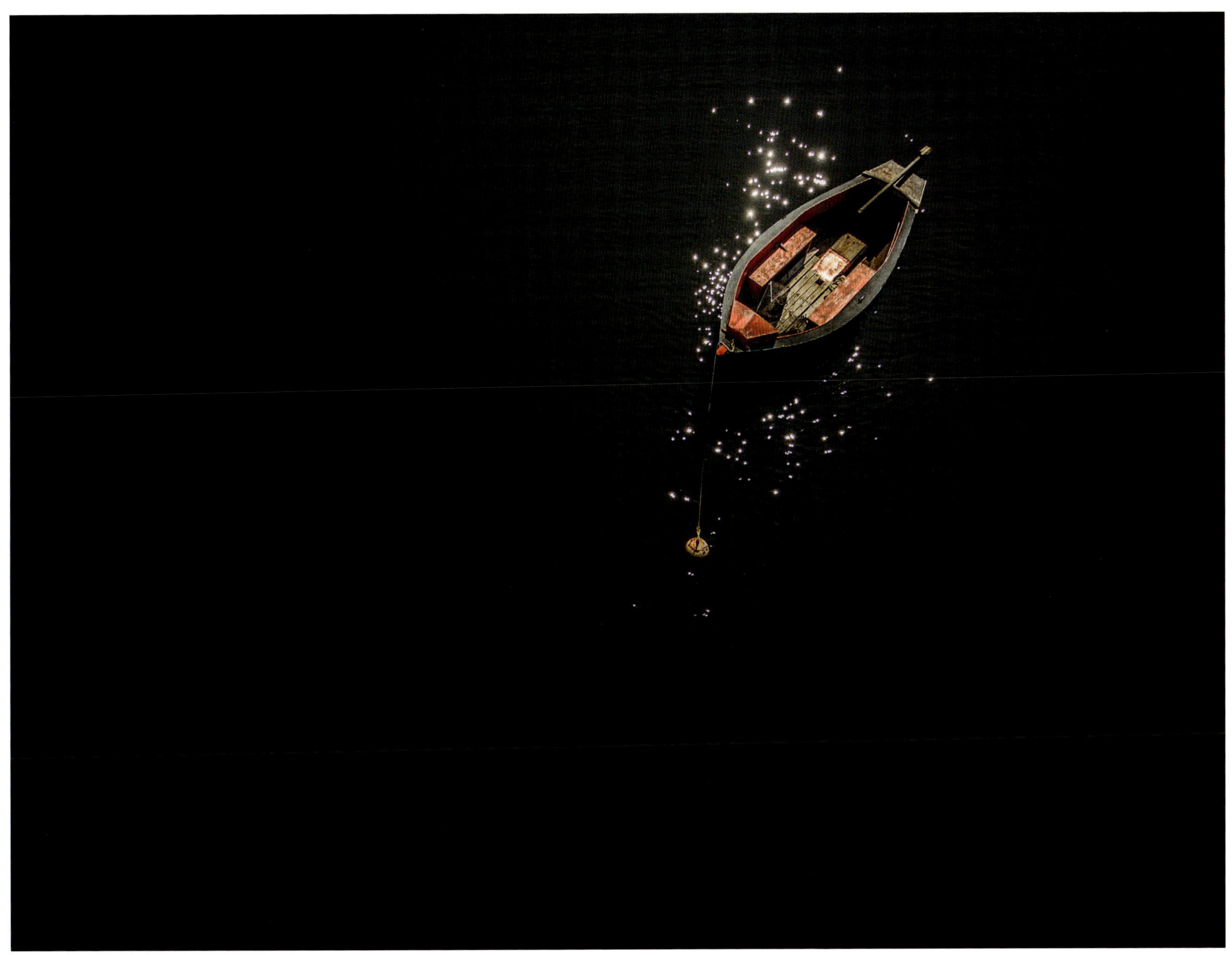

The sun reflects off the water like diamonds while *Hero* keeps watch on the Herring River.

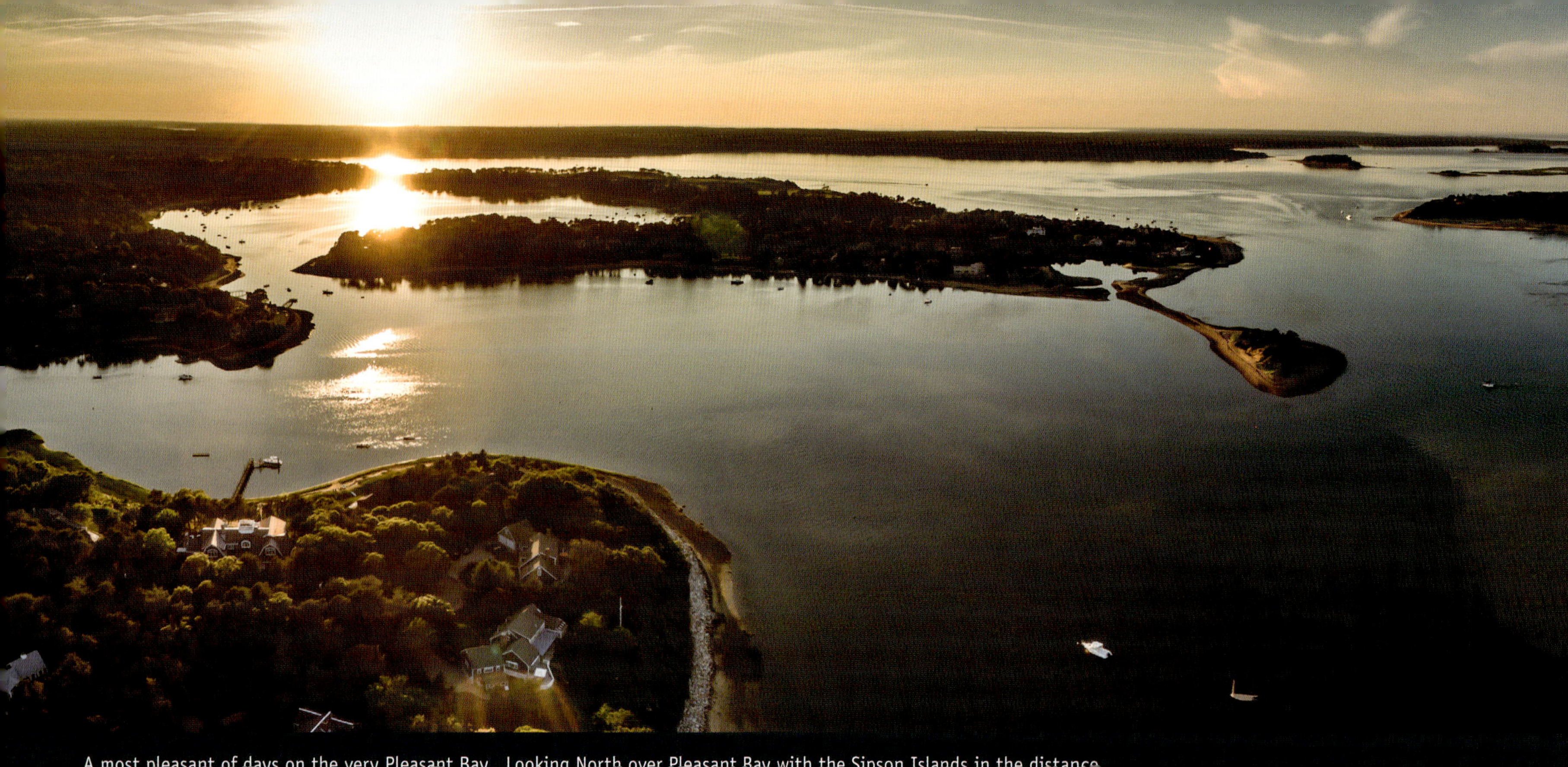

A most pleasant of days on the very Pleasant Bay. Looking North over Pleasant Bay with the Sipson Islands in the distance.

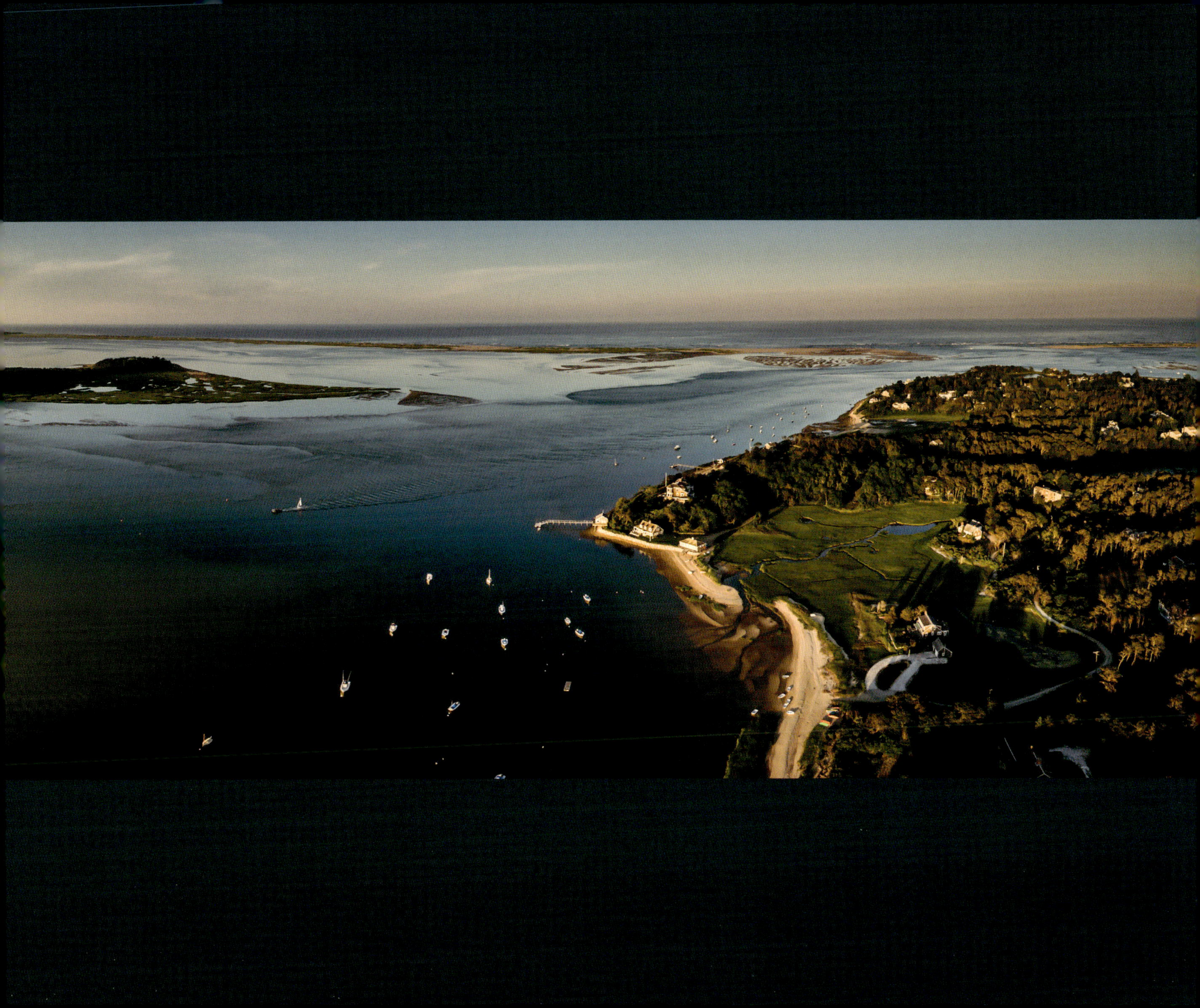

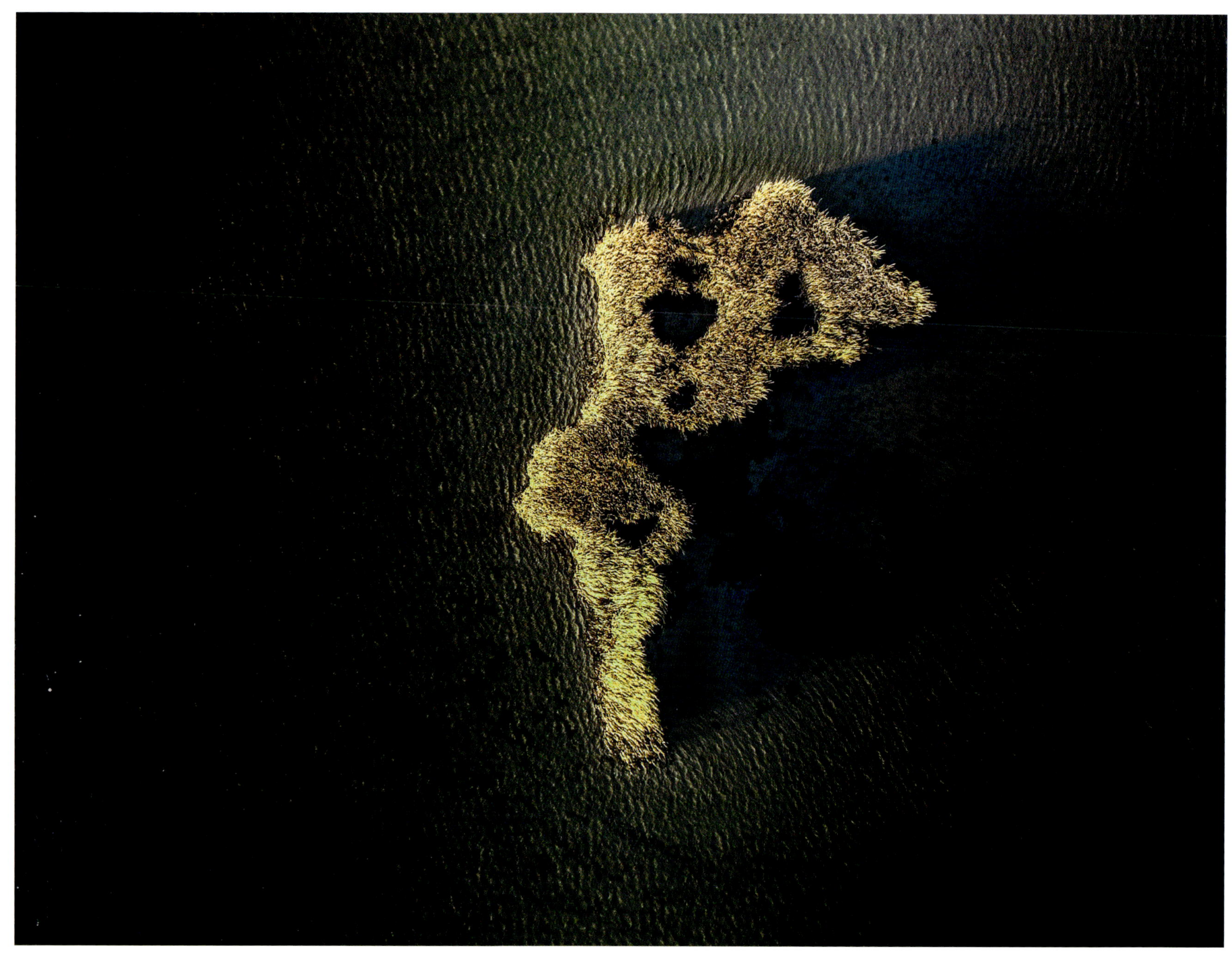

"Into the Jungle" - Looking down over a lone patch of seagrass rising above the tide in the salt marshes of Eastham.

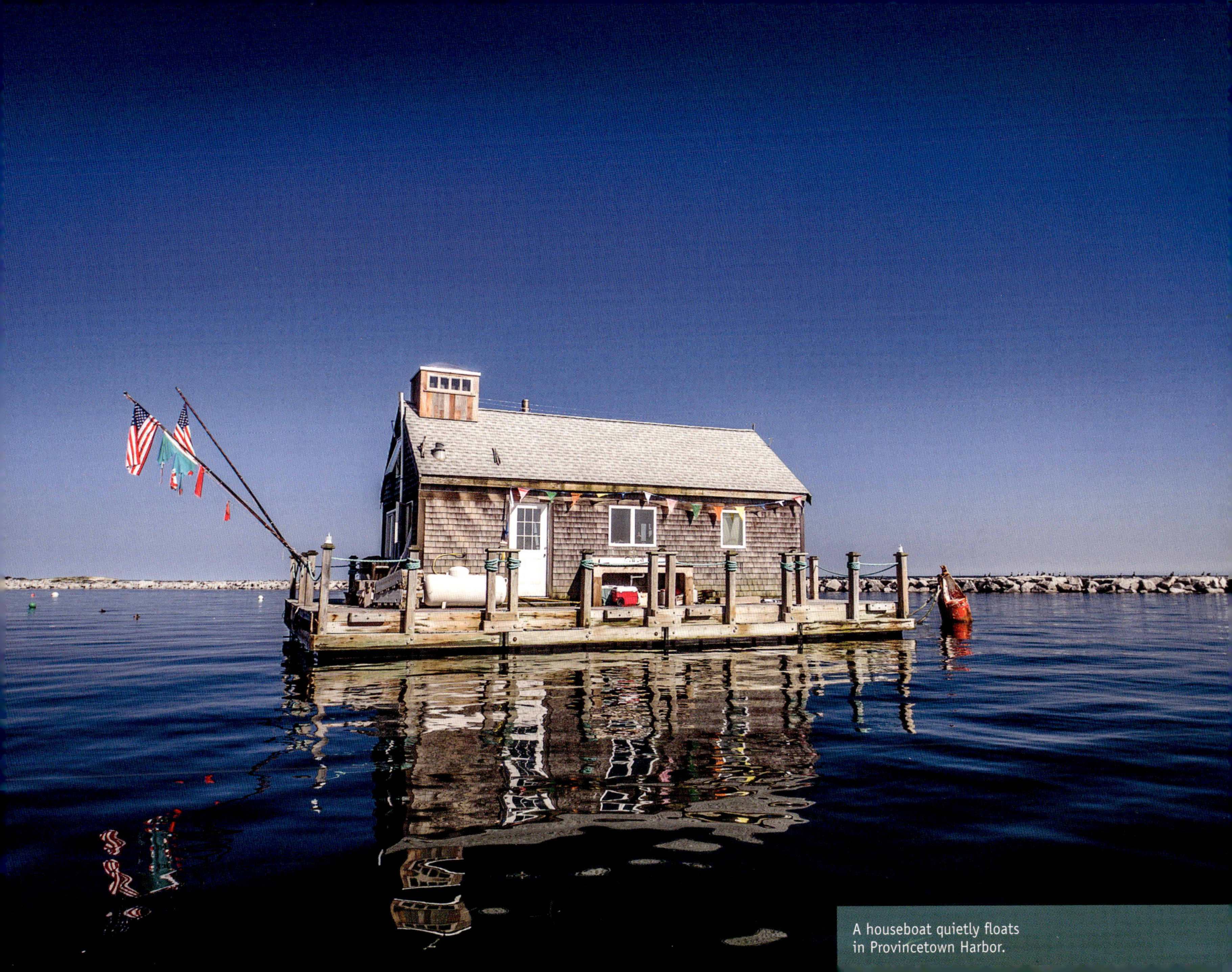

A houseboat quietly floats in Provincetown Harbor.

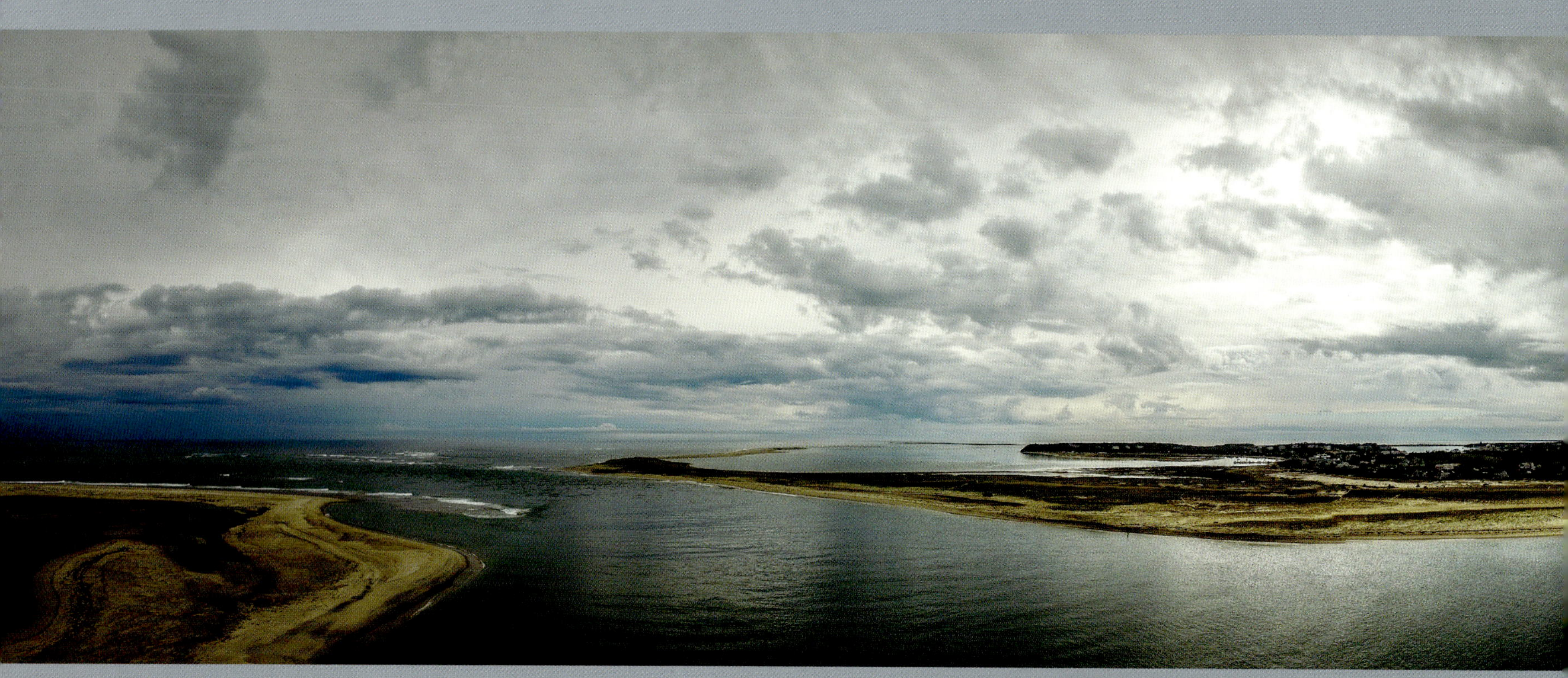

A storm approaches from the west over Monomoy. Time to head home.

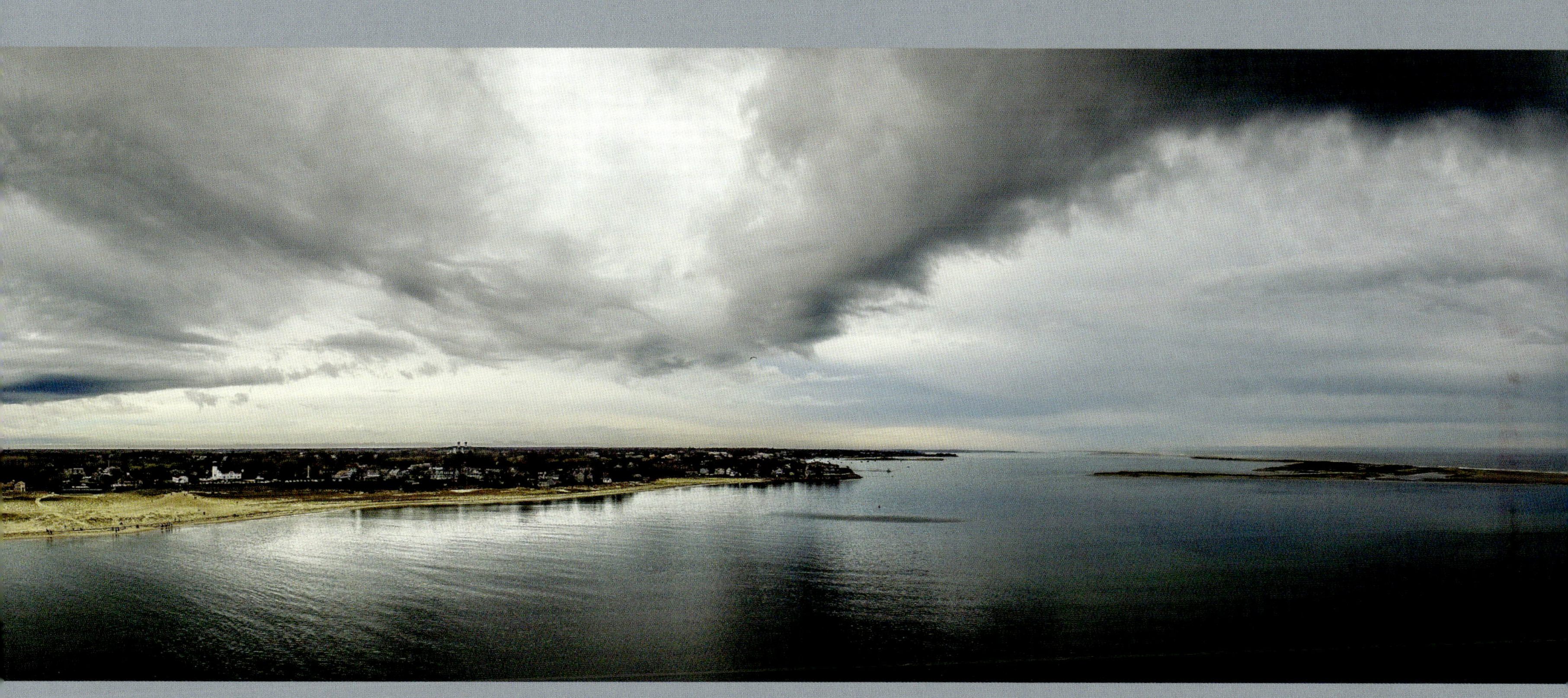

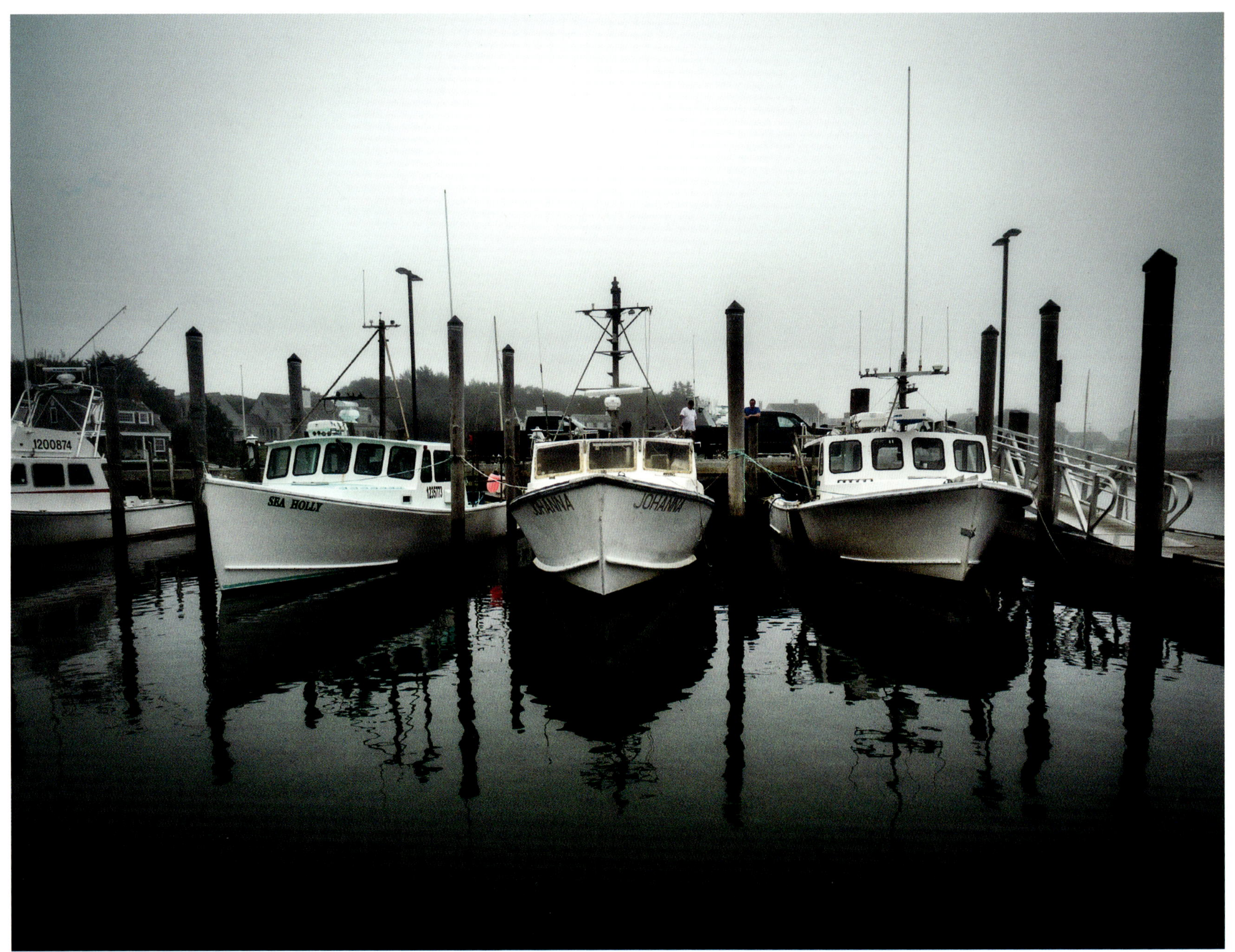

Johanna tied up alongside her two sisters on a foggy day in Harwichport.

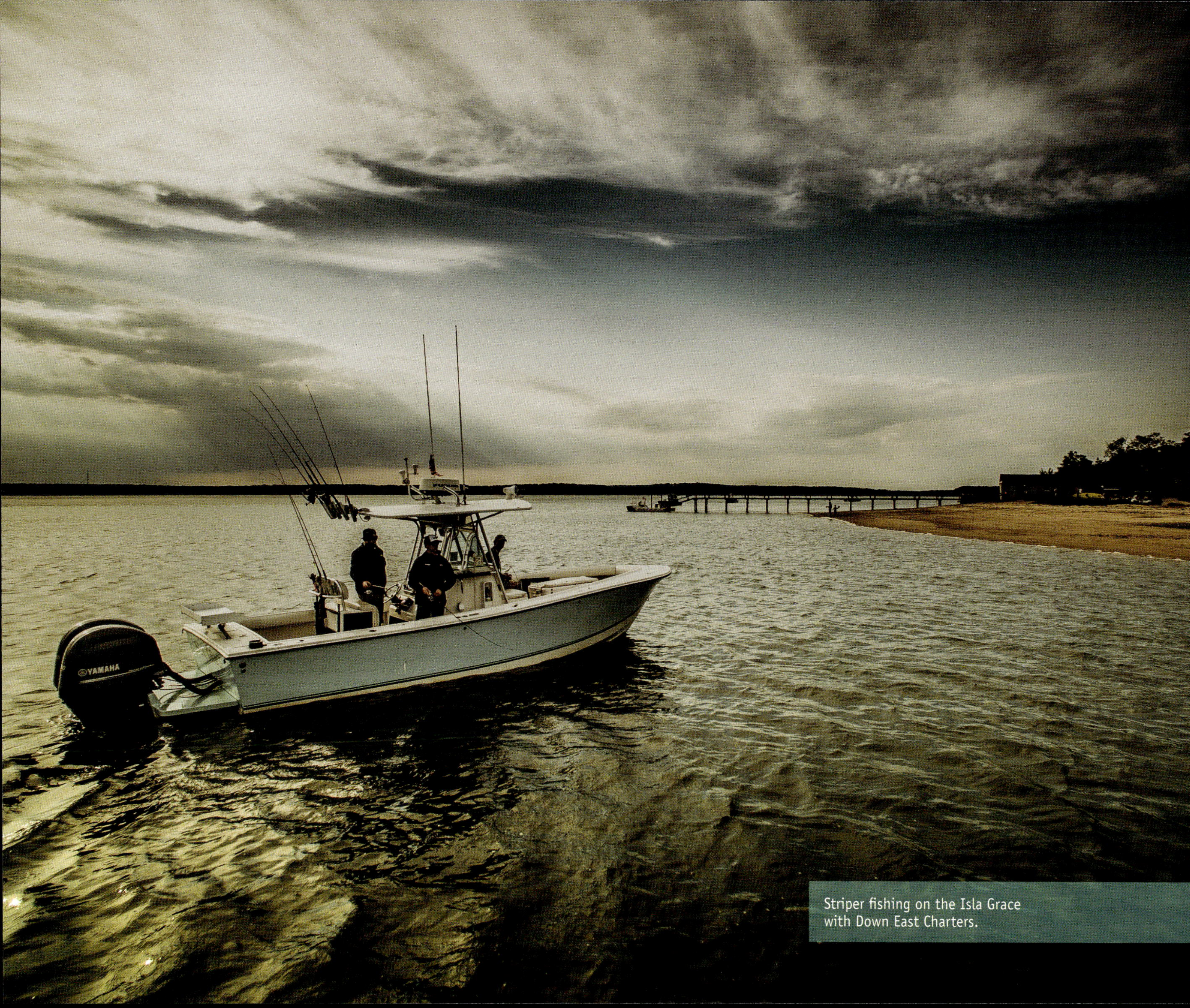

Striper fishing on the Isla Grace with Down East Charters.

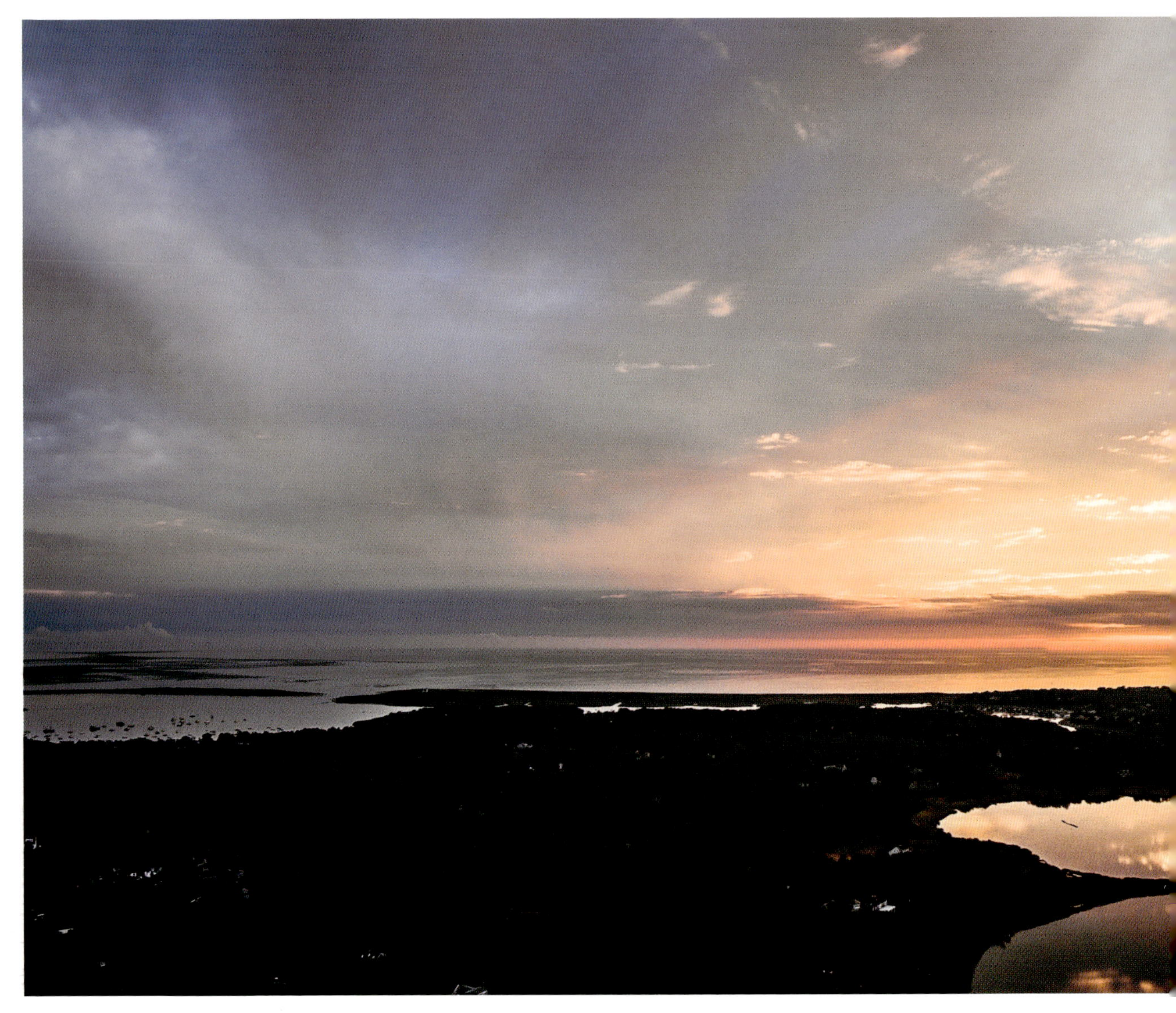

A single beam of sunlight fires down onto Oyster Pond at sunset.

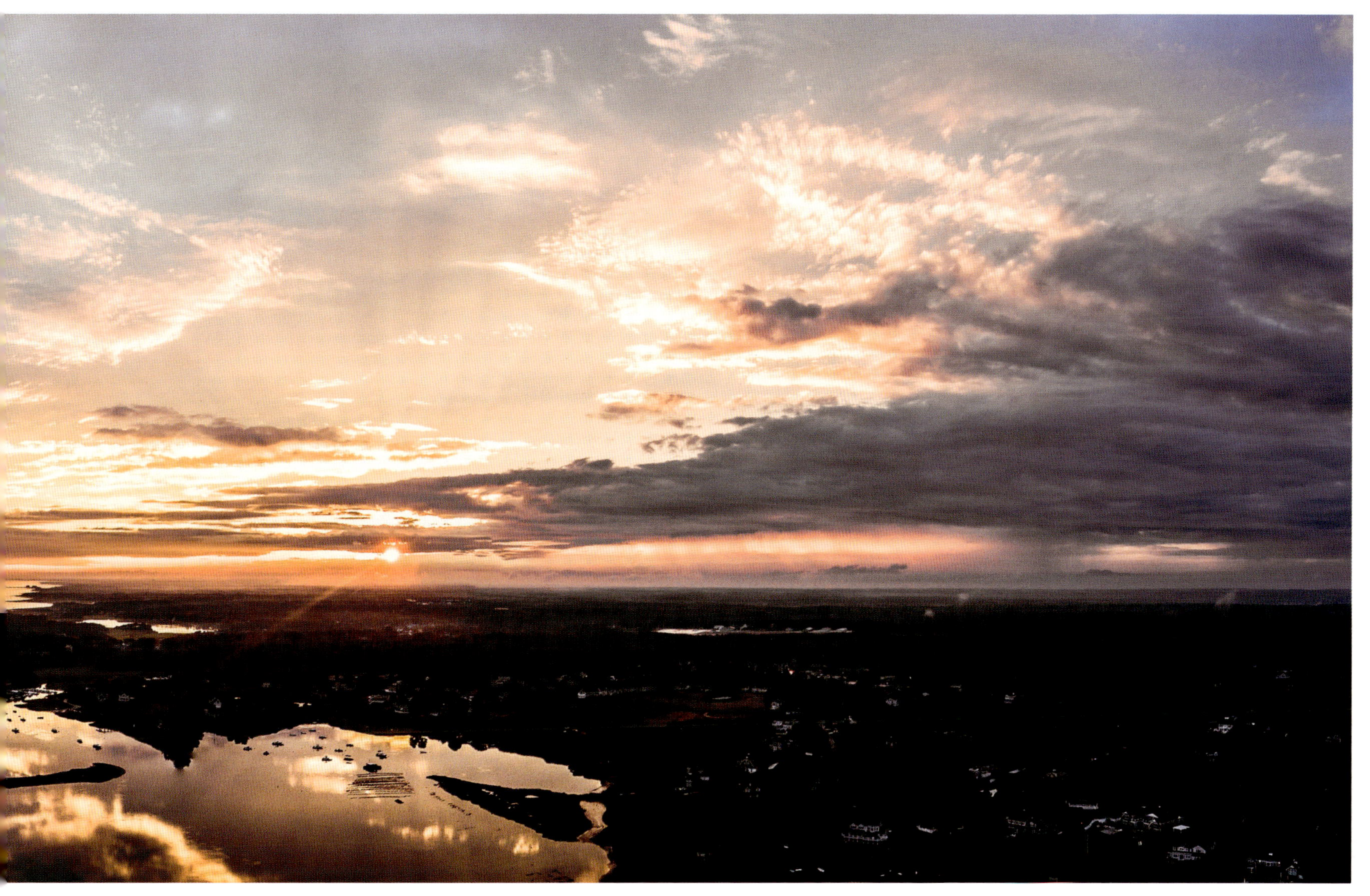

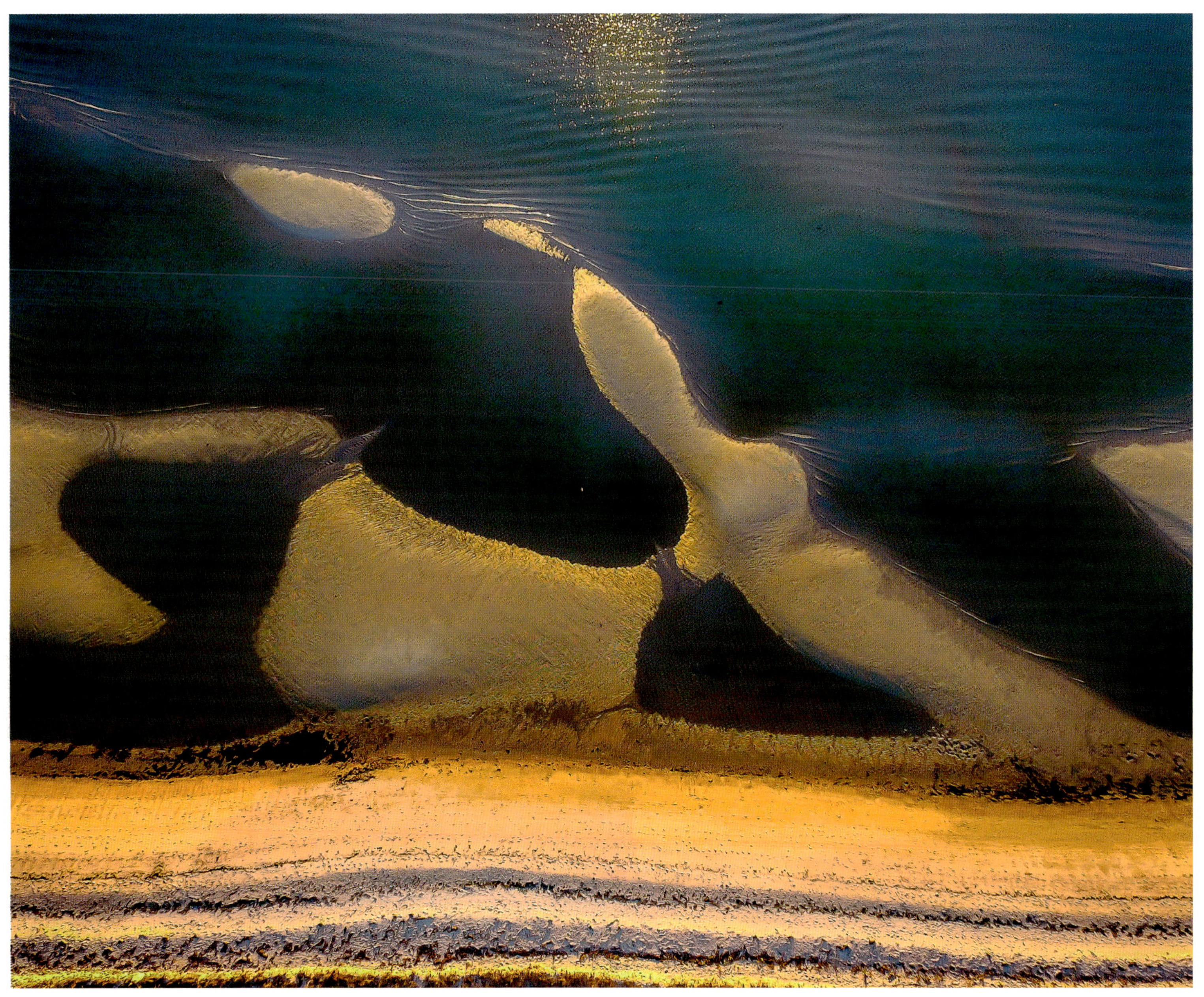

Shoals rising from the Atlantic as the tide drops with the sun.

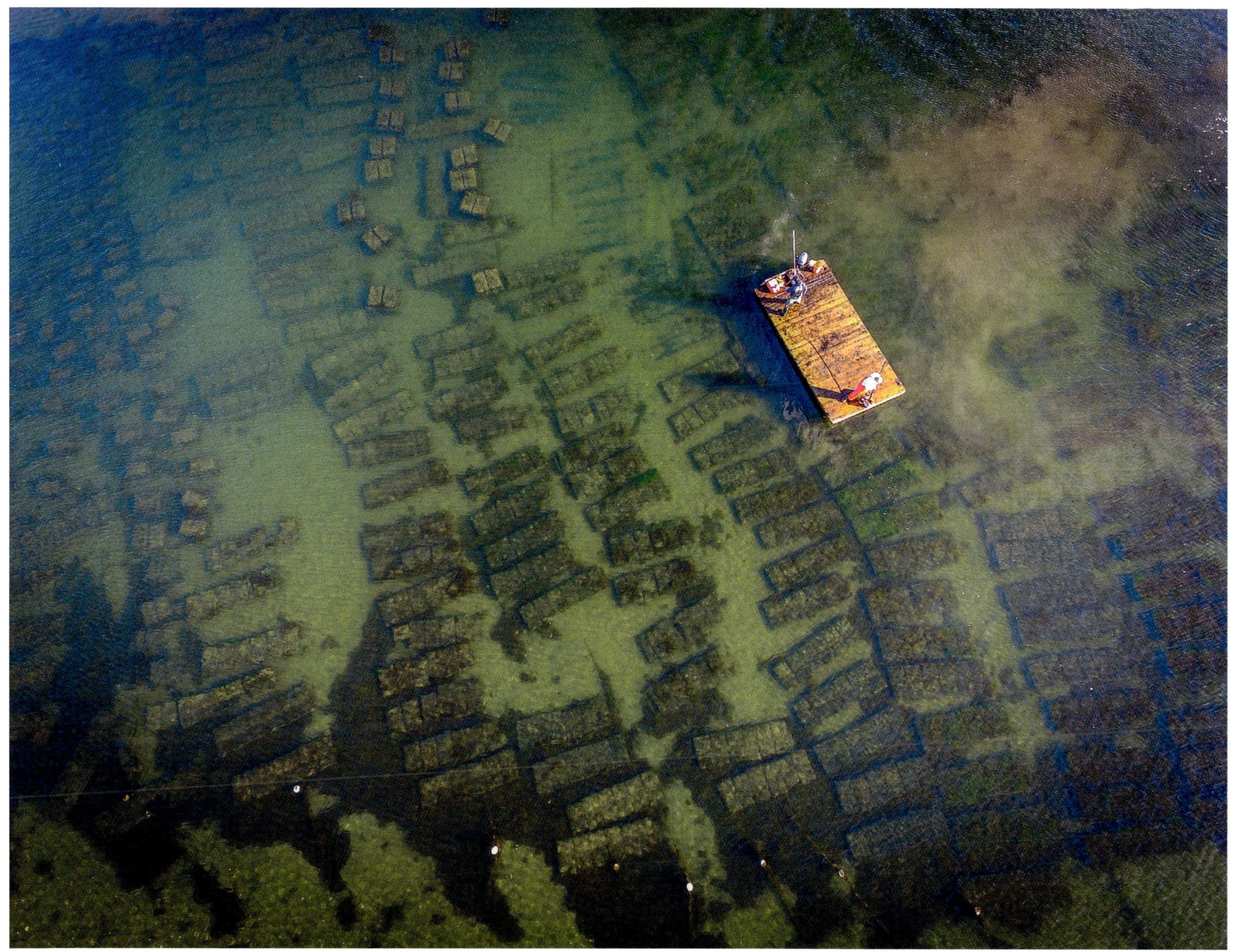

“Lay ‘em Down” - The men of the Chatham Shellfish Company grind away on racks of oysters in March.

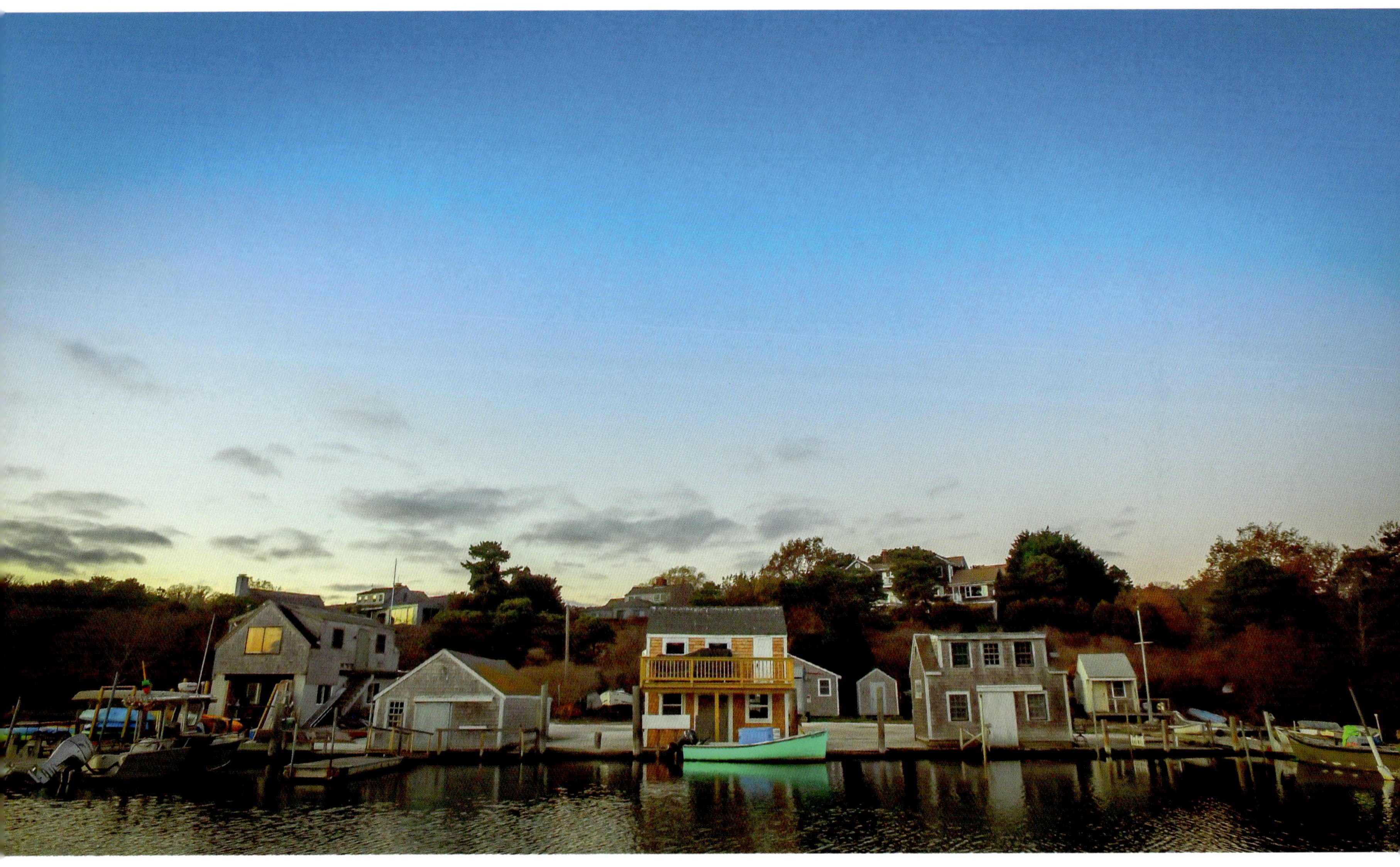

The shanties of Oyster River are not only supply and gear maintenance buildings but also the source of generations of wild lore and local history.

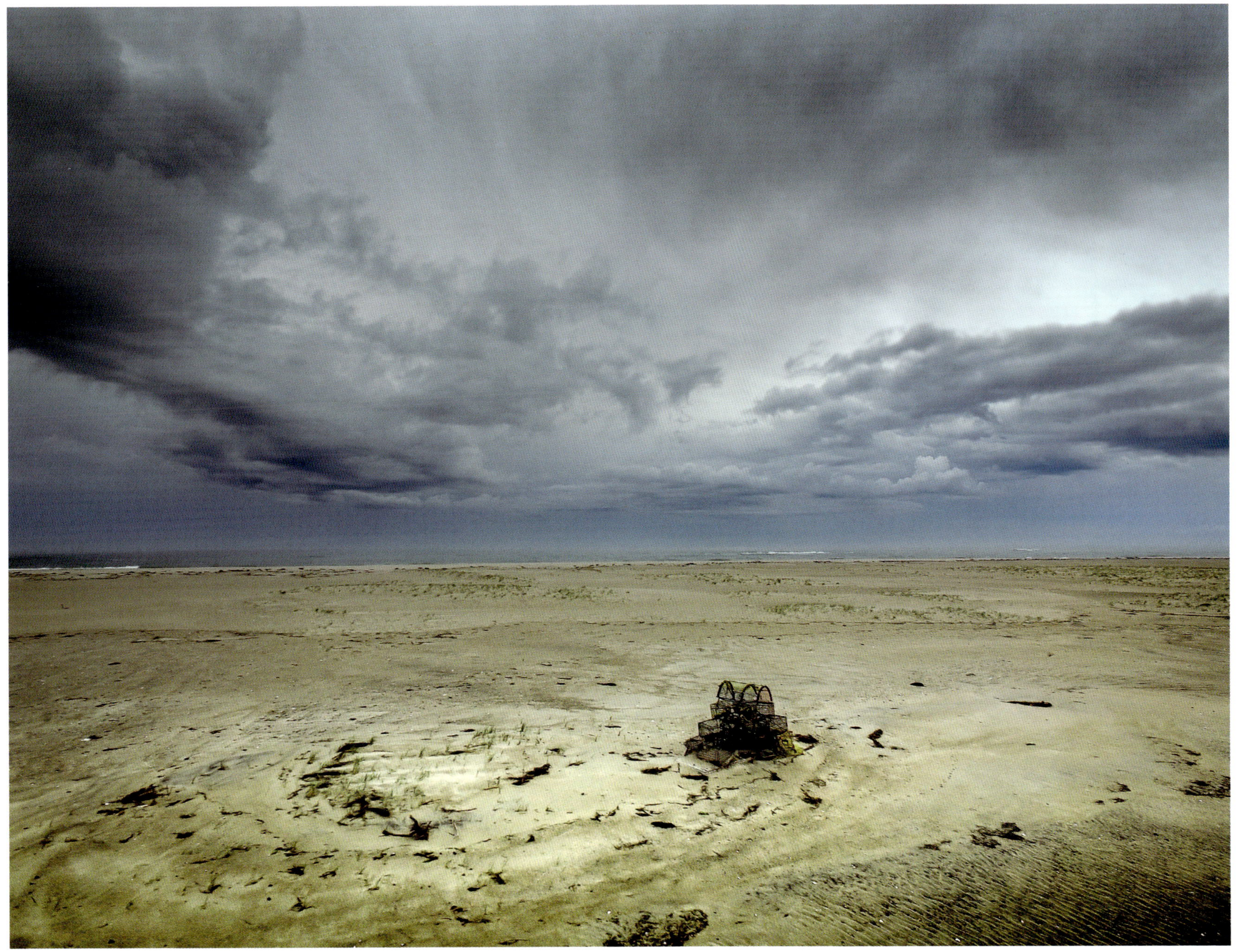

A pile of abandoned lobster pots that people have collected and neatly stacked over the years, accessible only by boat and away from the tide on North Beach Island.

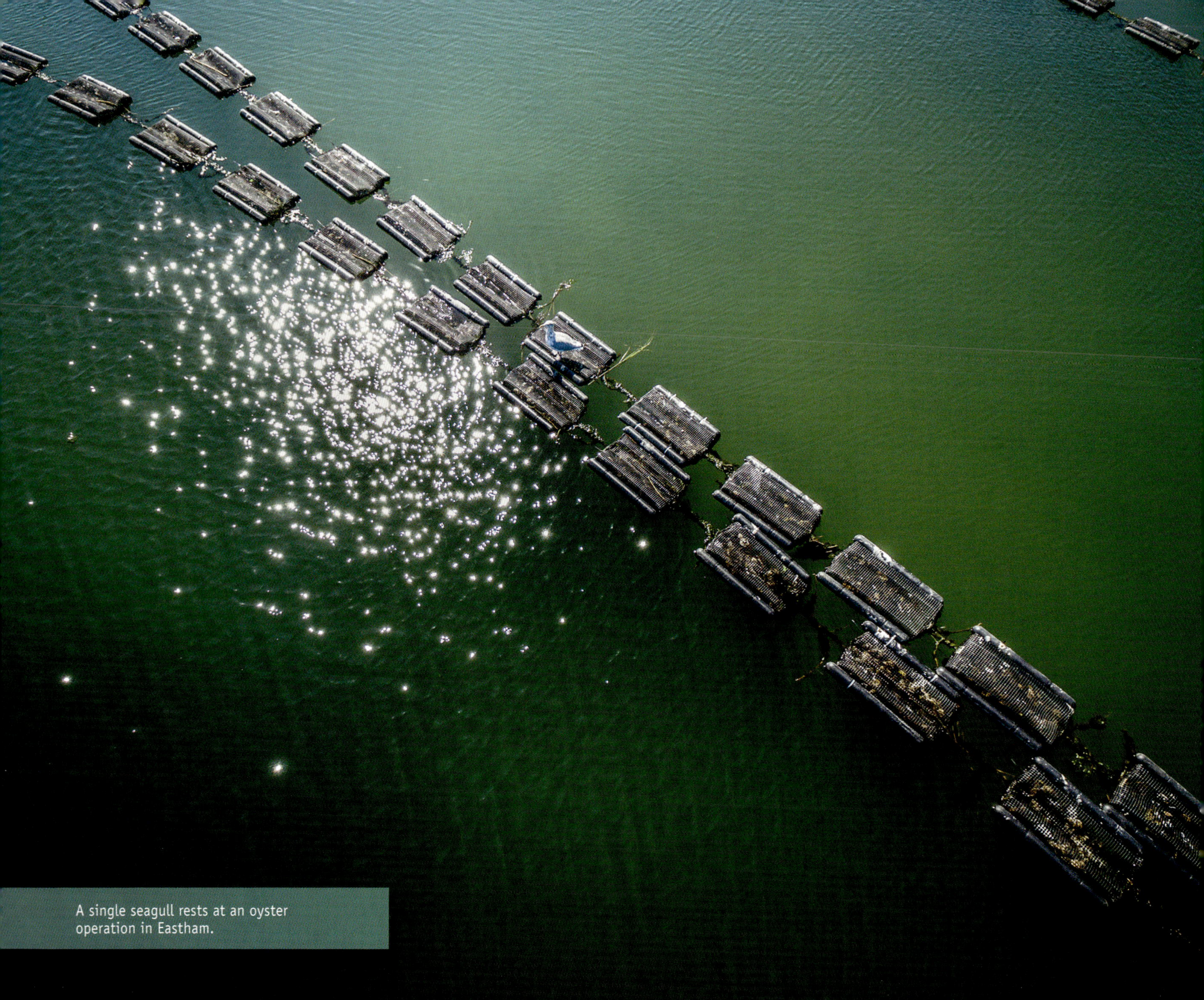

A single seagull rests at an oyster operation in Eastham.

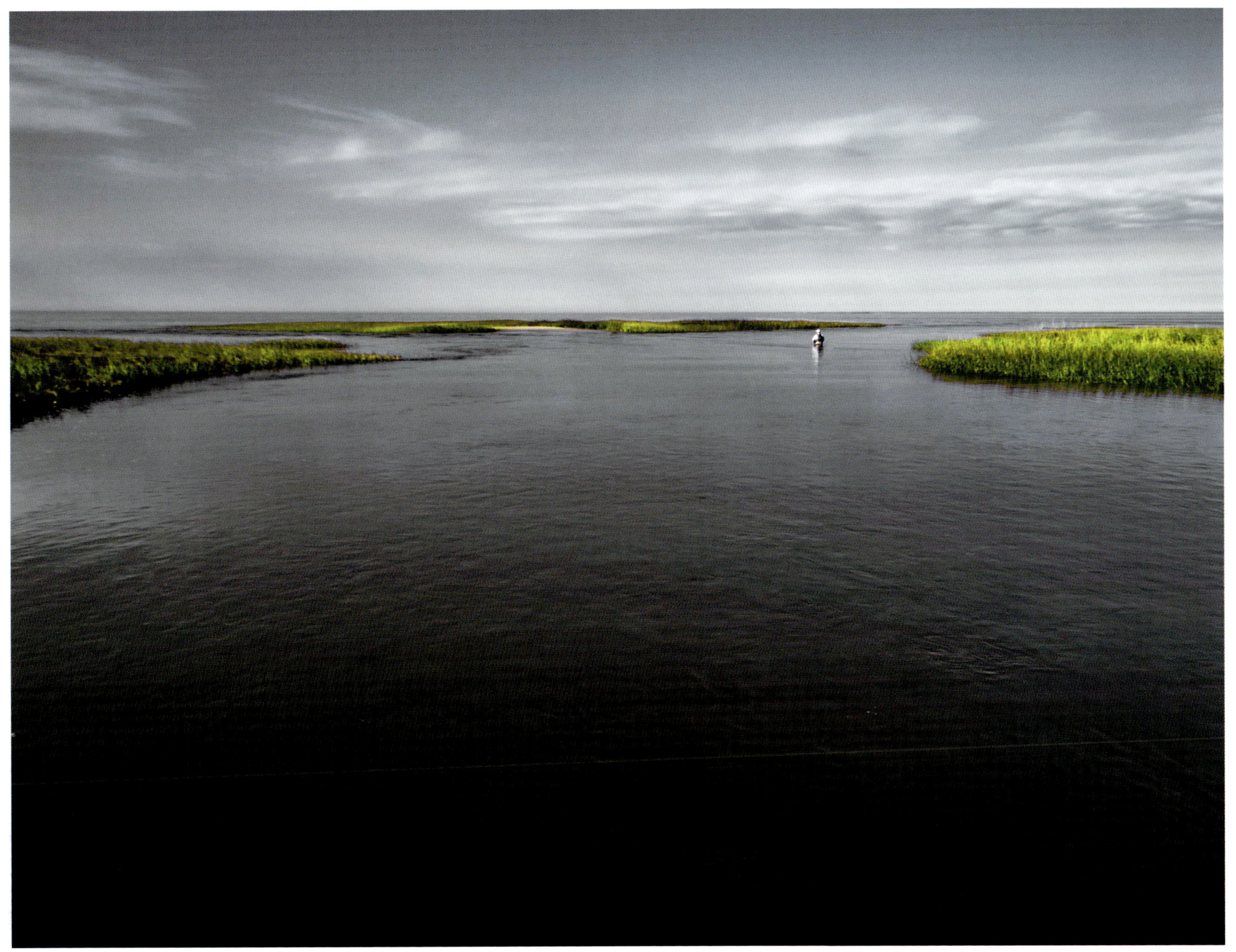

"The Lone Warrior" - A fisherman uses the retreating tide at Paine's Creek in Brewster.

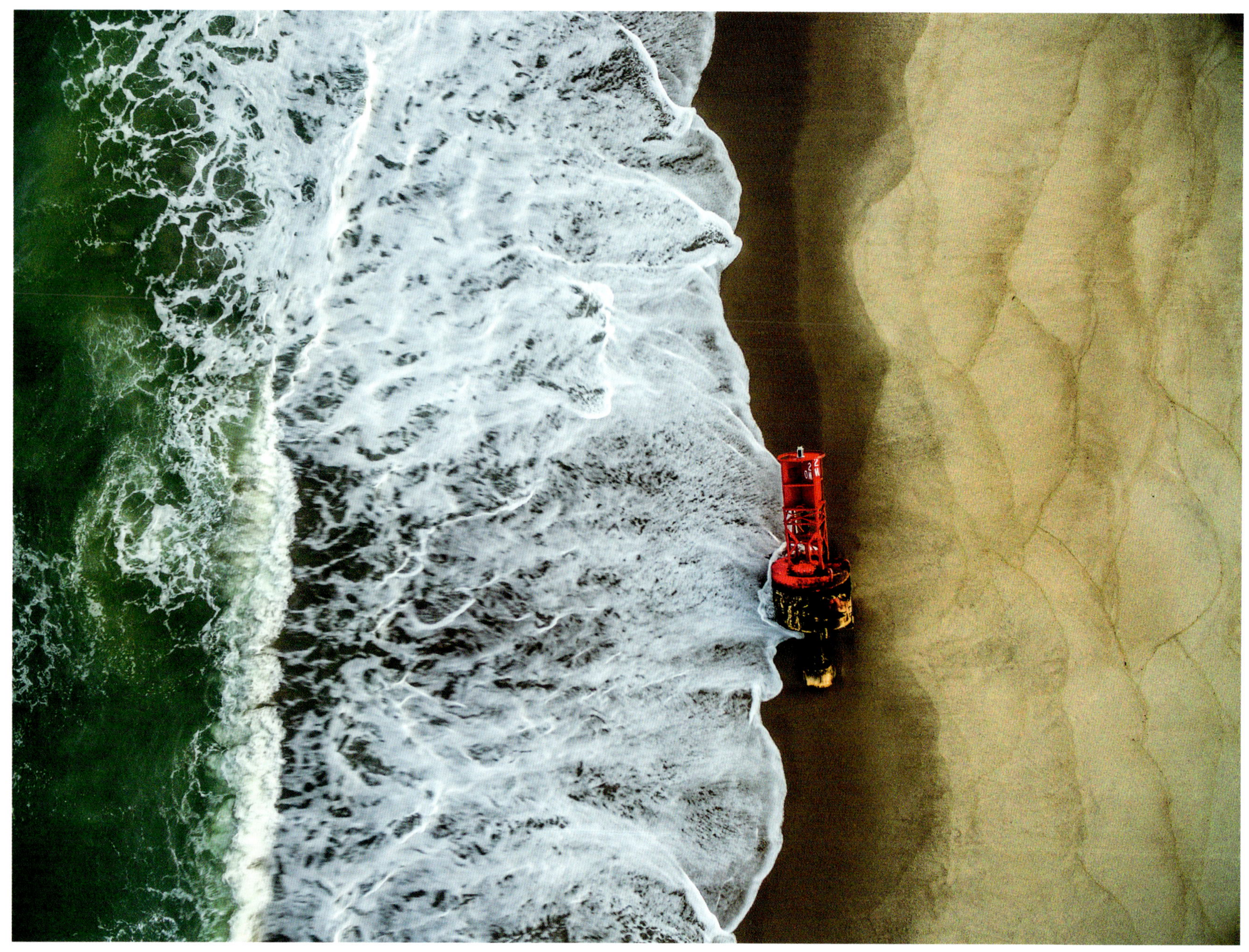

"Lost and Found" - Buoy 20M broke free of its mooring and made the lonely, 155-mile journey from Muscongus, Maine, to the shore of South Beach in Chatham. A National Guard Chinook helicopter lifted the 12,000-pound buoy onto a Coast Guard Cutter so it could be returned home.

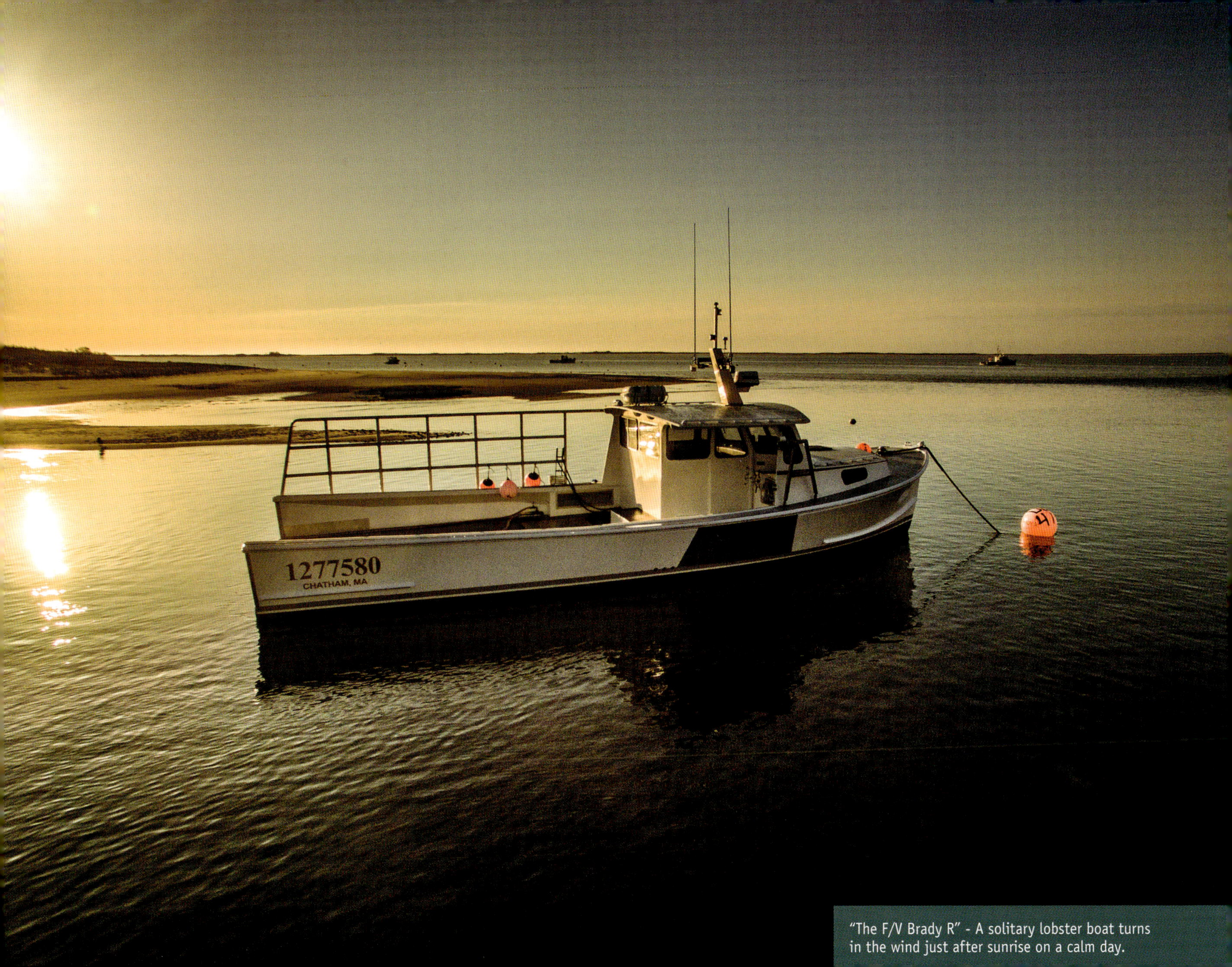

"The F/V Brady R" - A solitary lobster boat turns in the wind just after sunrise on a calm day.

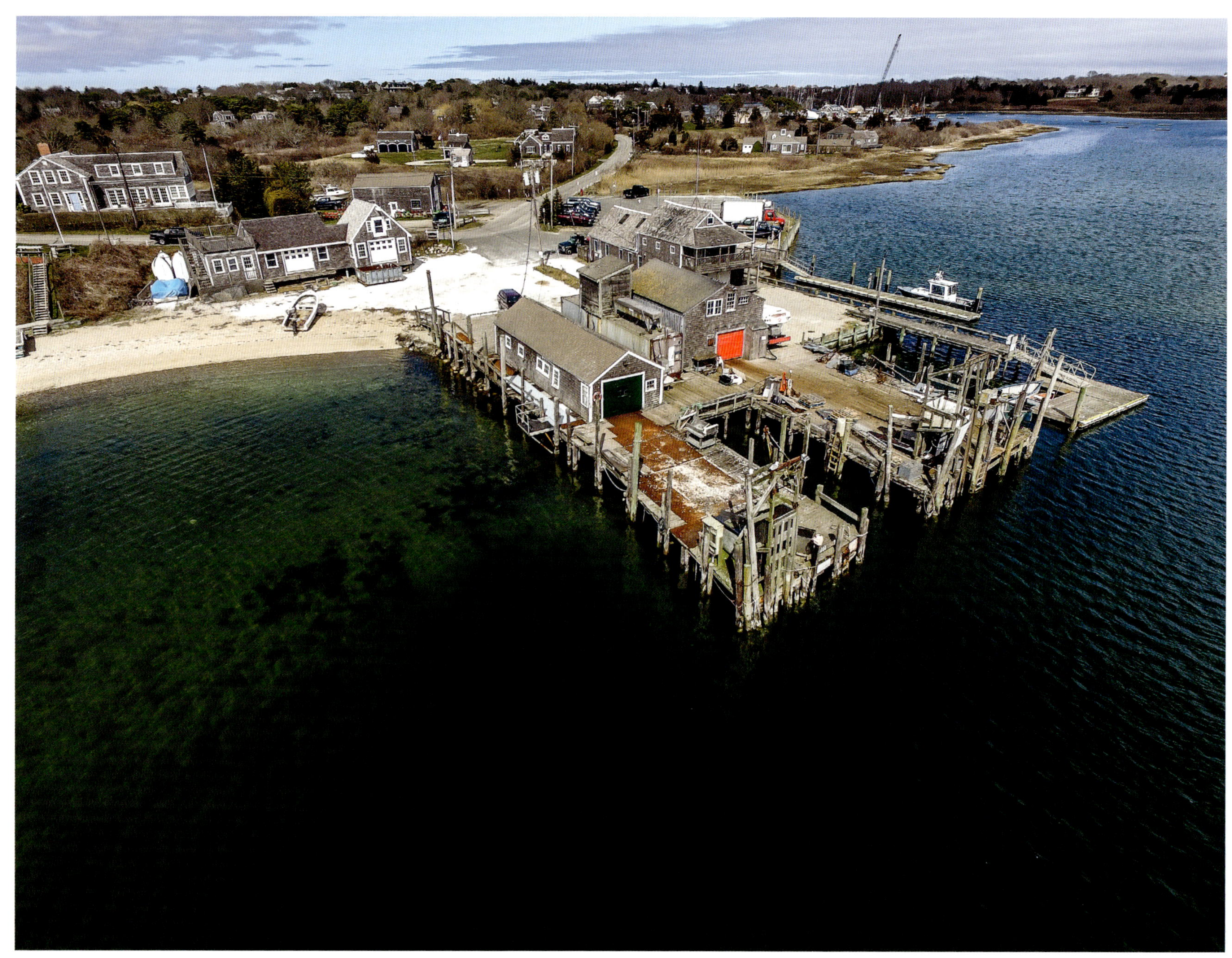

Looking northeast with the brand new Mitchell River Bridge in the background.

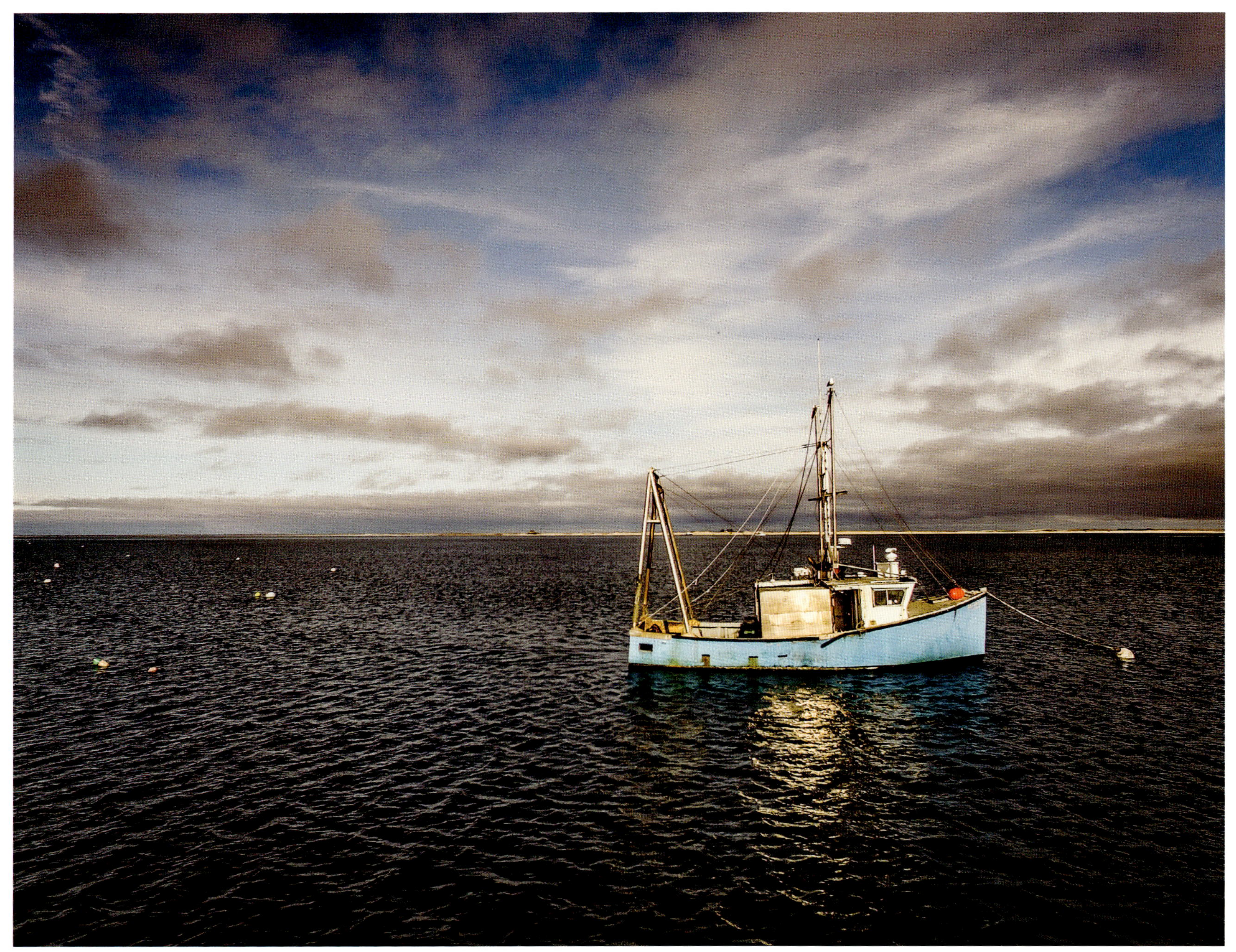

"Miss Rockville" - One of the most photogenic boats on Cape Cod.

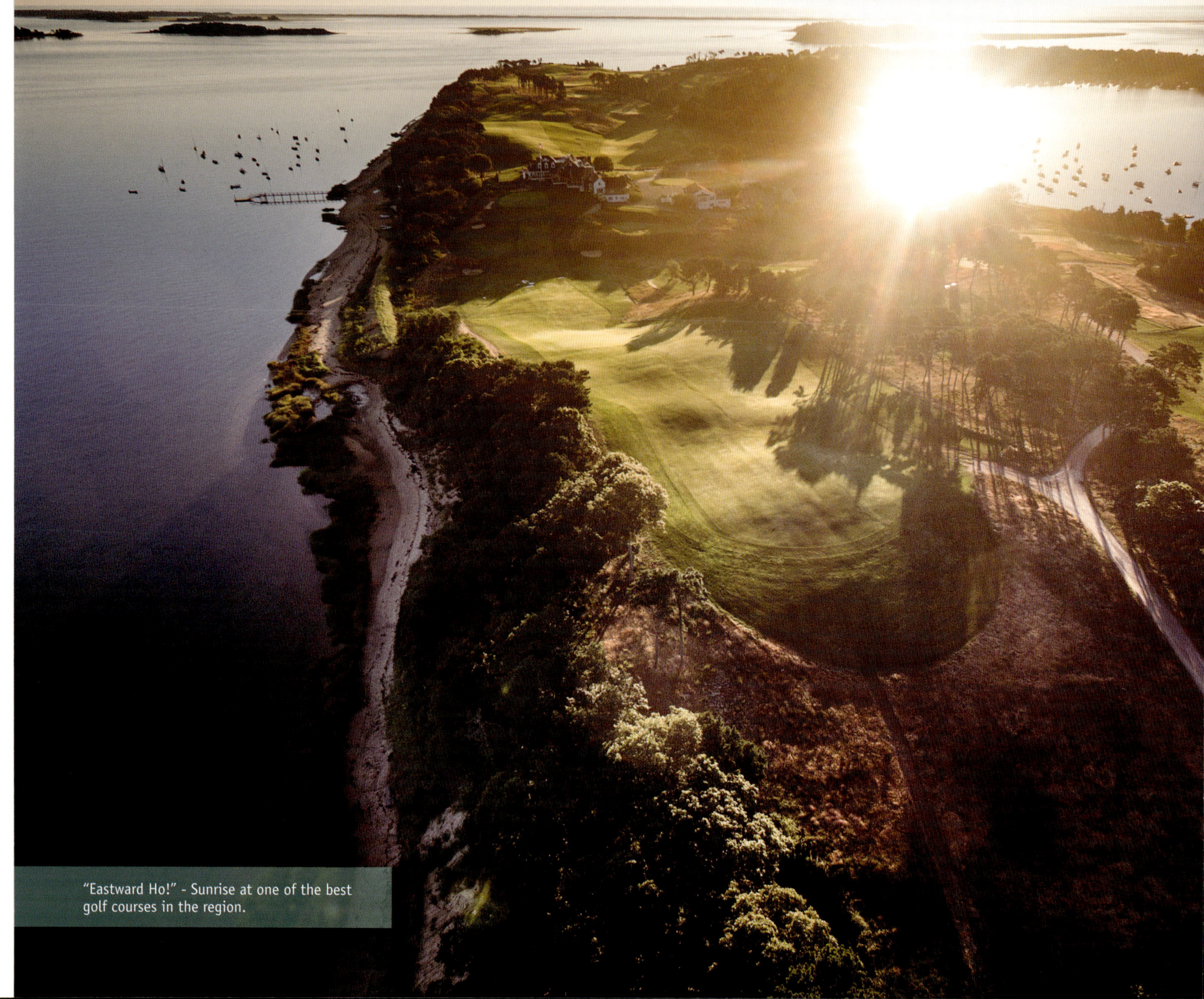

"Eastward Ho!" - Sunrise at one of the best golf courses in the region.

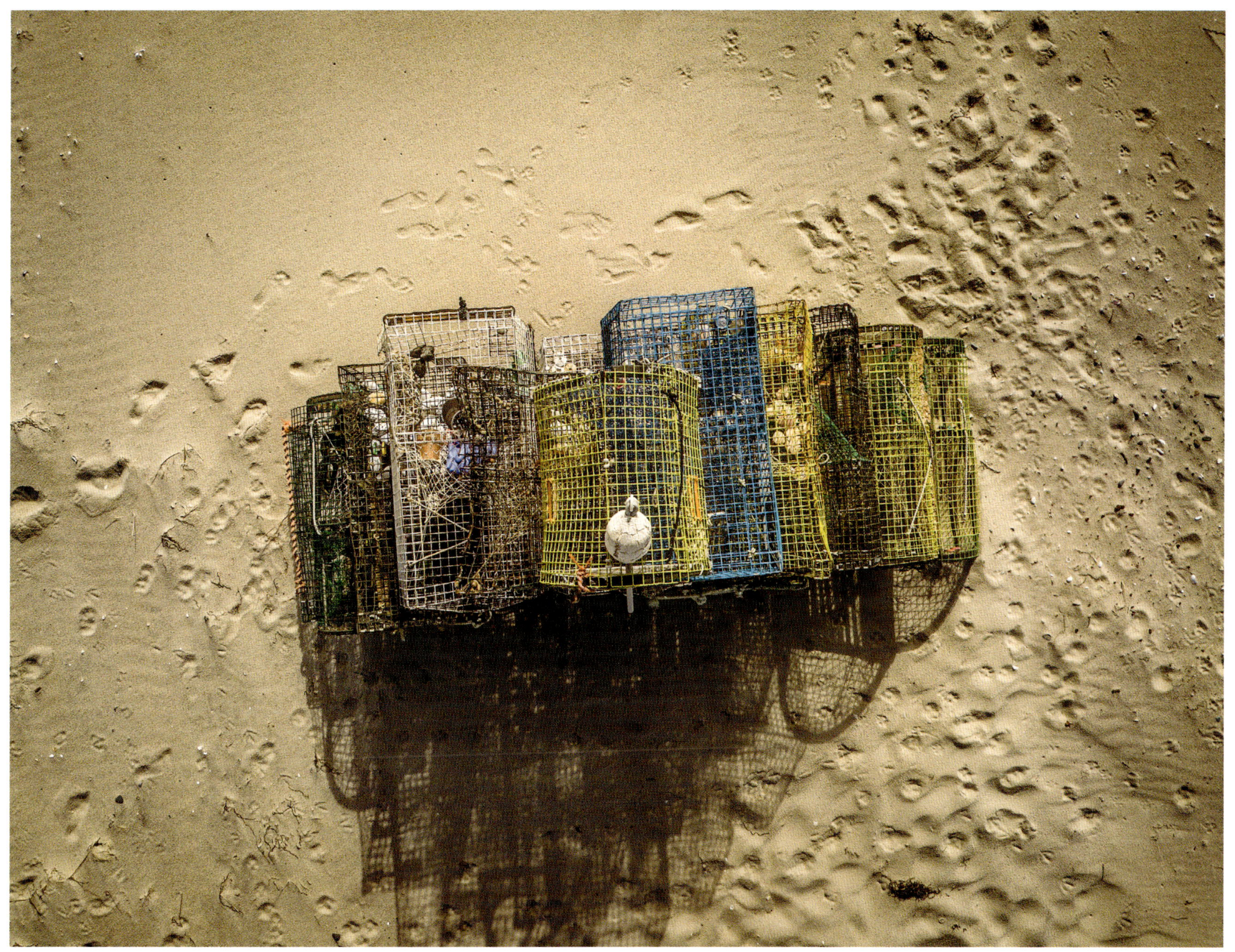

Lobster pots neatly stacked on the shore near Woods Hole.

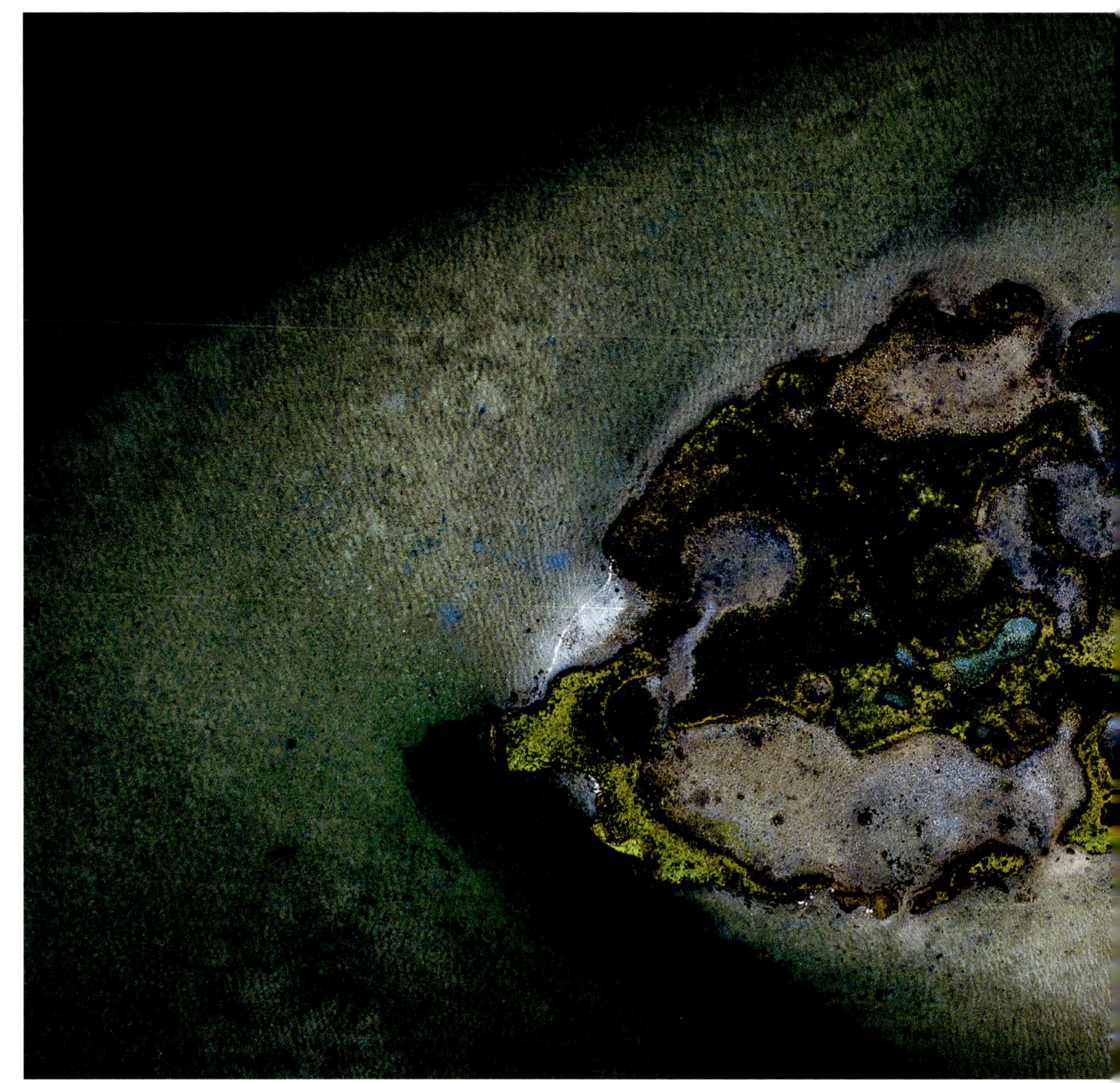

A marsh discovered on an aerial haunt with friends. Naturally, I claimed it for myself.

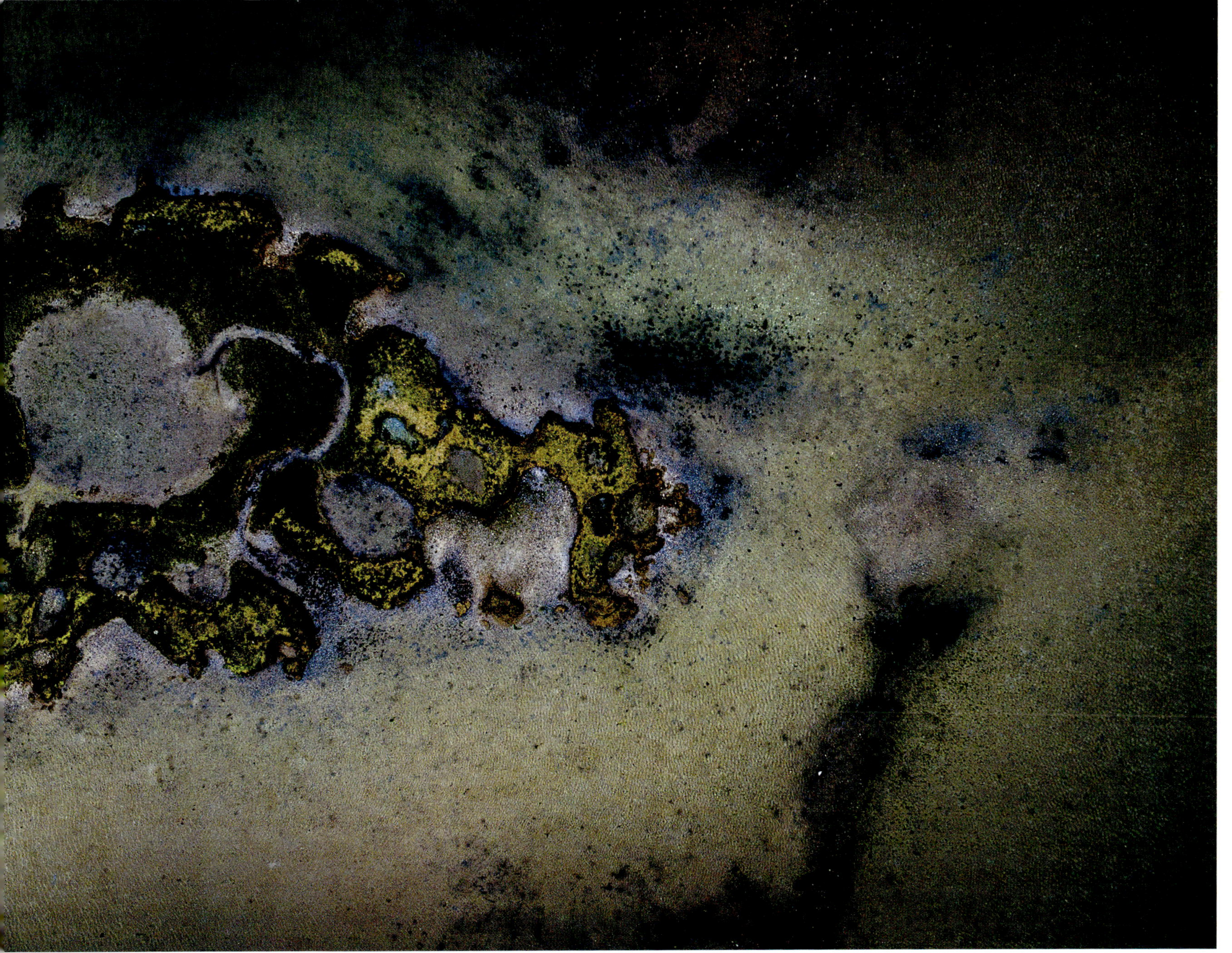

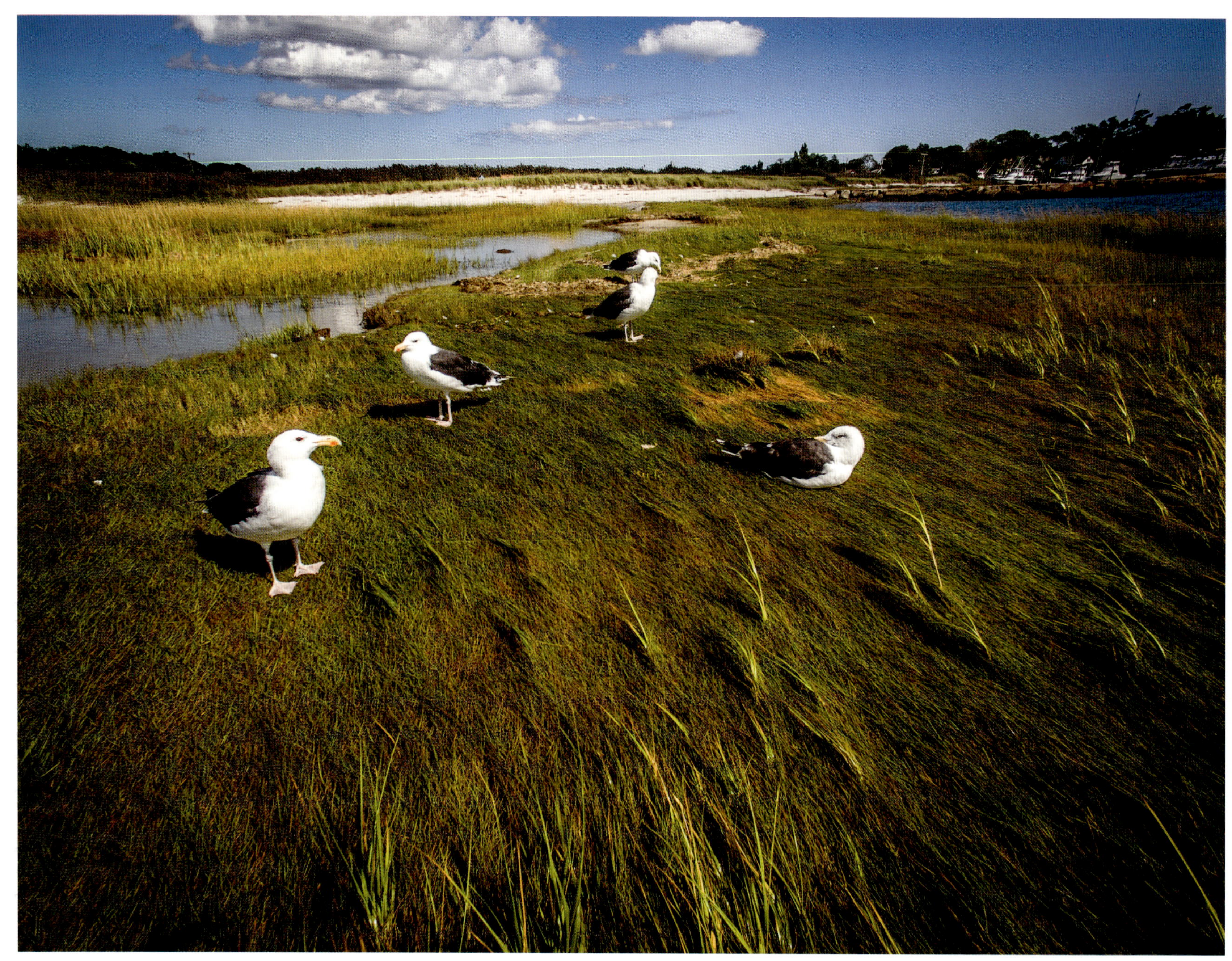

The gulls seemed extraordinarily unimpressed with my flying skills.

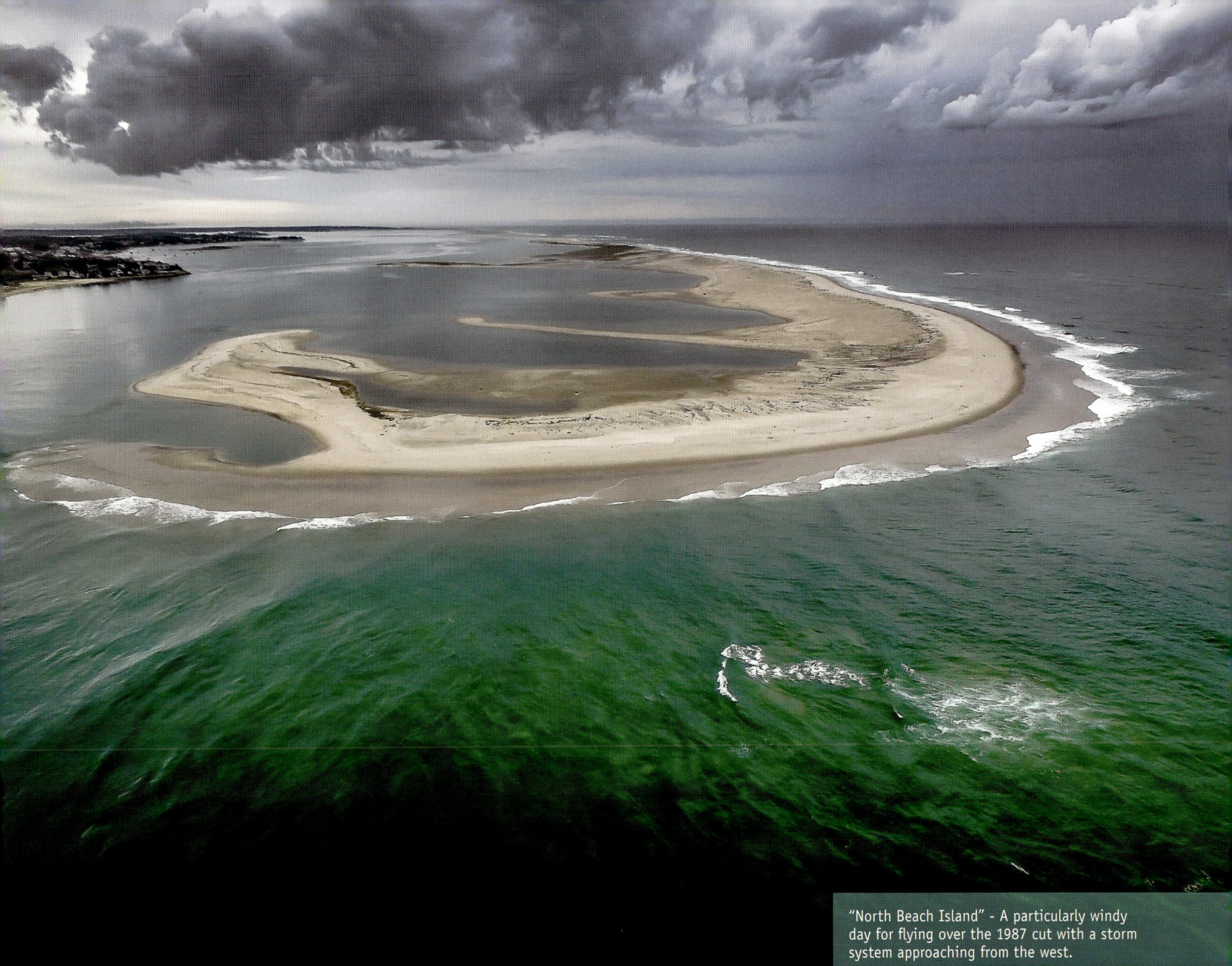

"North Beach Island" - A particularly windy day for flying over the 1987 cut with a storm system approaching from the west.

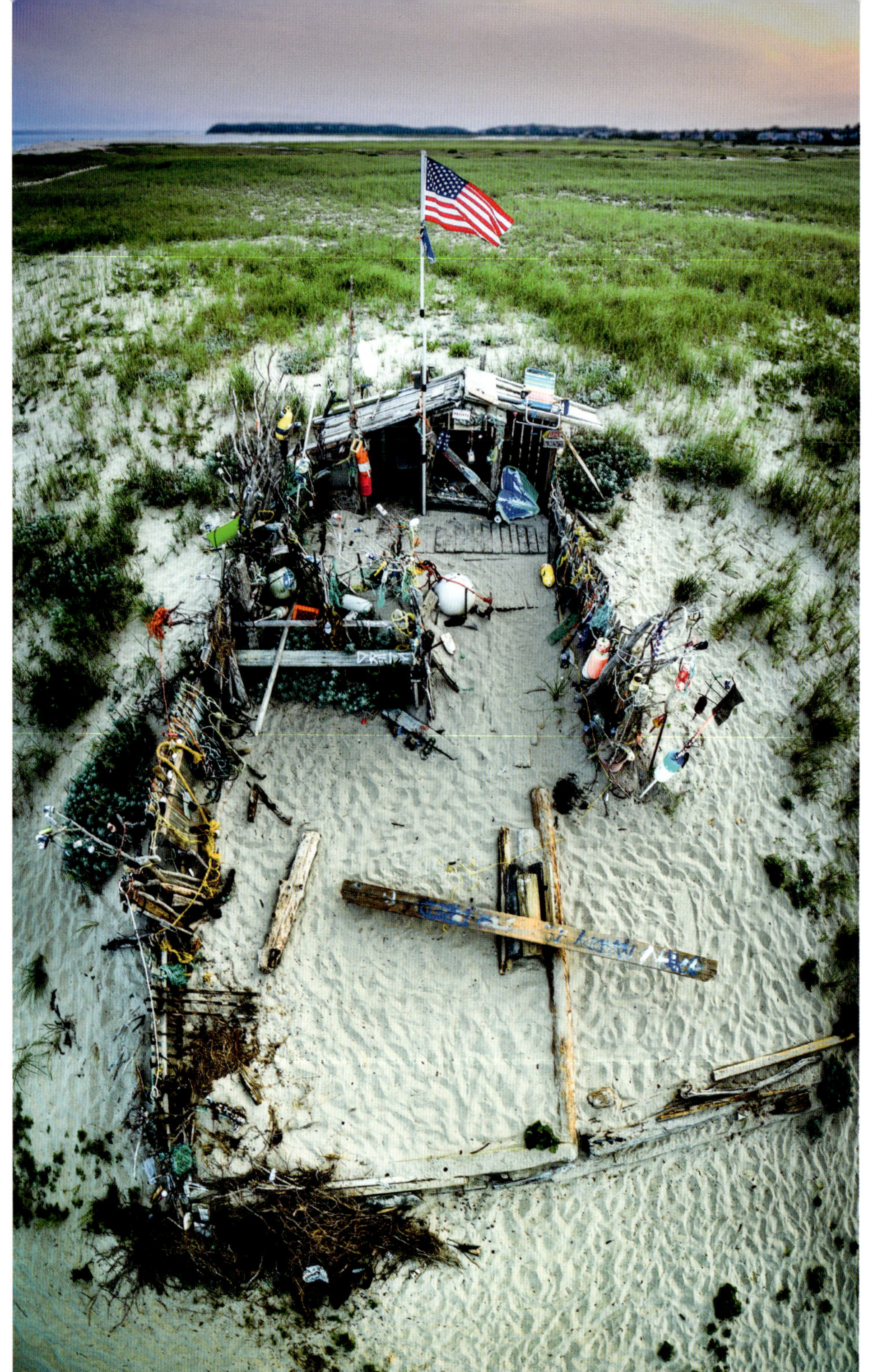

The shack at Lighthouse Beach is constructed almost entirely of debris that washed ashore or been left behind. It's a popular attraction and even has its own Facebook page: Occupy South Beach.

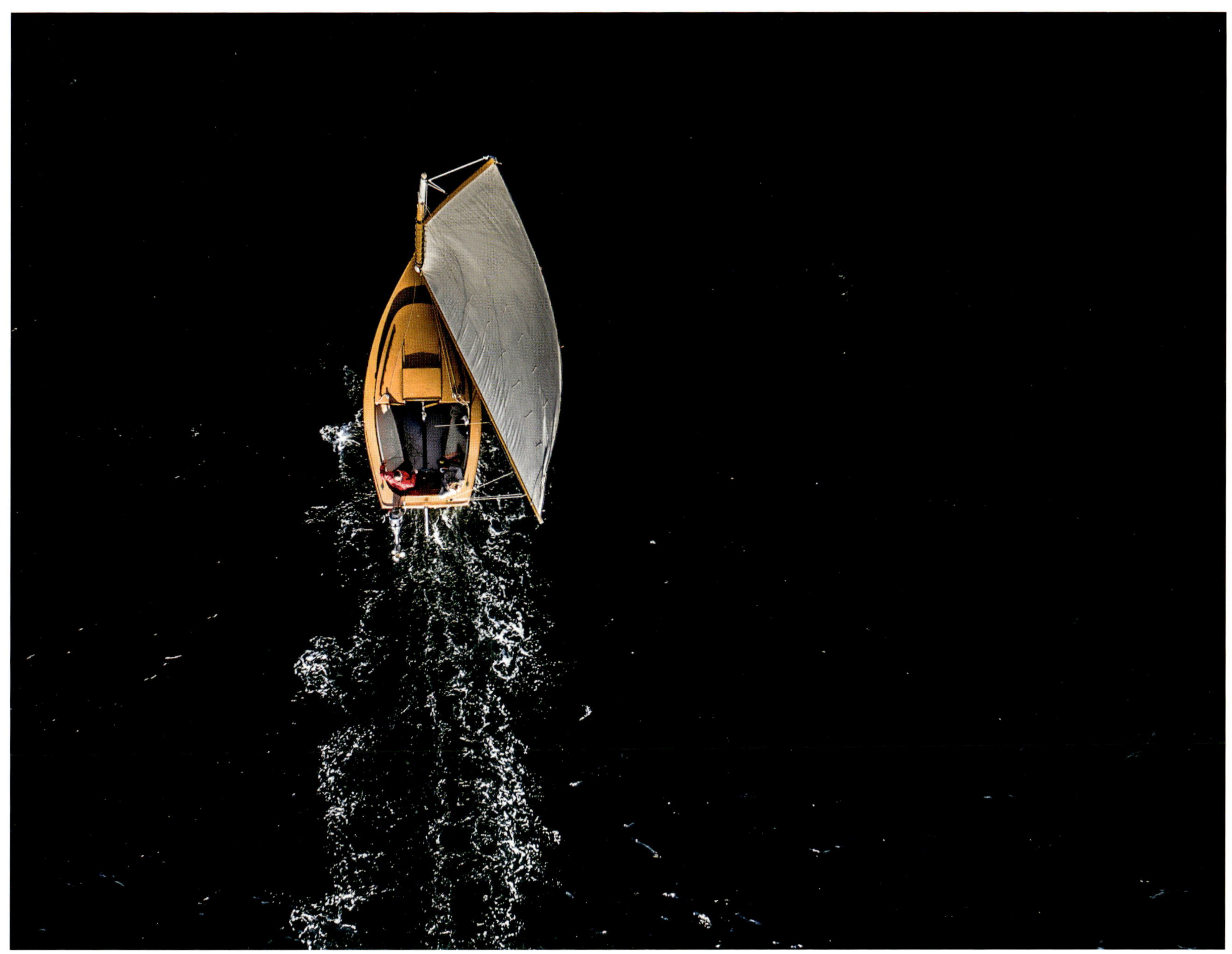

A gaff-rigged cat cranking eastward far off West Dennis Beach.

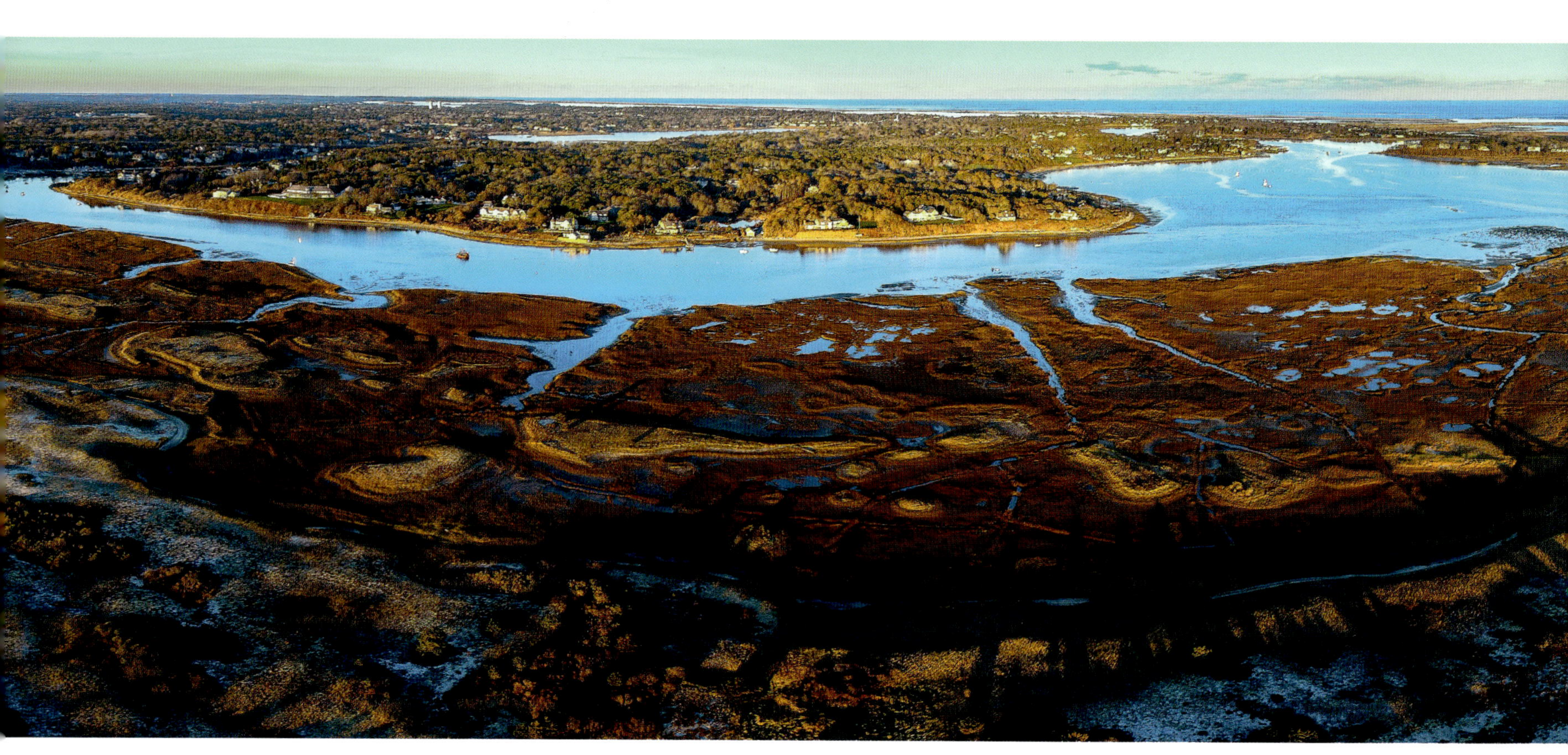

Orange hues in the vegetation pop under the late afternoon sky.

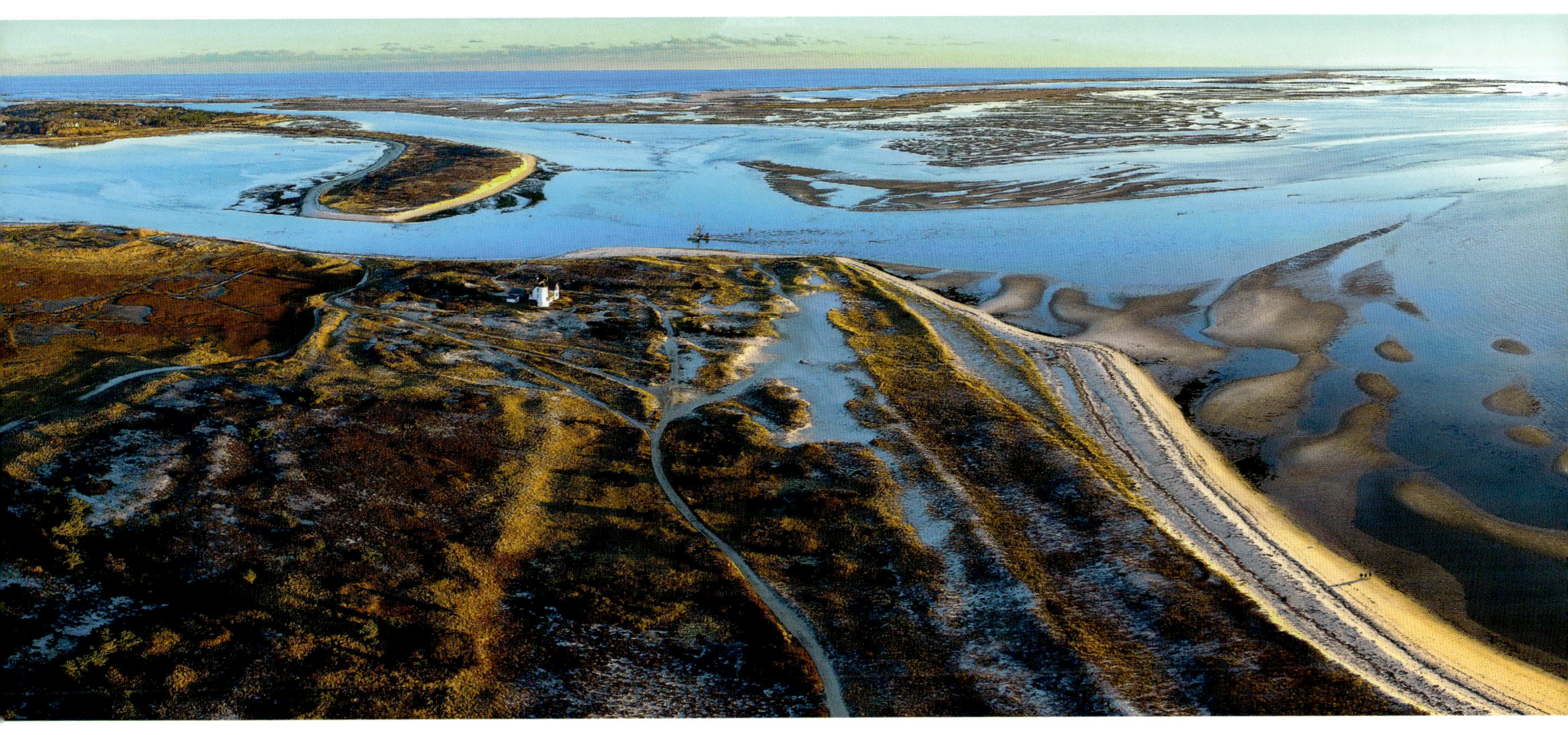

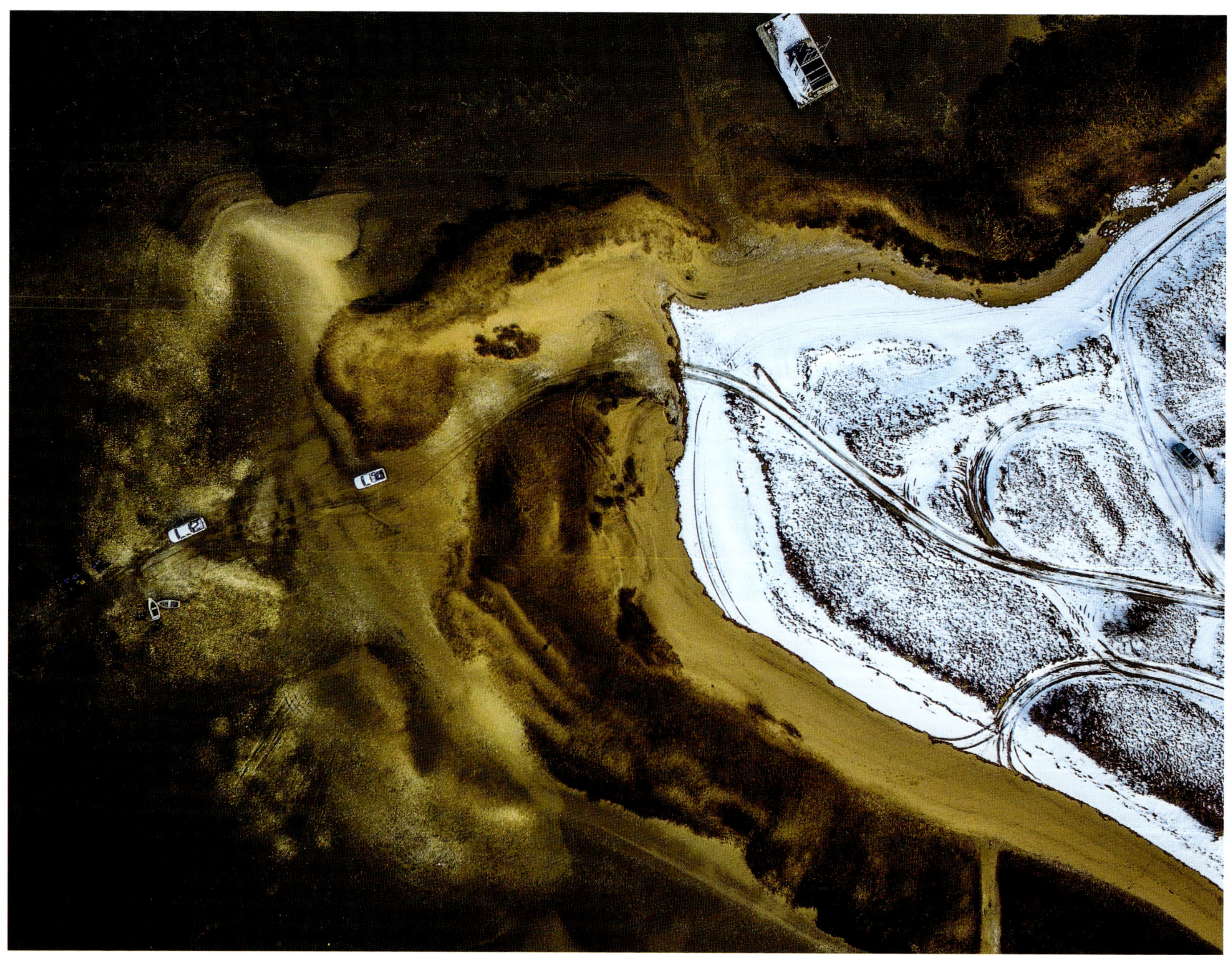

Trucks go off-road down to the oyster racks at low tide to tend the crop.

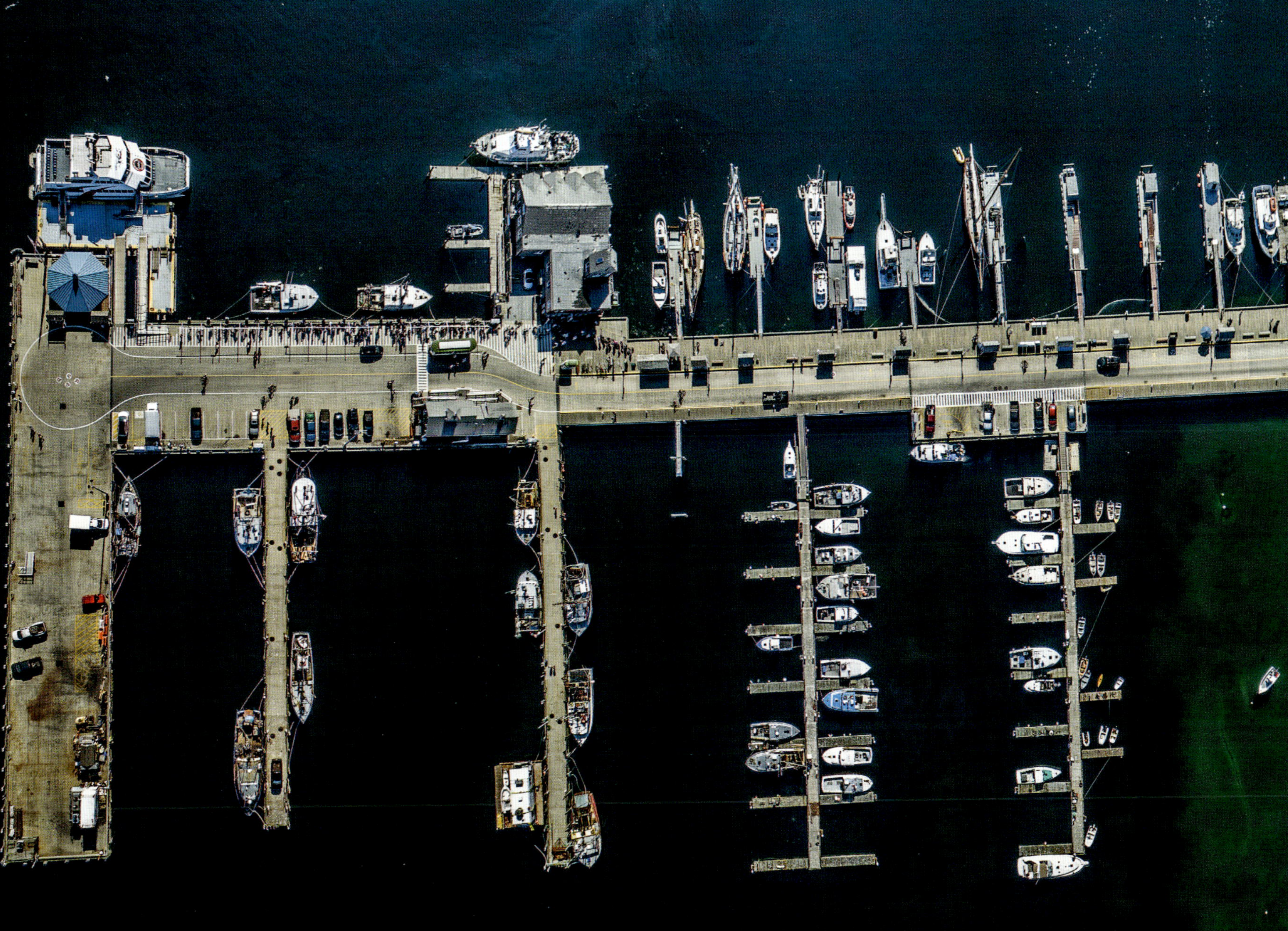

“Tourists and locals mill about the town pier in Provincetown. Six photos are stitched together to give the illusion of a higher altitude and to fit the whole pier in the frame.

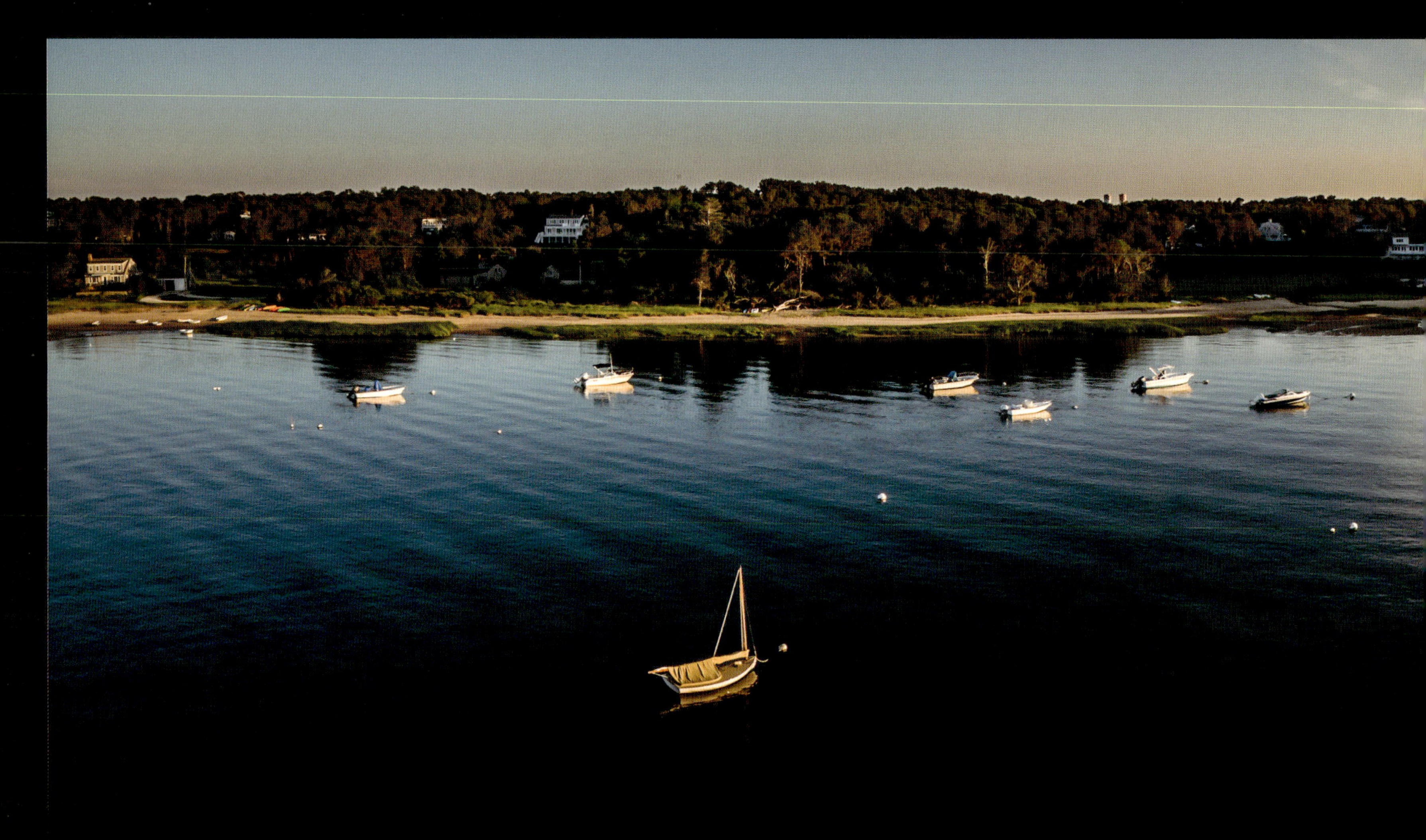

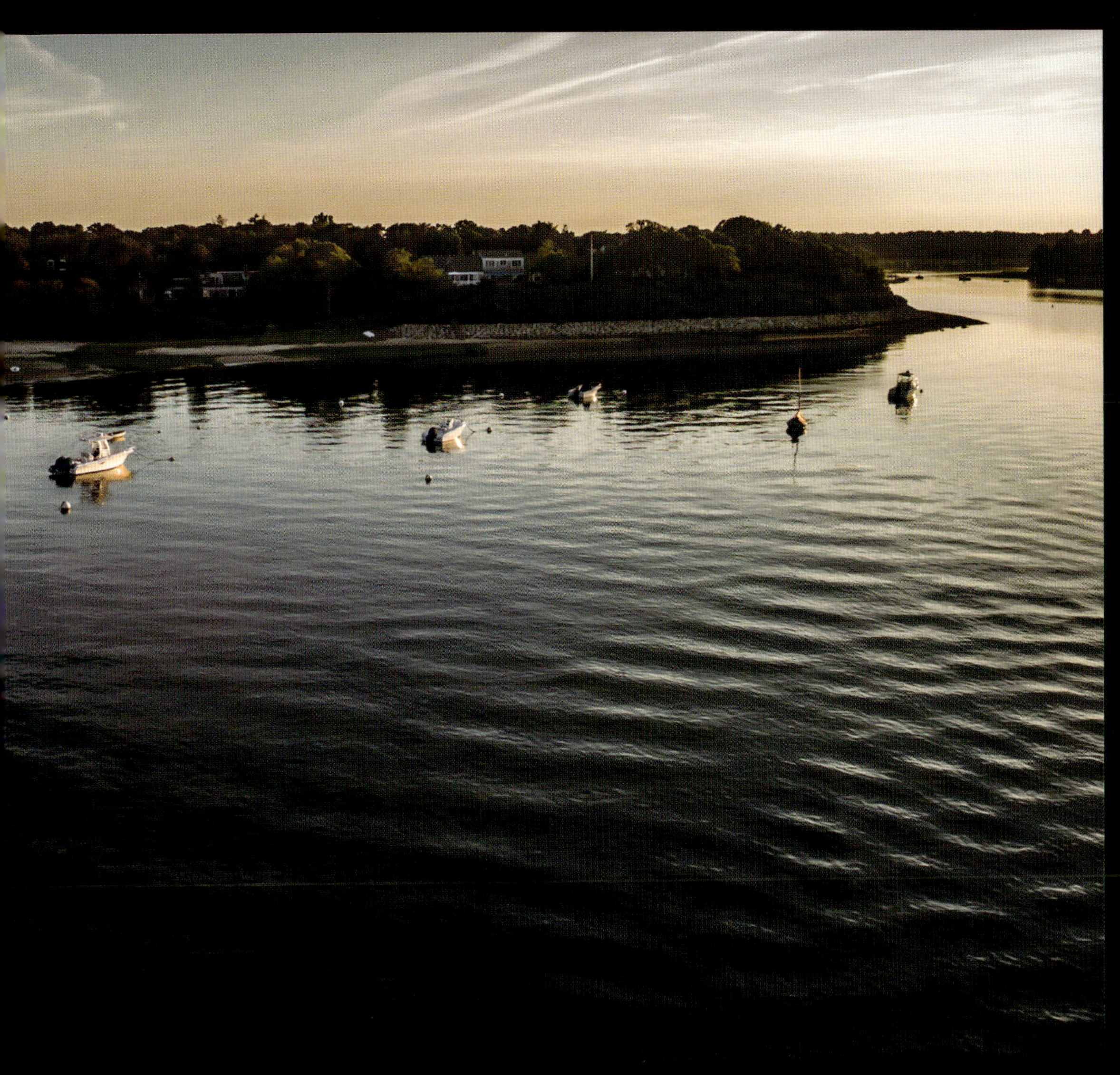

A Beetle Cat resting in the stillness of Pleasant Bay.

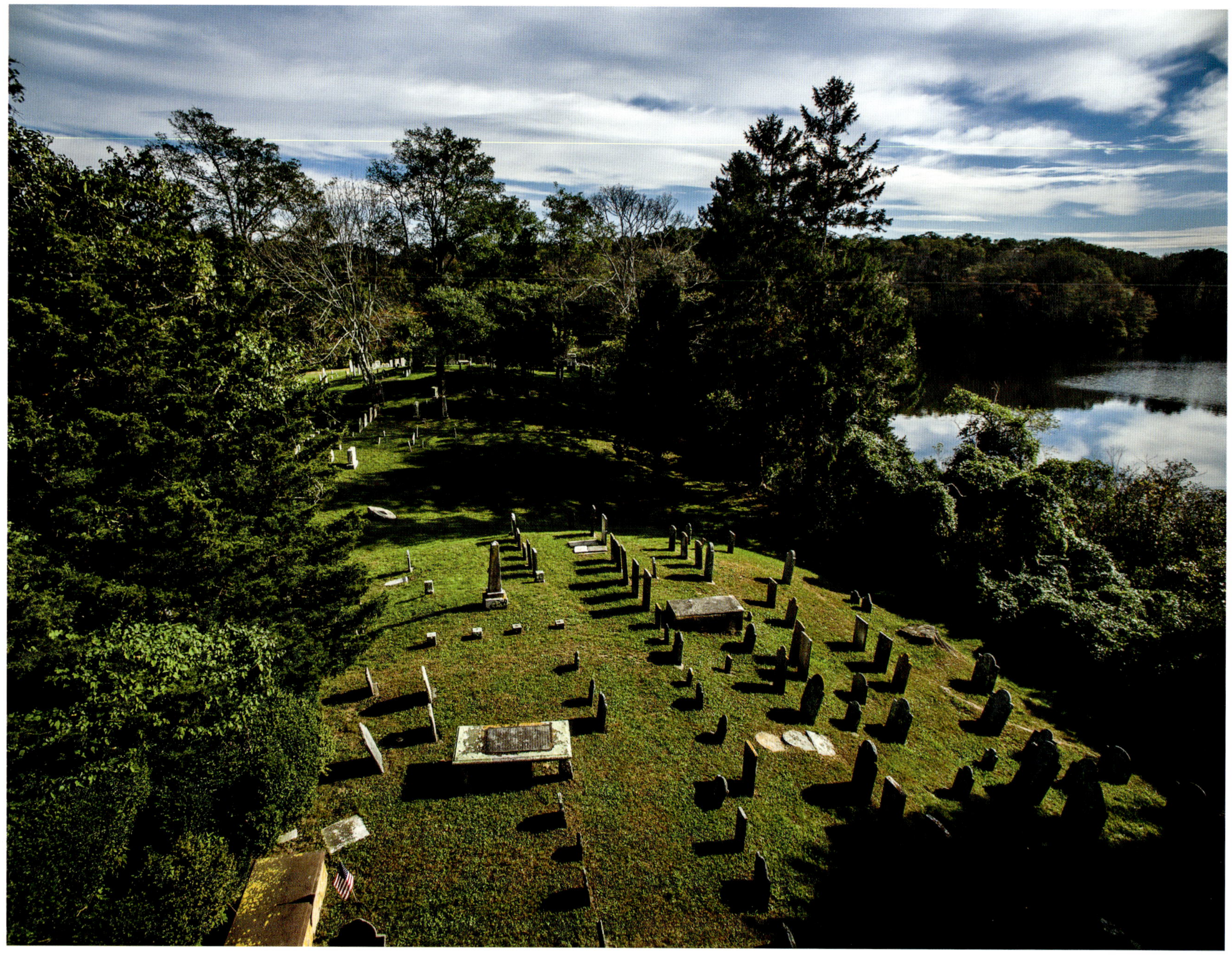

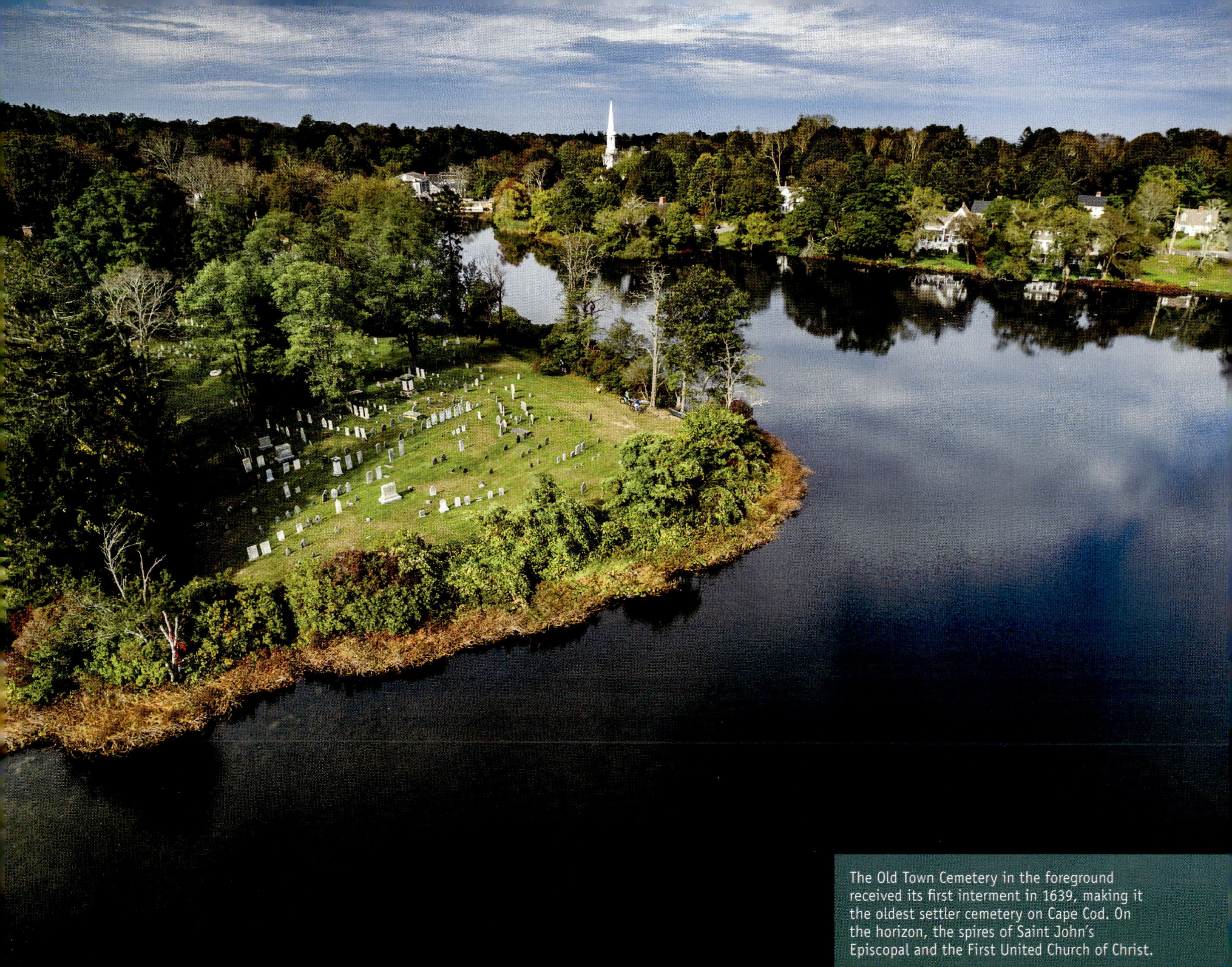

The Old Town Cemetery in the foreground received its first interment in 1639, making it the oldest settler cemetery on Cape Cod. On the horizon, the spires of Saint John's Episcopal and the First United Church of Christ.

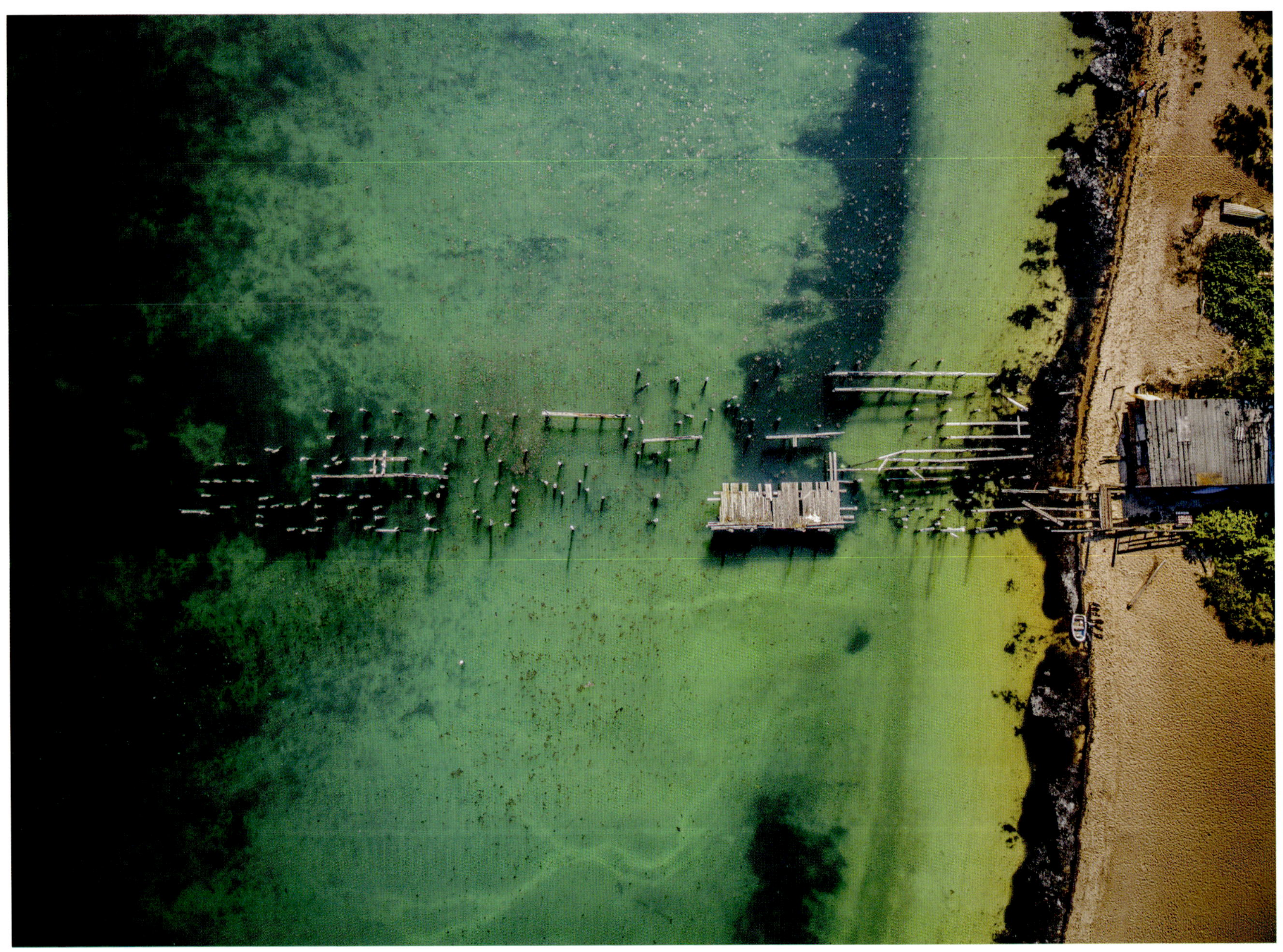

All that remains of the old wharf in Provincetown.

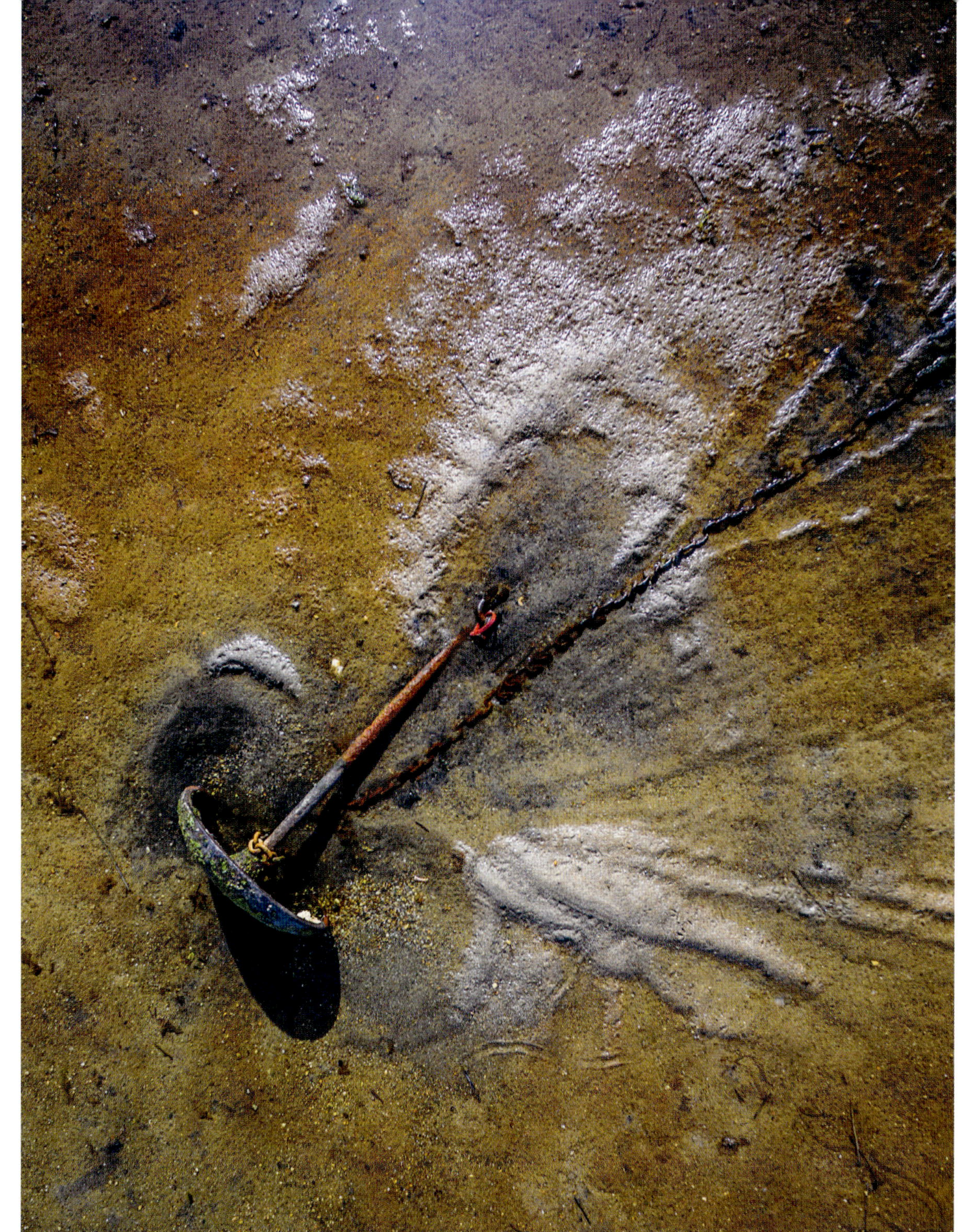

A 2,000-pound mushroom sinks into the mud at low tide.

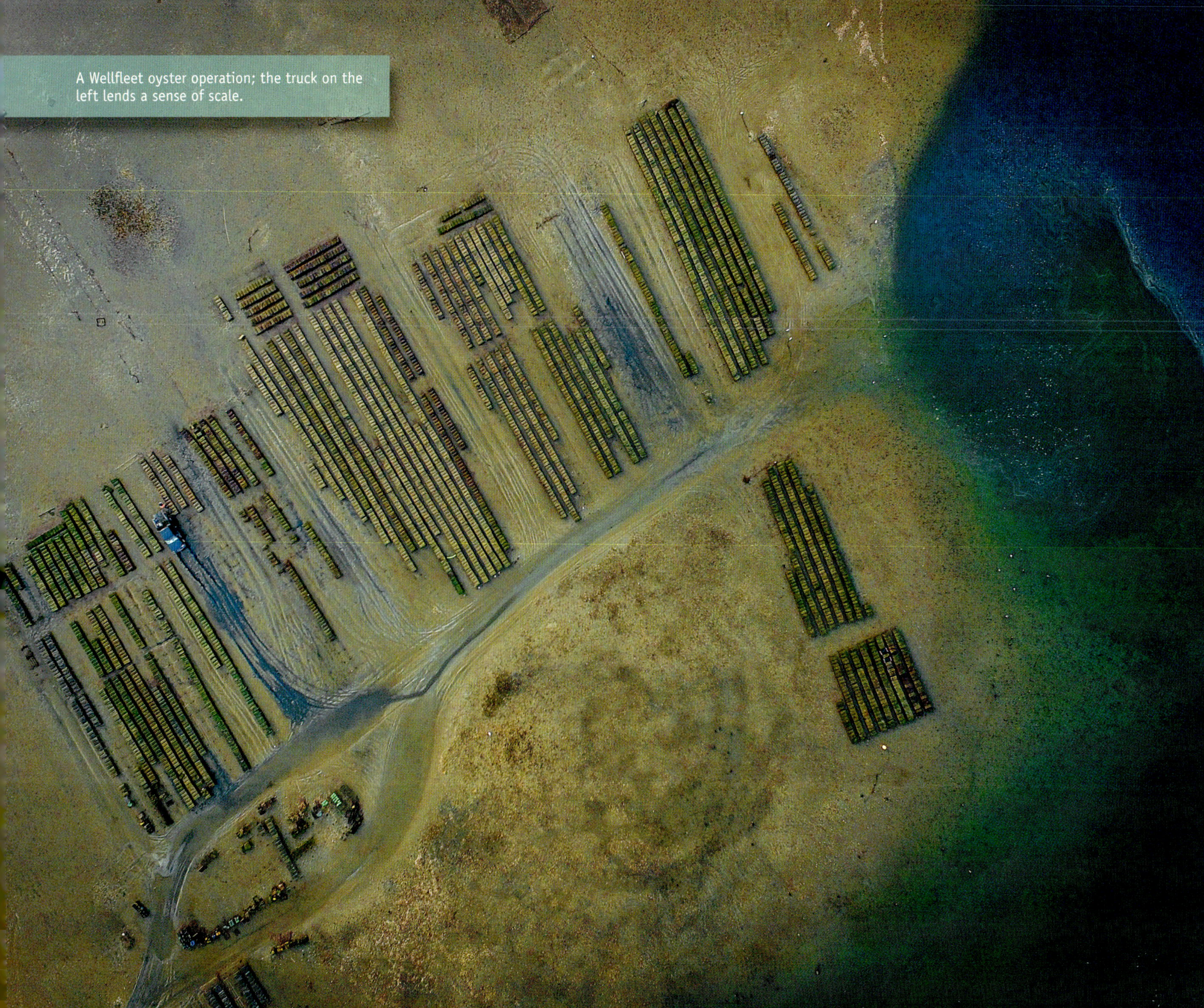

A Wellfleet oyster operation; the truck on the left lends a sense of scale.

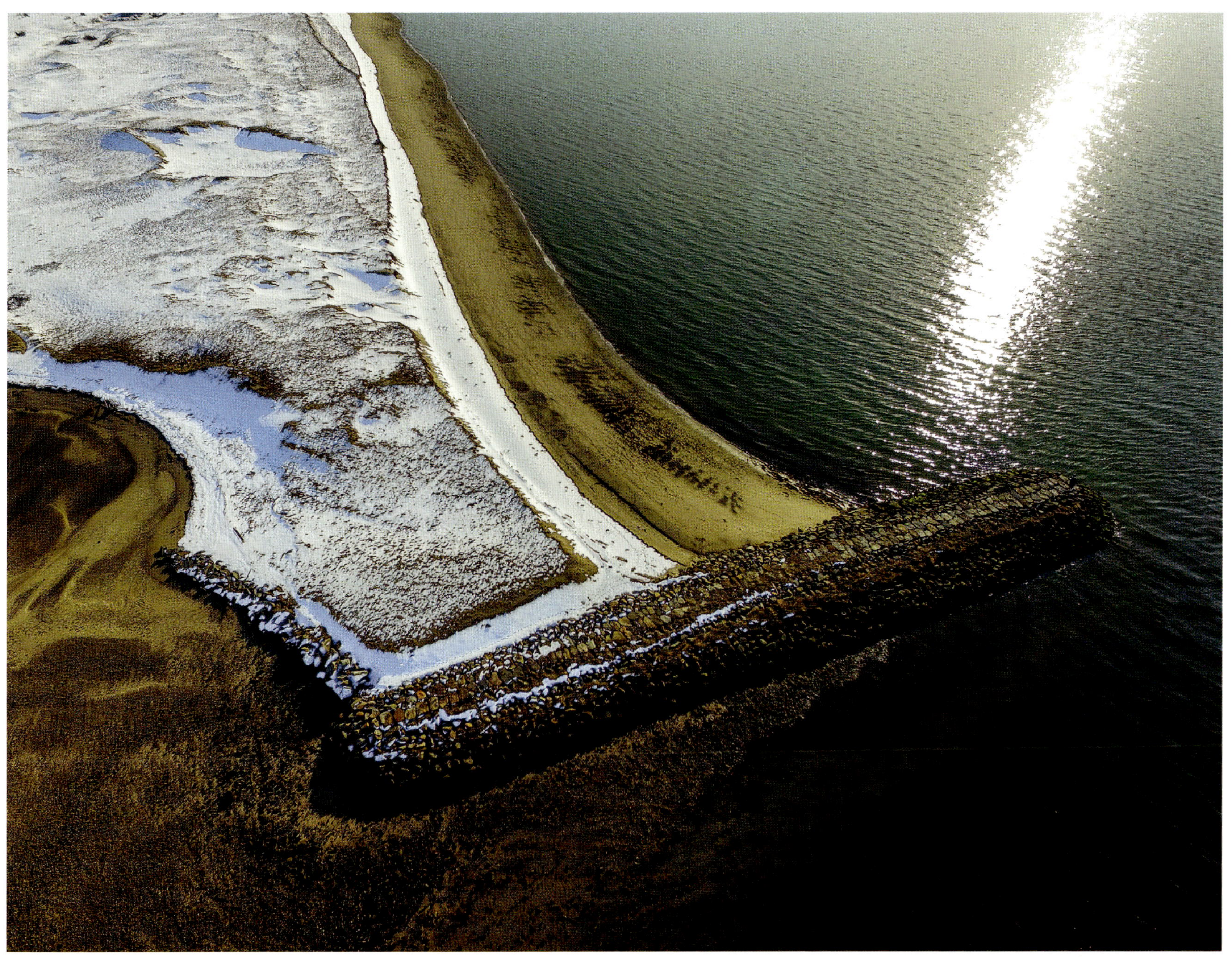

Snow-covered dunes at the southern breakwater of Pamet Harbor just before sunset.

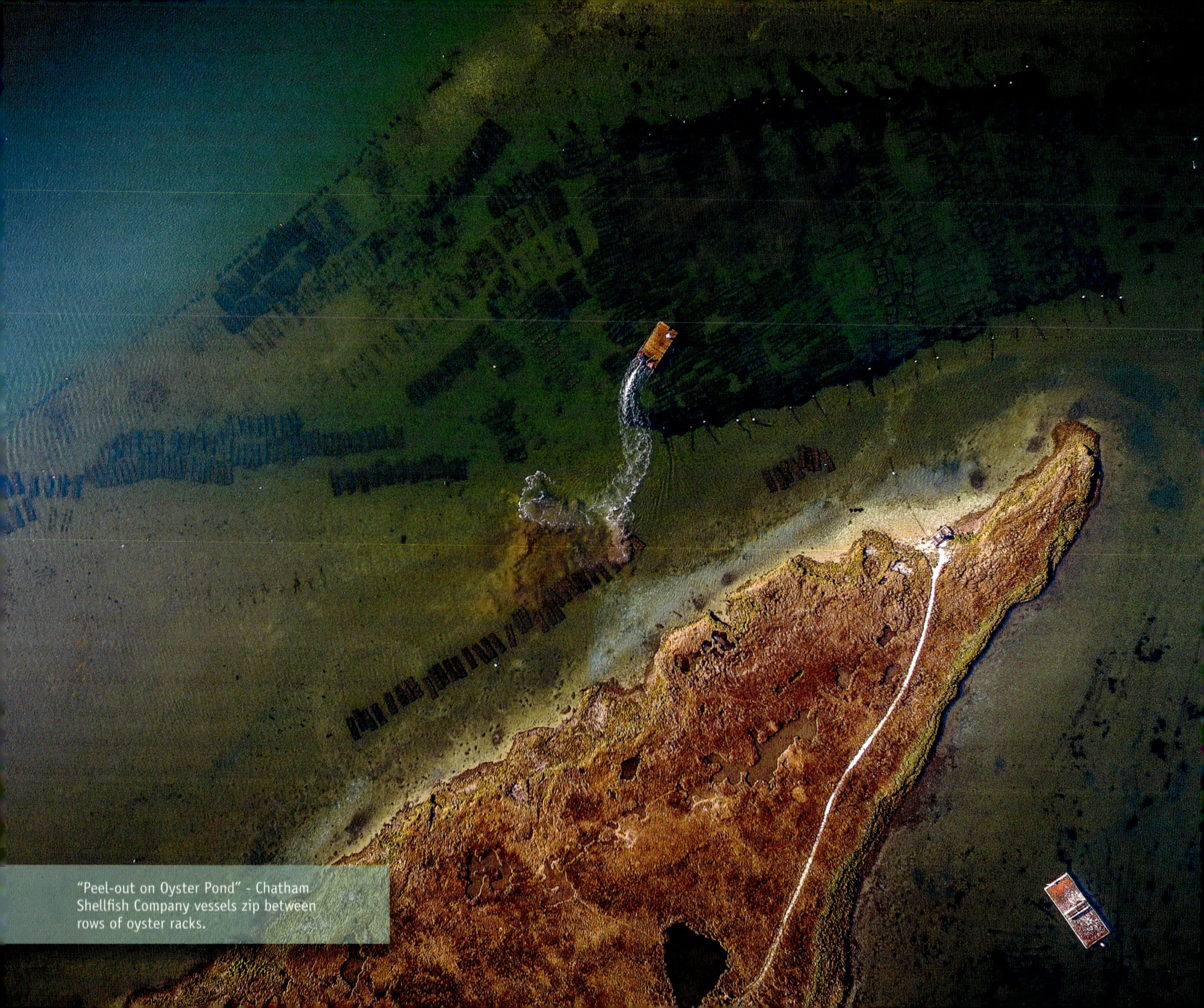

"Peel-out on Oyster Pond" - Chatham Shellfish Company vessels zip between rows of oyster racks.

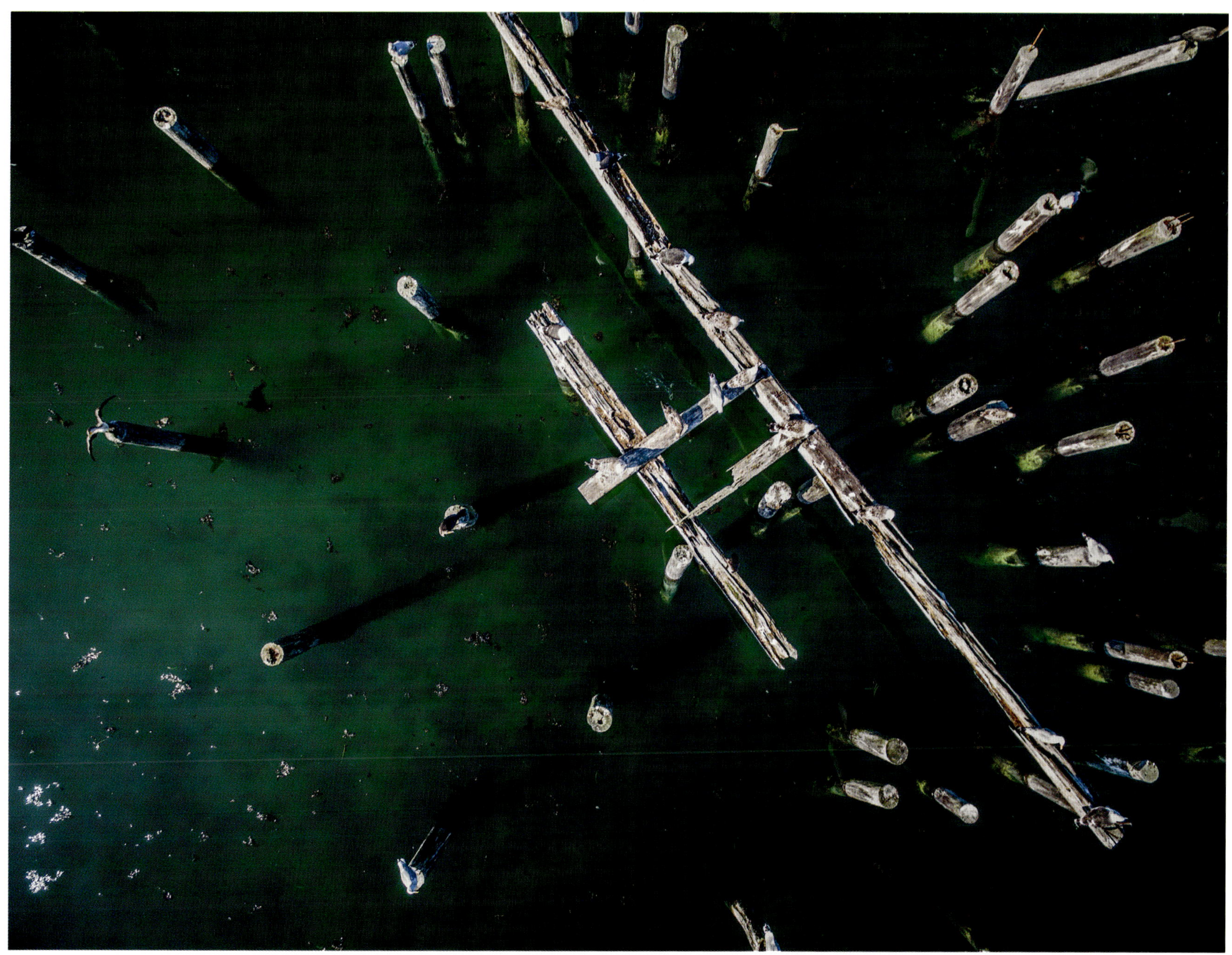

The skeletal remains of one of Provincetown's more ancient piers.

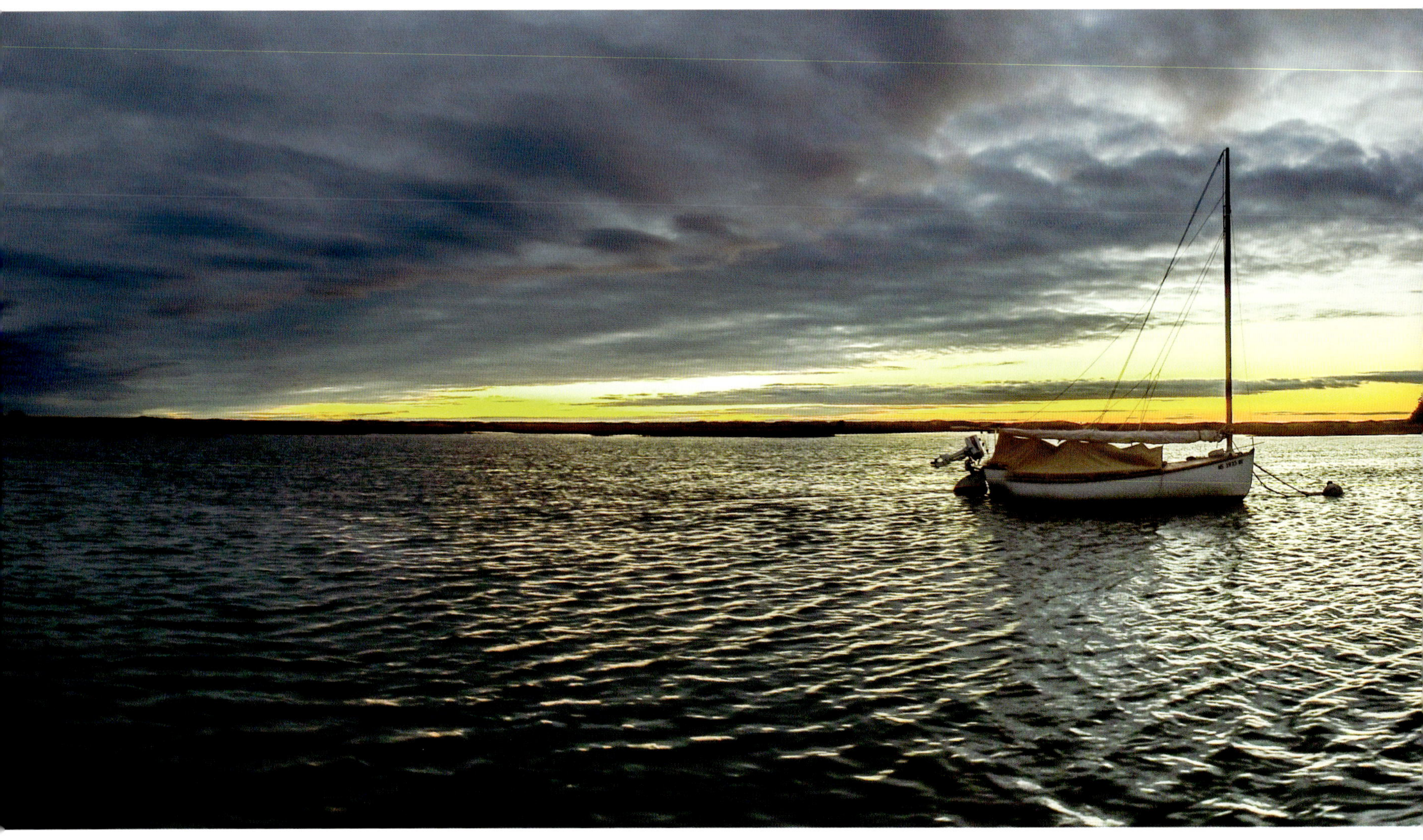

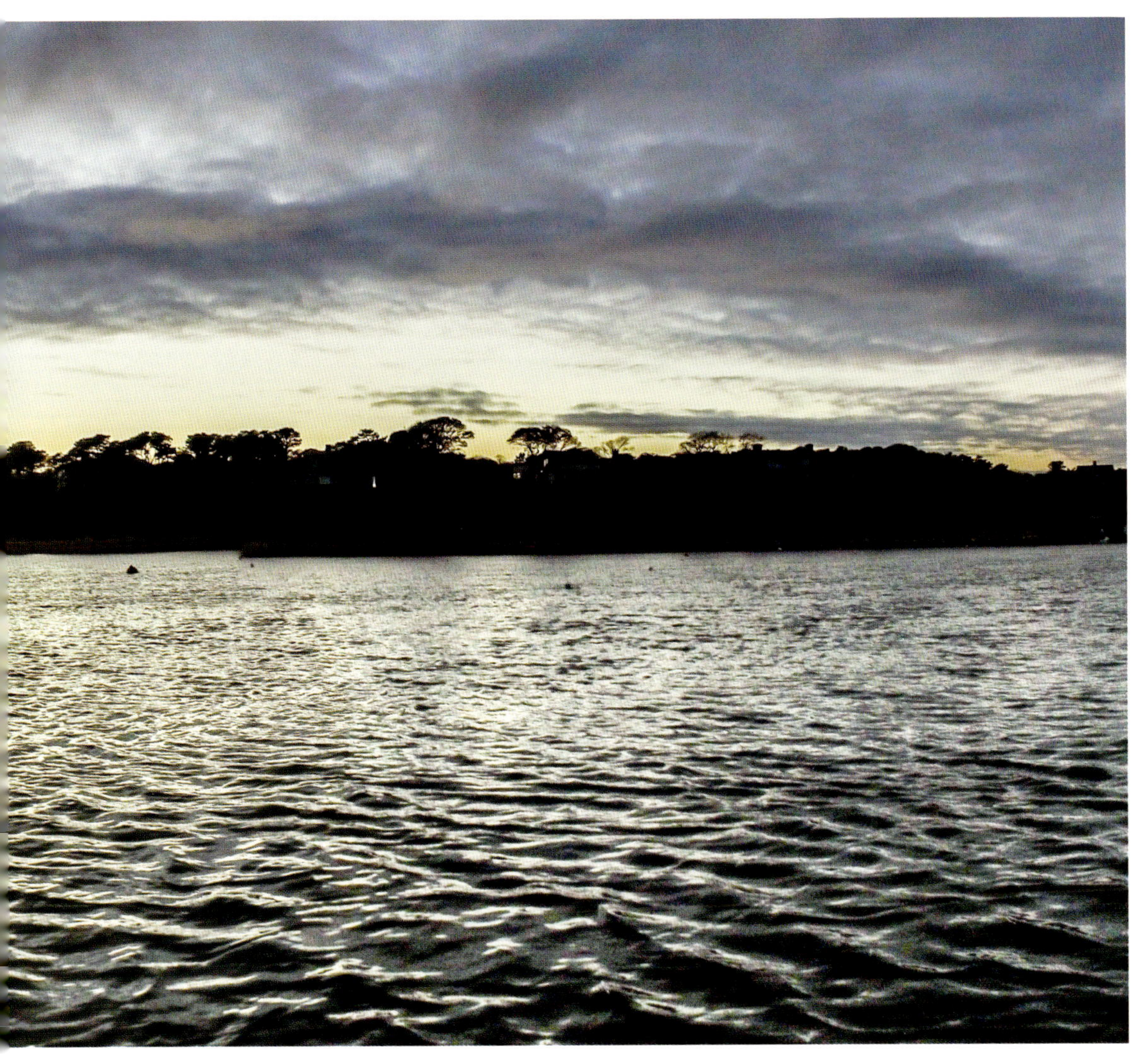

A solitary gaff-rigged cat boat remains in the river at the end of the season.

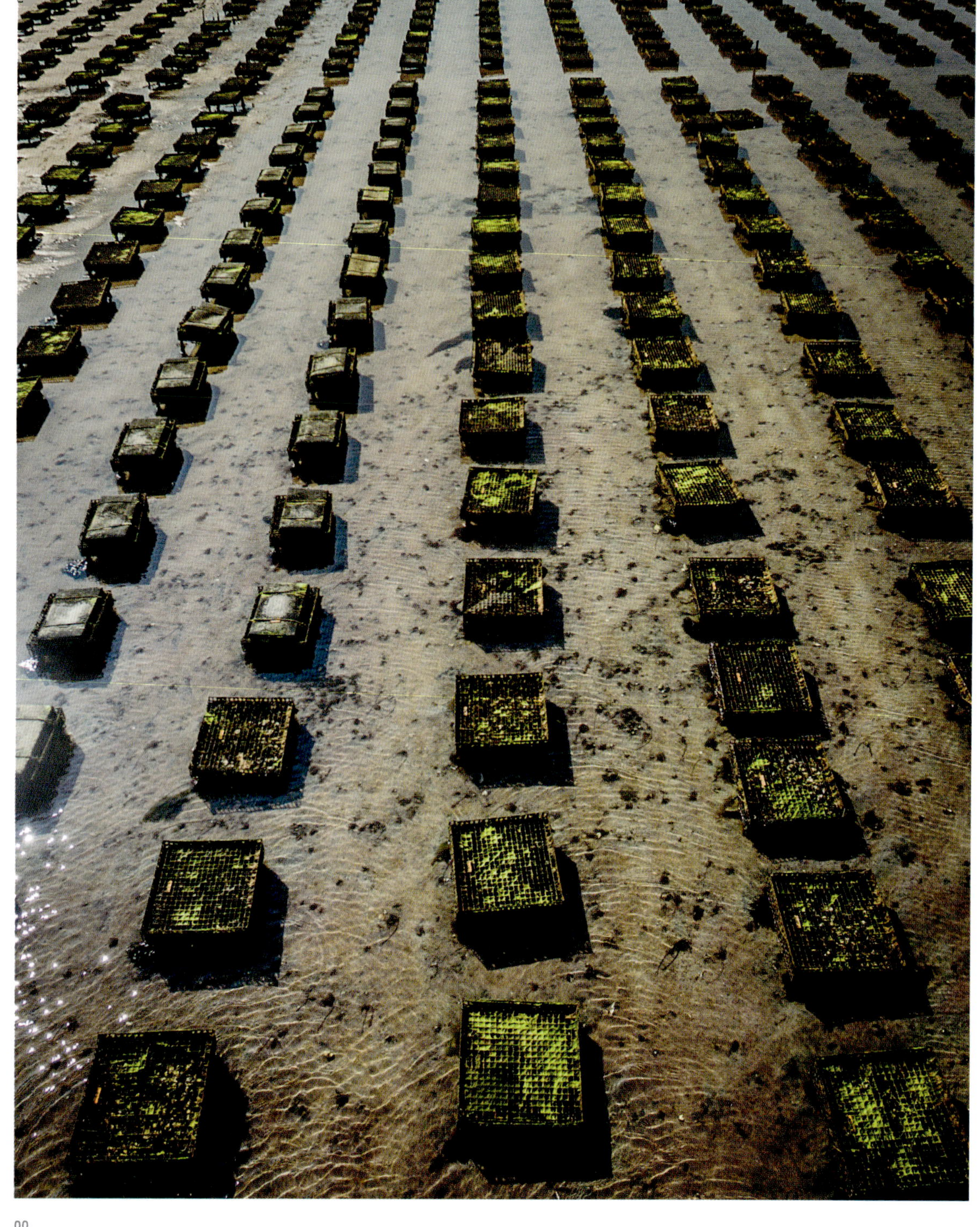

Endless rows of perfectly aligned oyster racks.

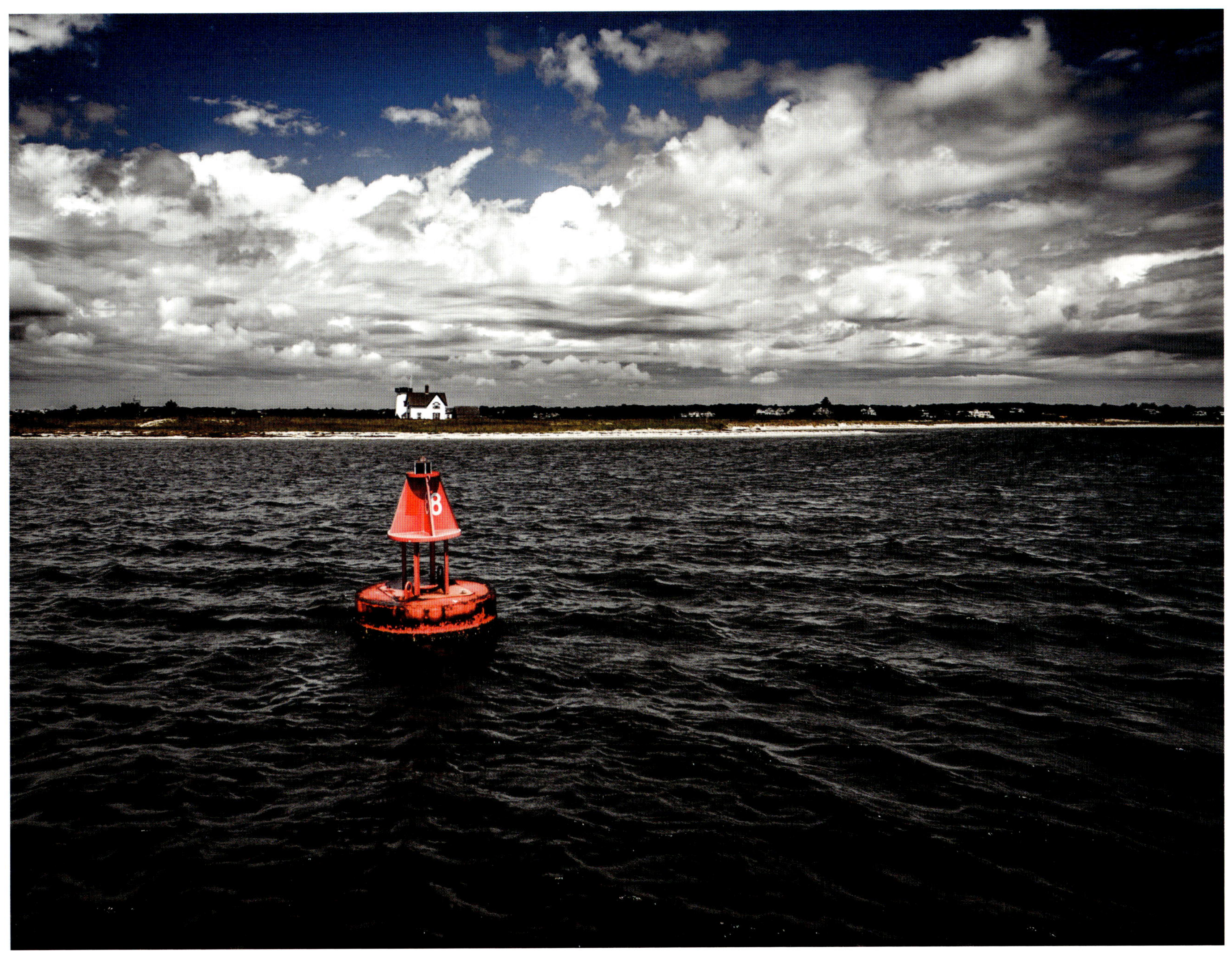

The red nun channel marker with Stage Harbor Lighthouse in the background.

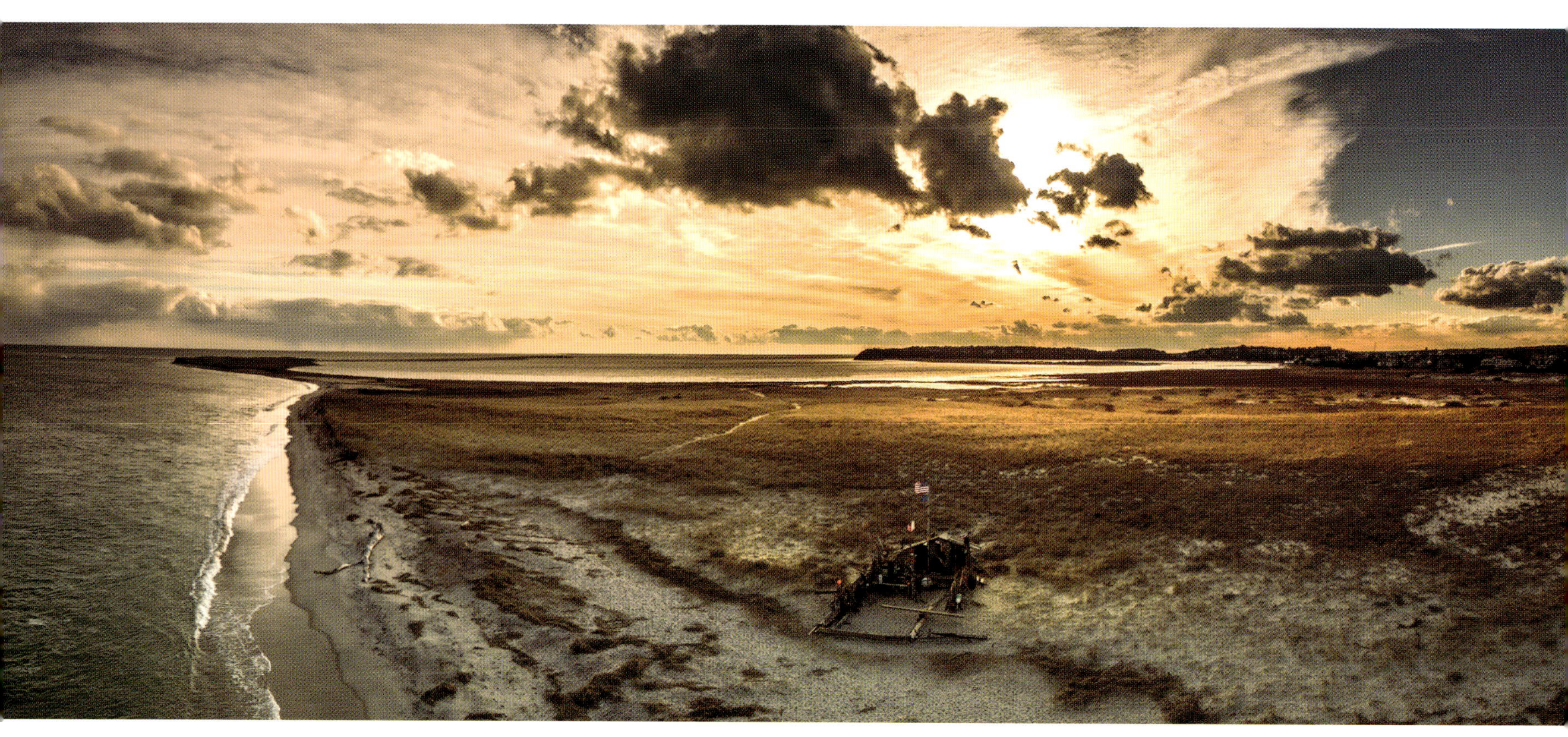

"Red, White, and Hue" - A blazing sunset behind the beach shack in Chatham with Old Glory waving at full-tilt.

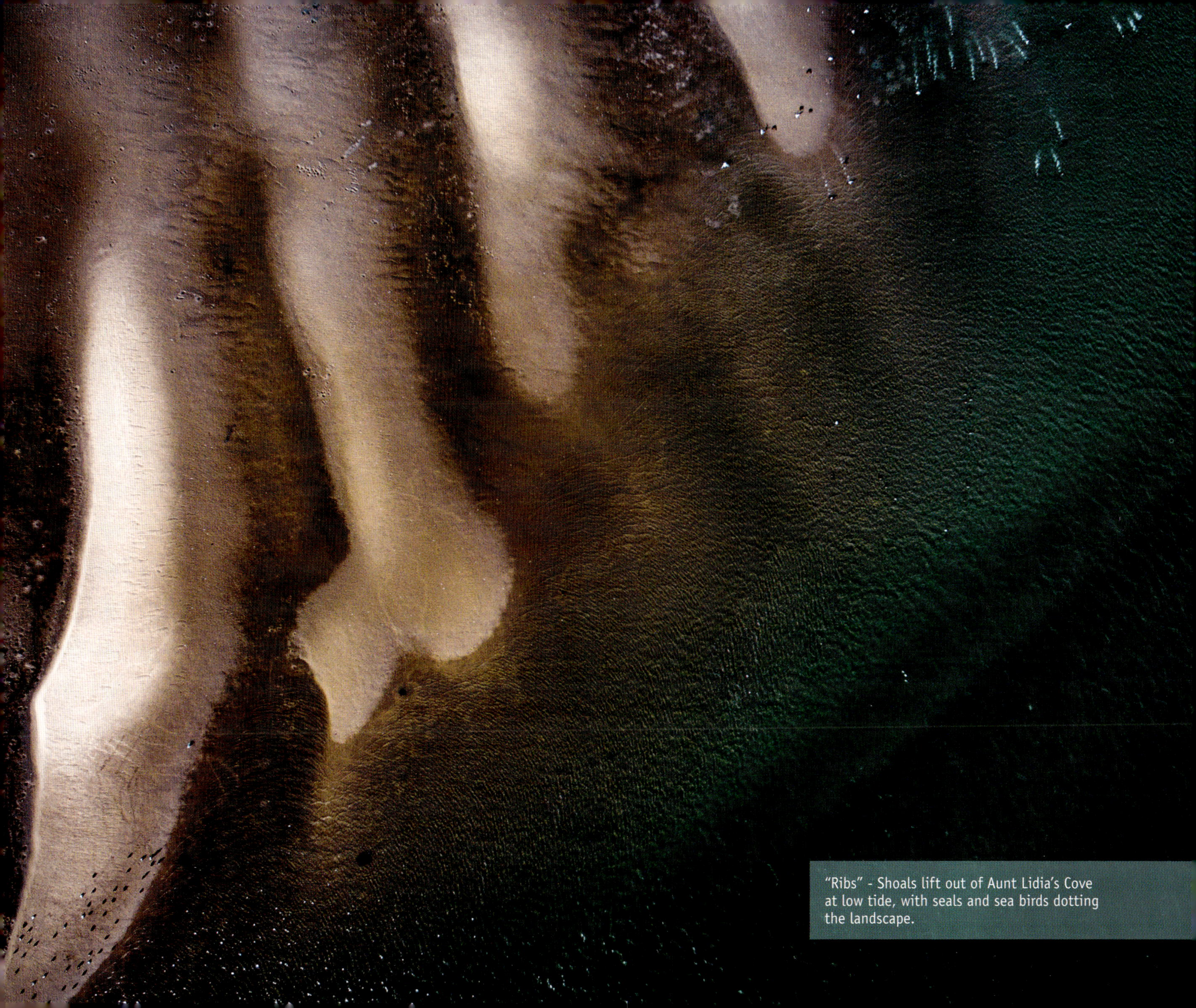

"Ribs" - Shoals lift out of Aunt Lidia's Cove at low tide, with seals and sea birds dotting the landscape.

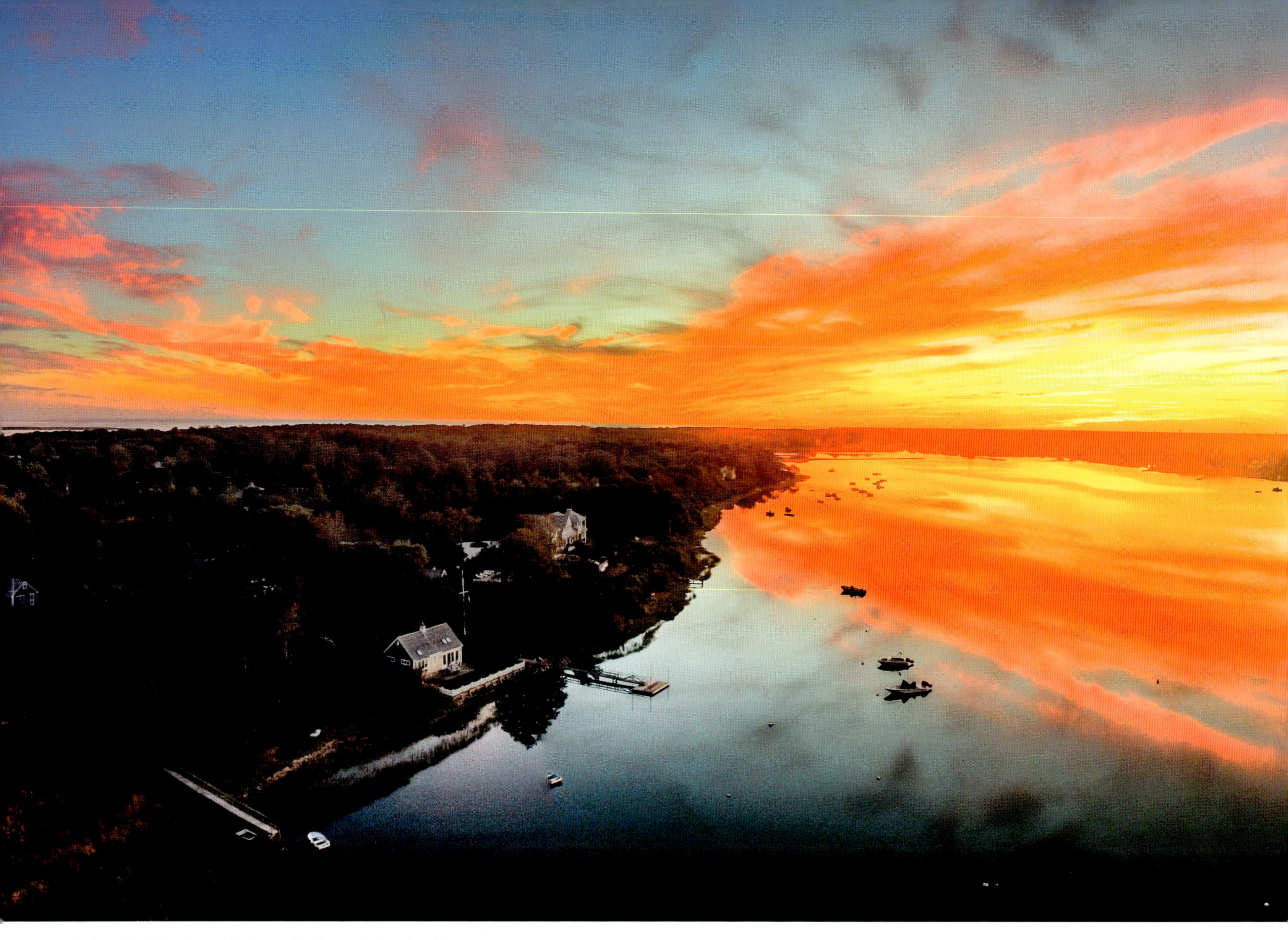

“Ribbon Candy” - A double dose of a fiery, pink-and-gold sunset.

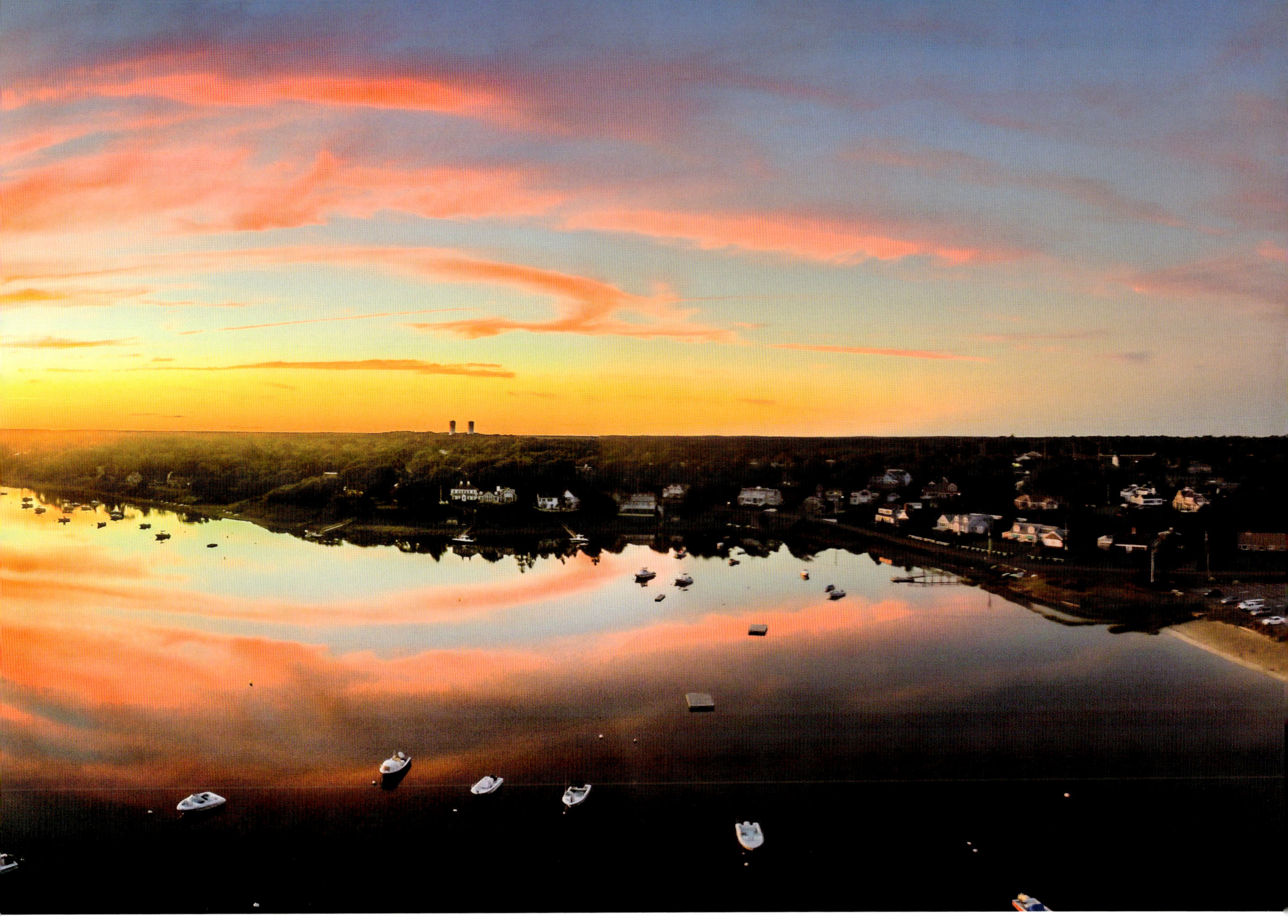

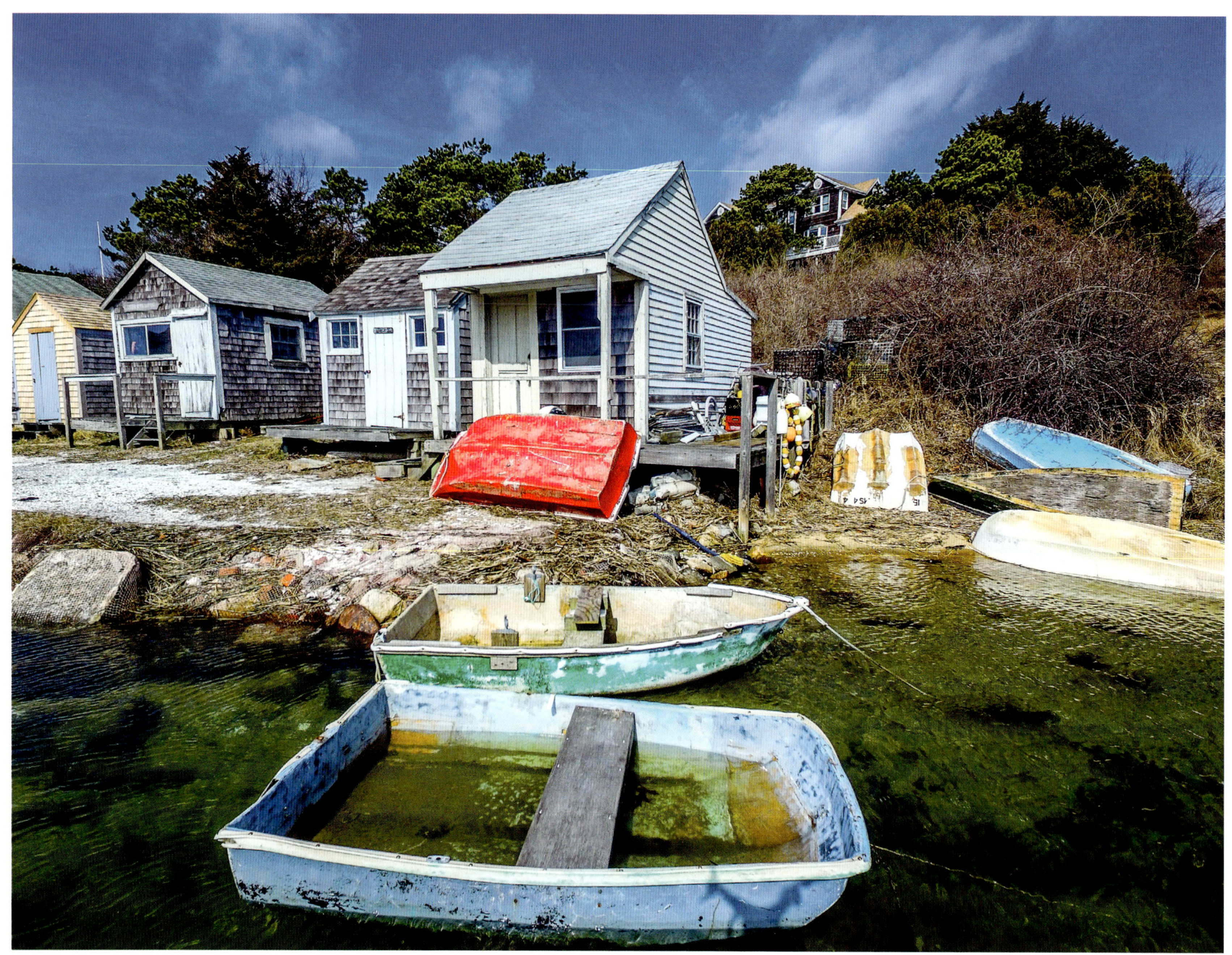

Driving down to the shanties on the Oyster River is like stepping back in time.

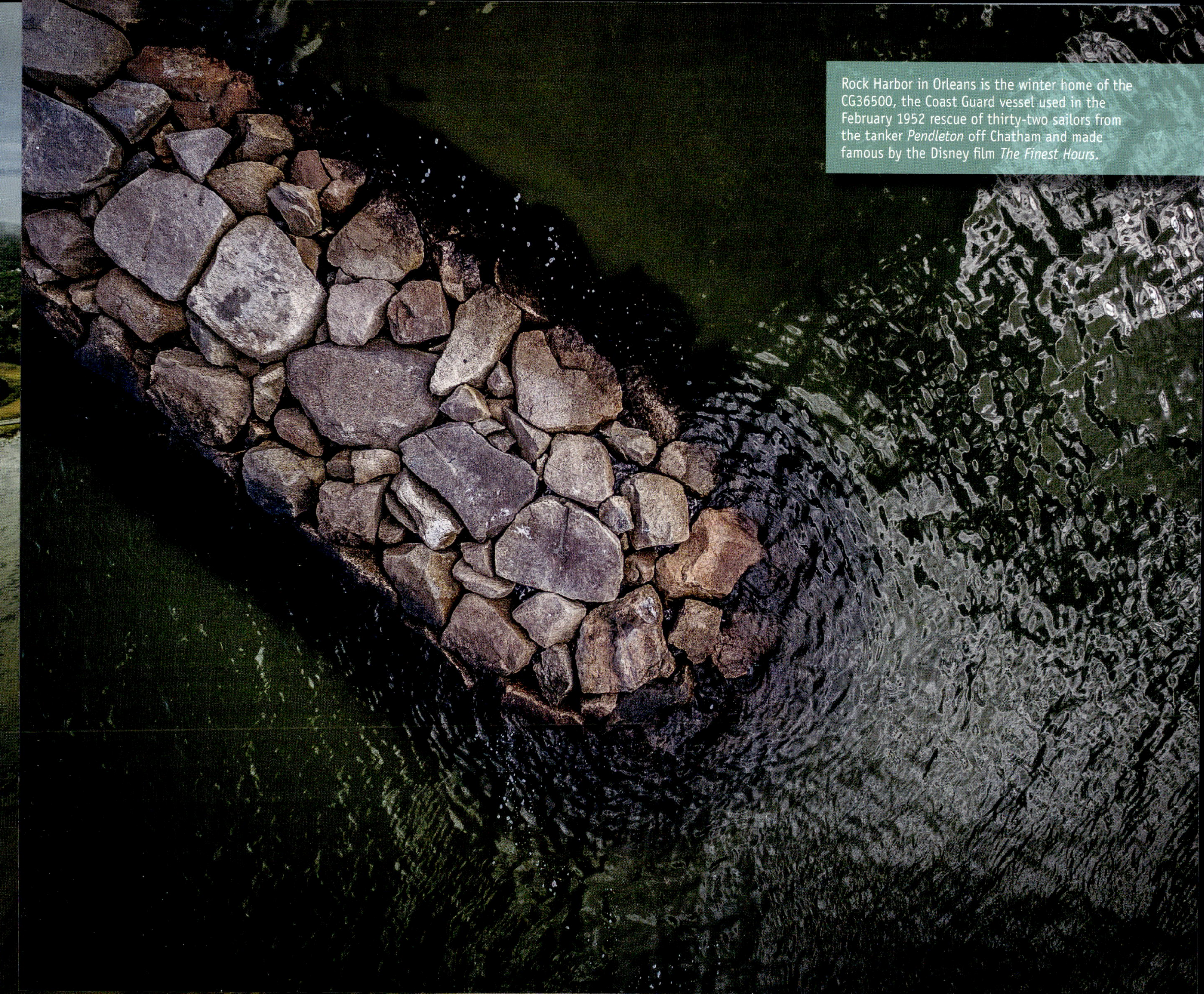

Rock Harbor in Orleans is the winter home of the CG36500, the Coast Guard vessel used in the February 1952 rescue of thirty-two sailors from the tanker *Pendleton* off Chatham and made famous by the Disney film *The Finest Hours*.

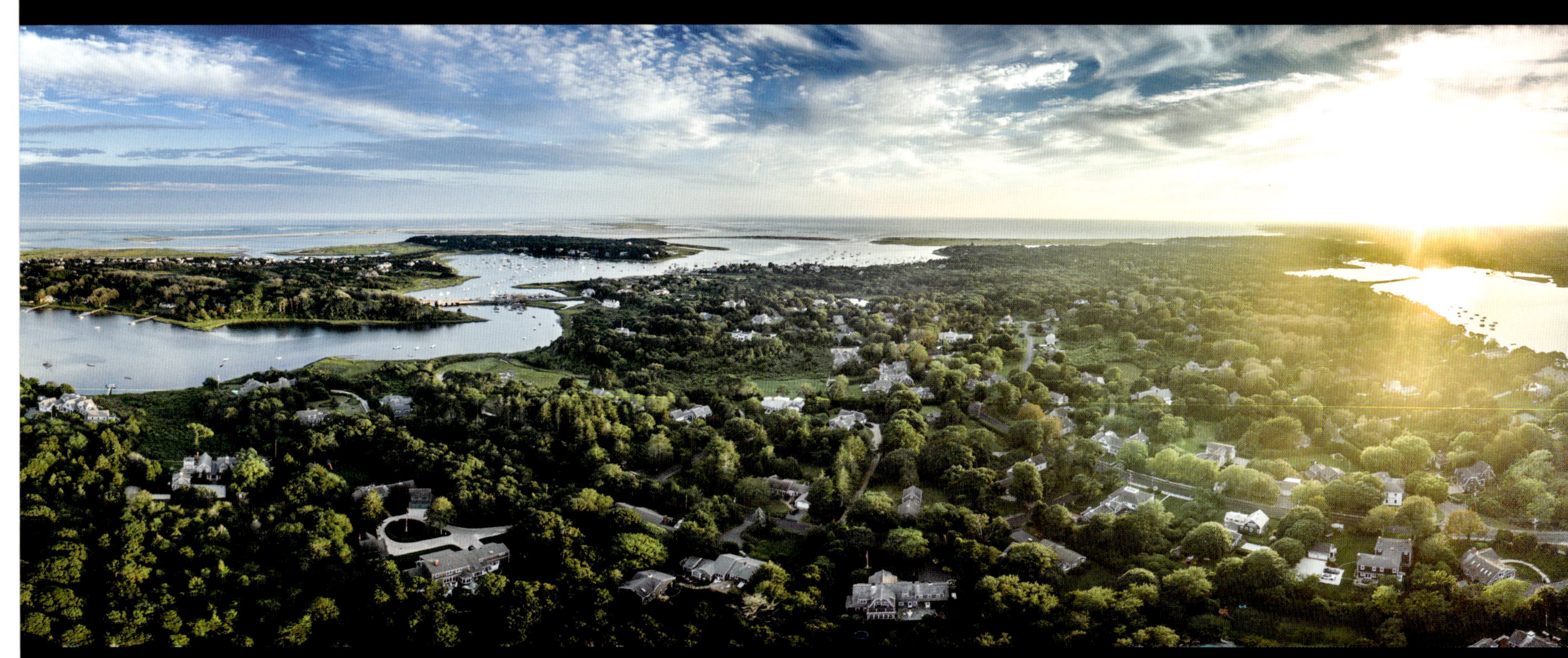

"Room with a View" - At 400 feet all is quiet, even on the Fourth of July.

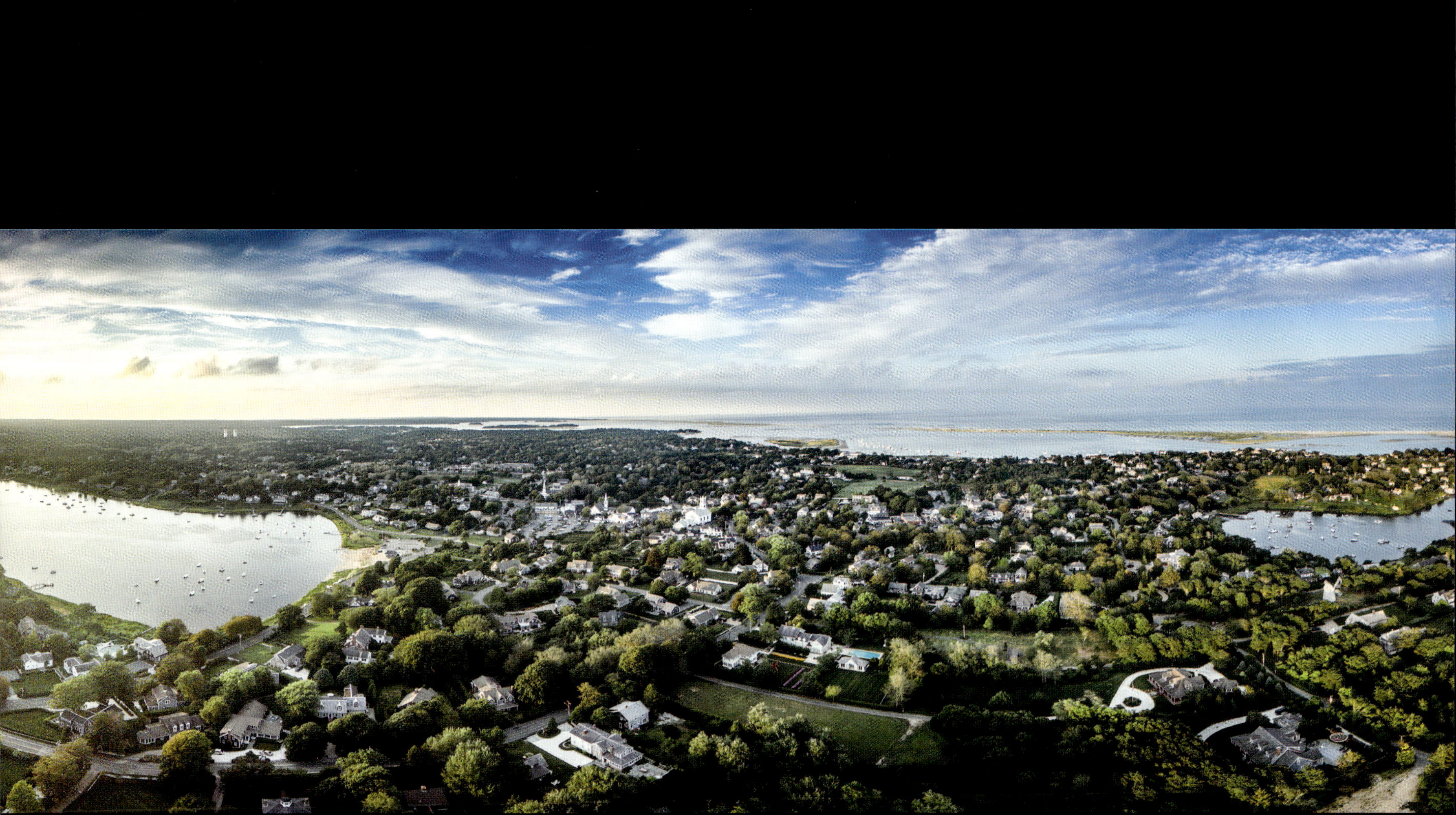

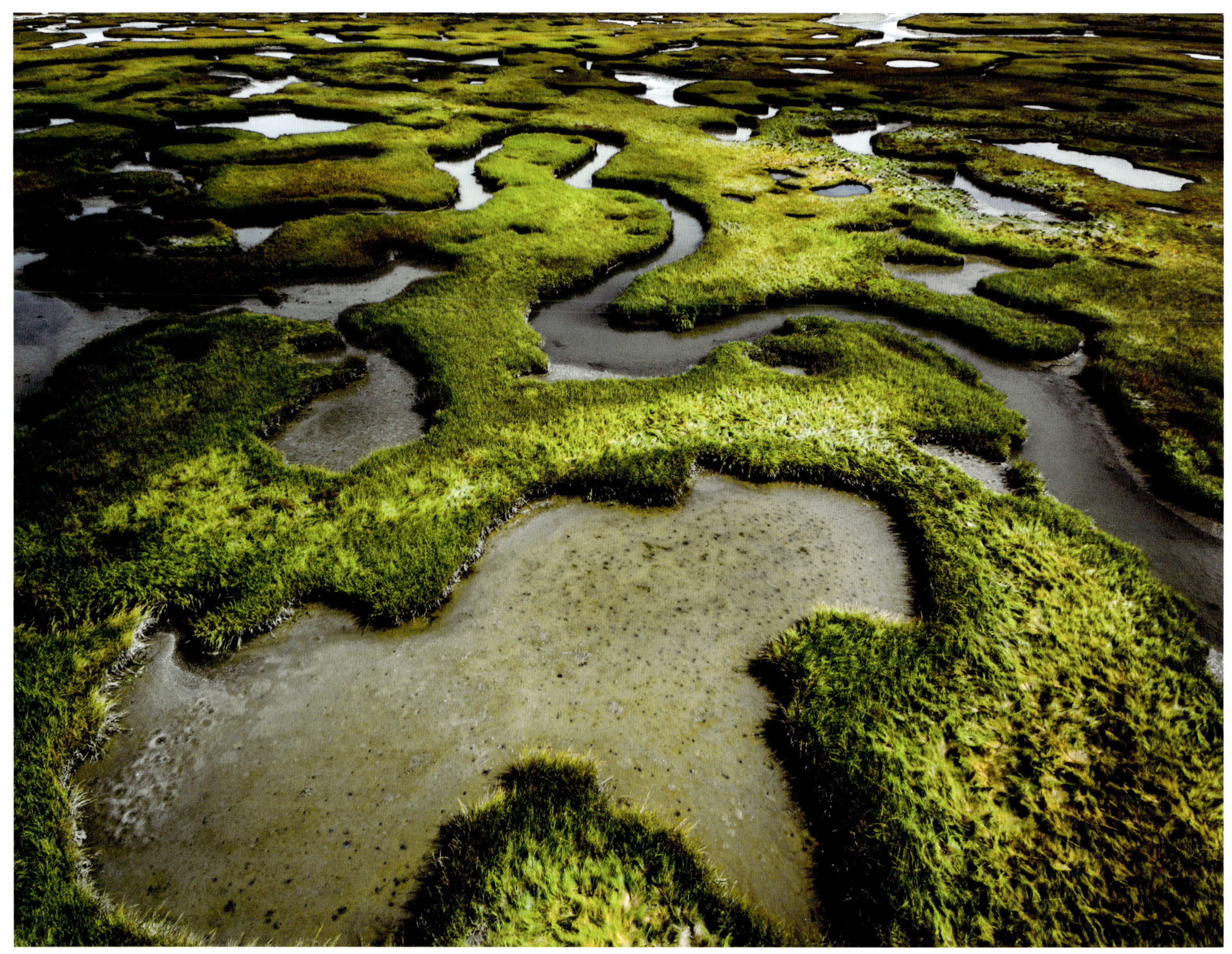

Coastal salt marshes like these are habitat for countless critters, including crabs, mussels, and birds of all types.

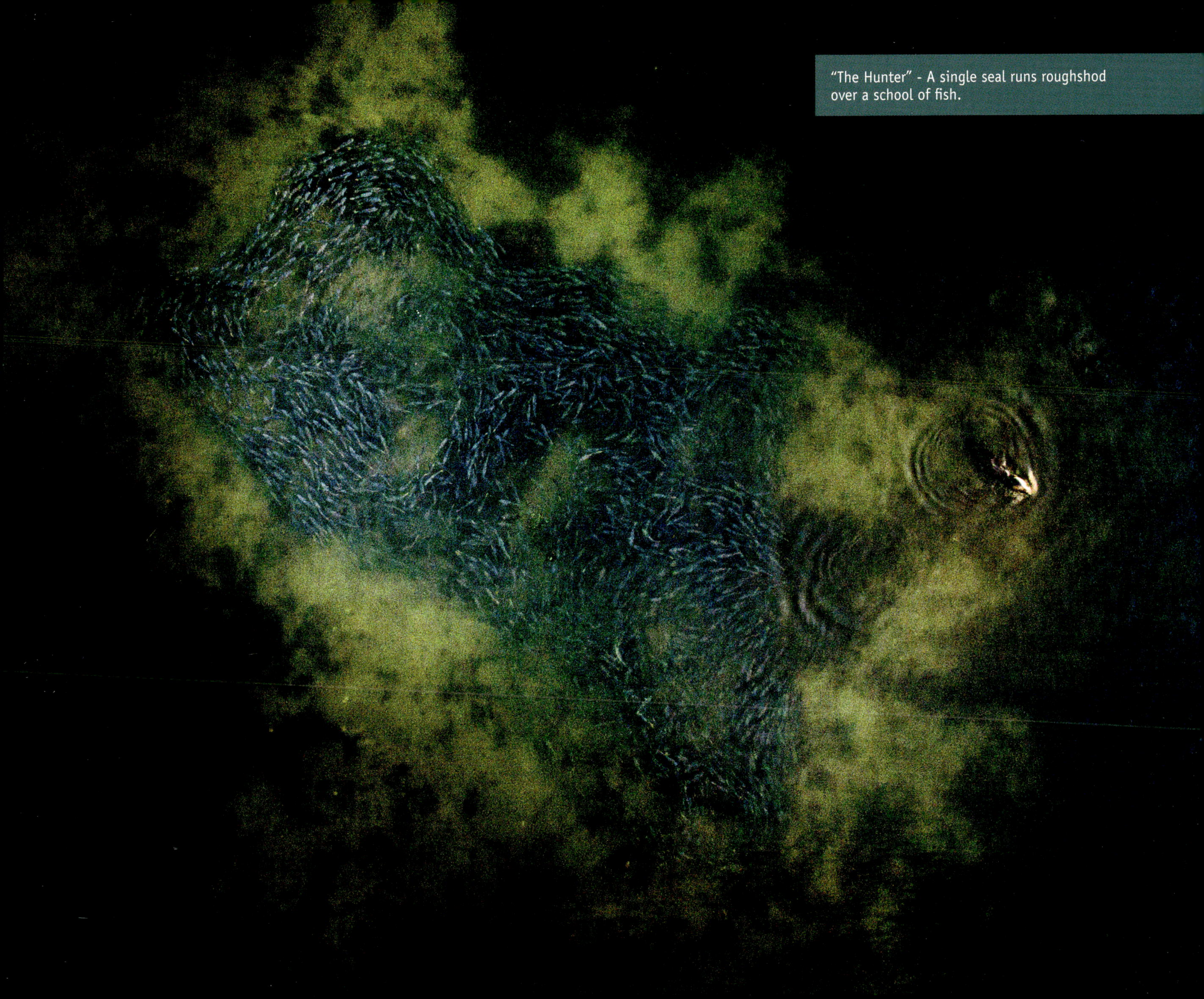

"The Hunter" - A single seal runs roughshod over a school of fish.

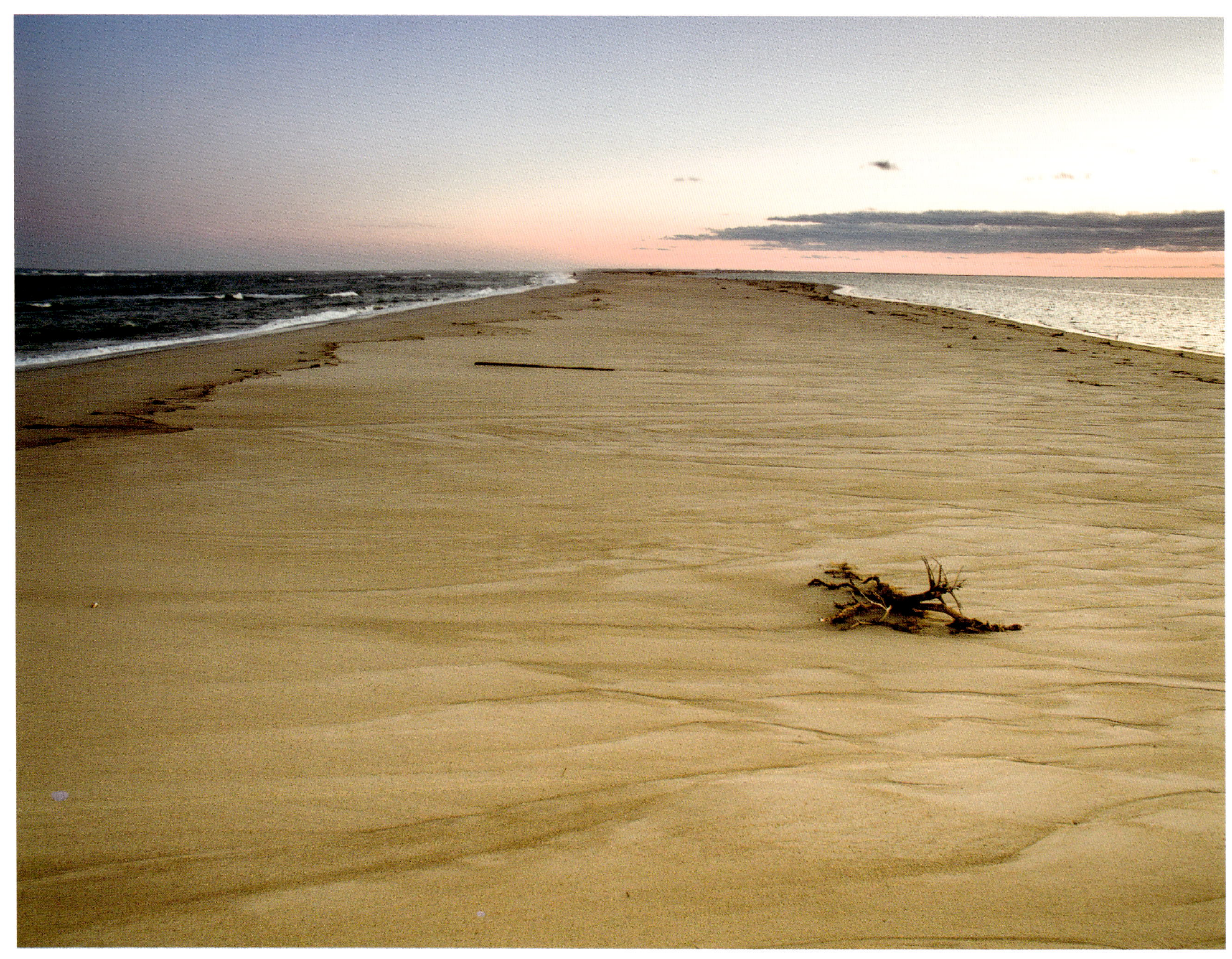

Driftwood that hasn't done any drifting in a very long time.

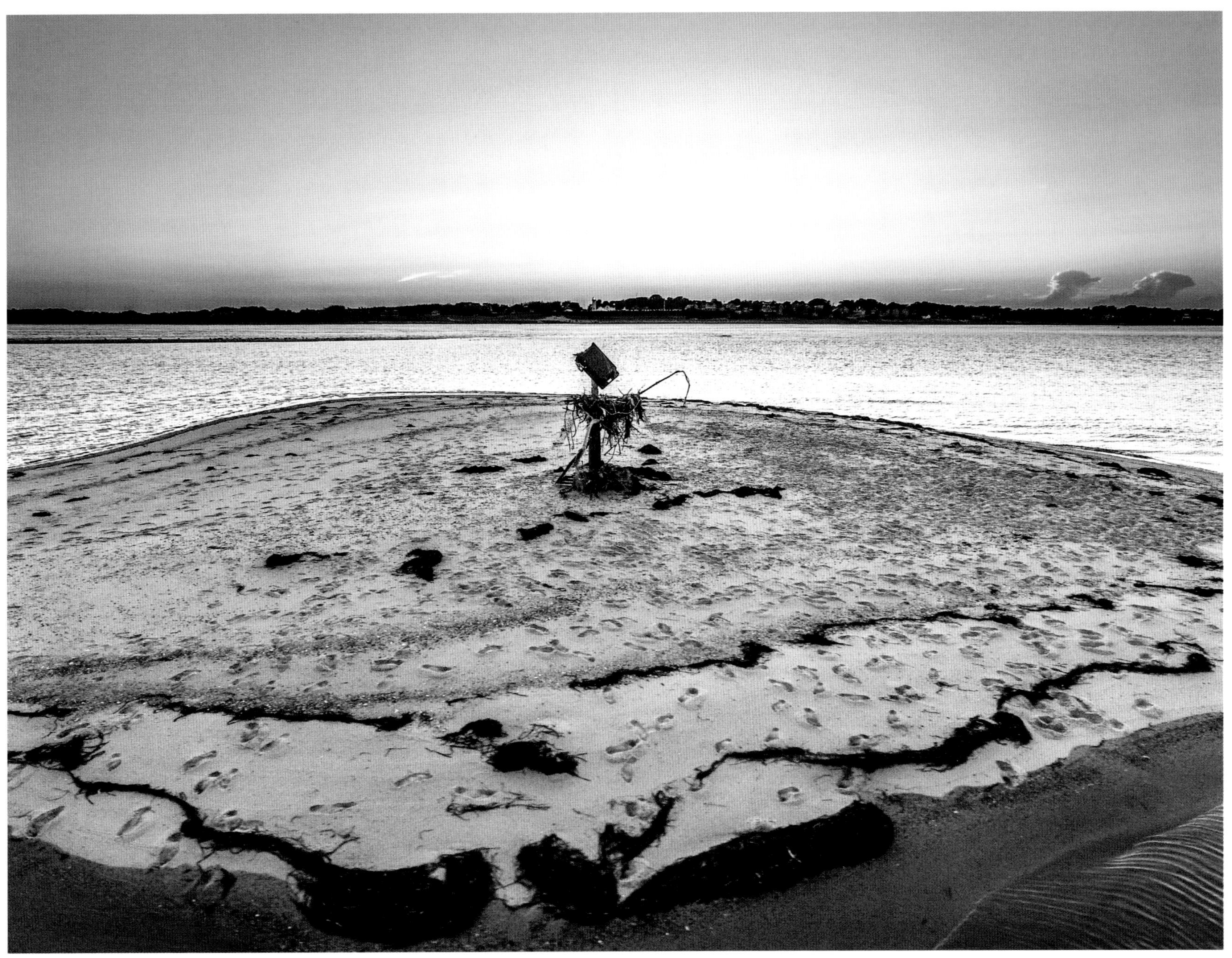

A makeshift monument is formed from debris that has washed ashore over the years.

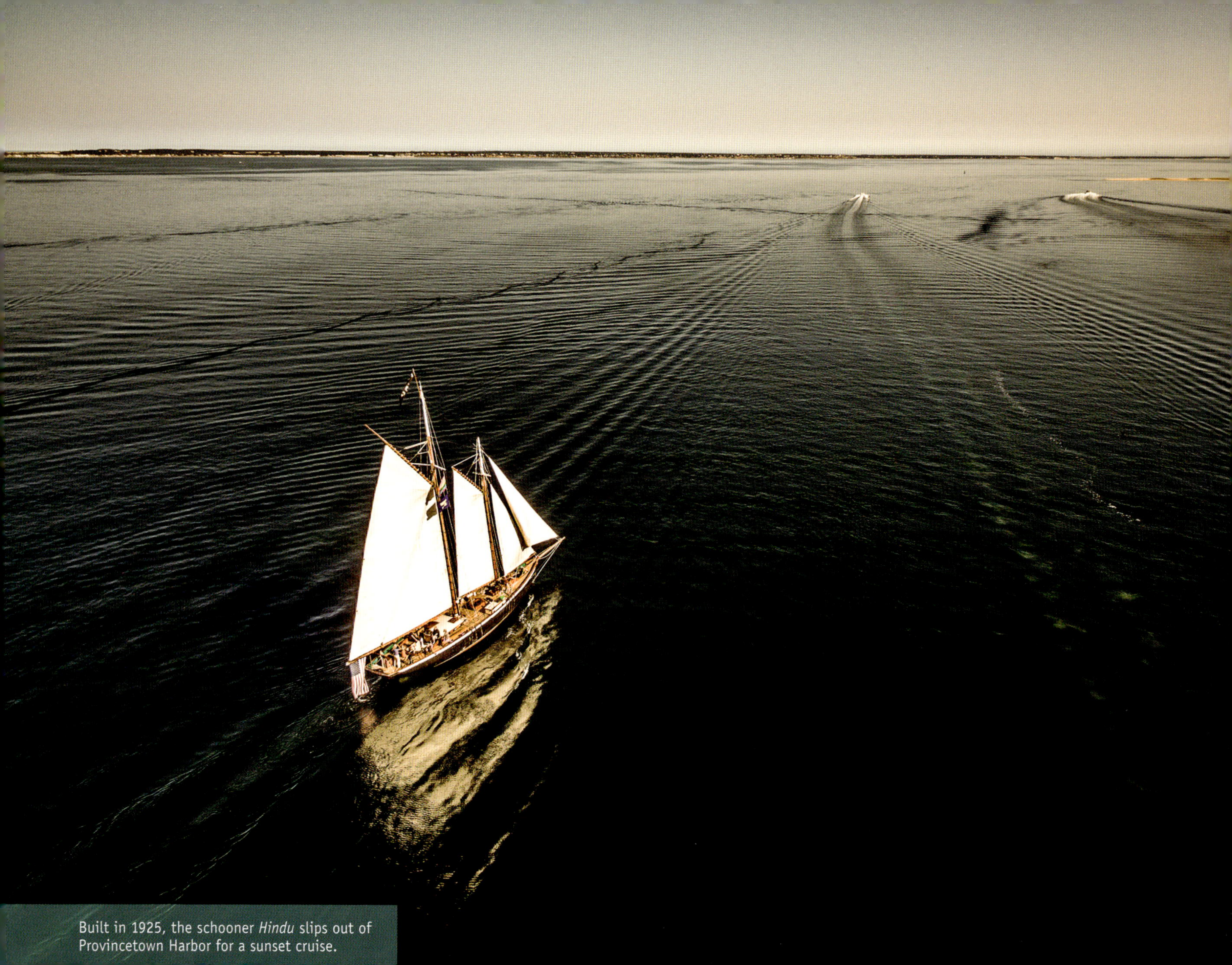

Built in 1925, the schooner *Hindu* slips out of Provincetown Harbor for a sunset cruise.

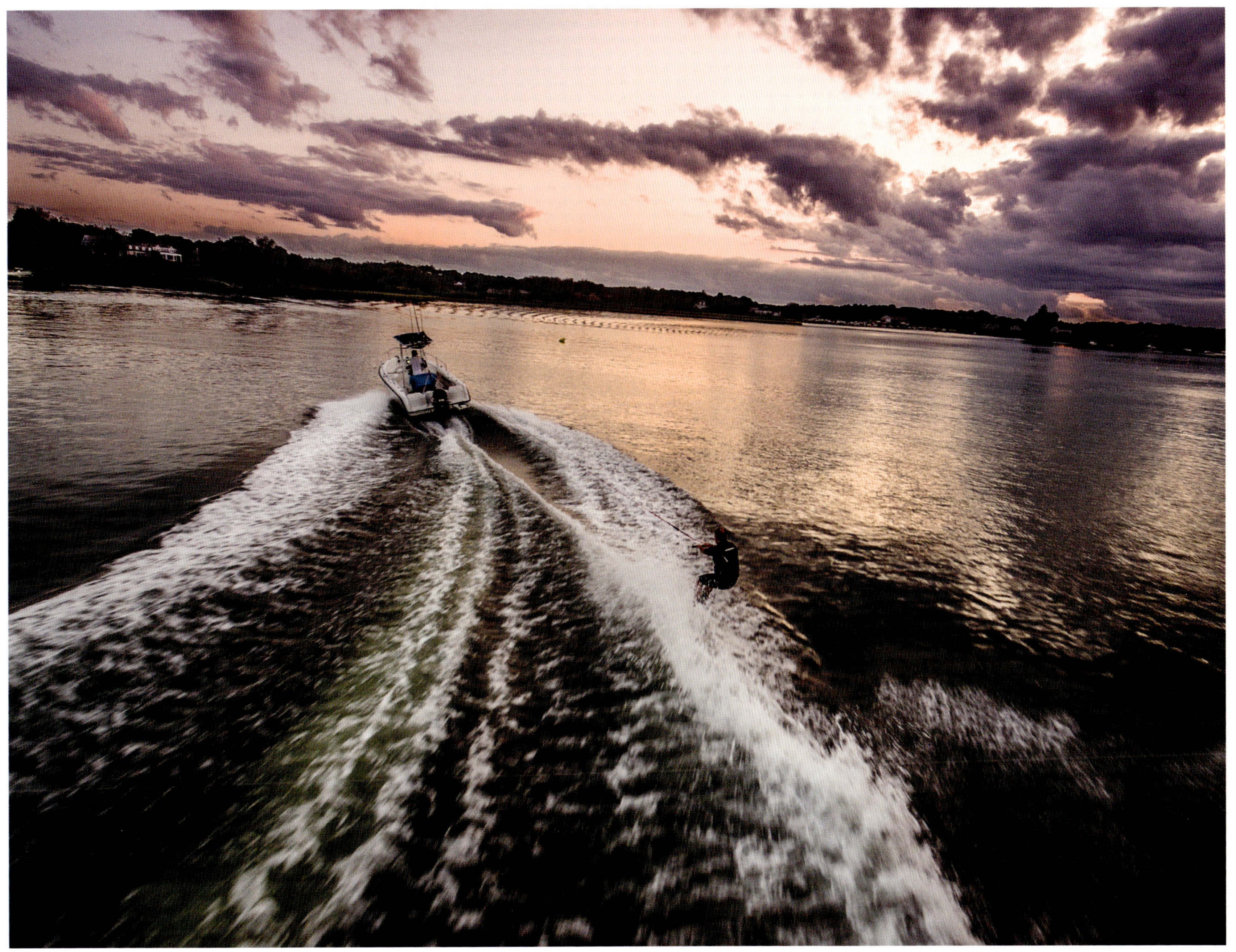

Waterskiers start the summer off right on Memorial Day.

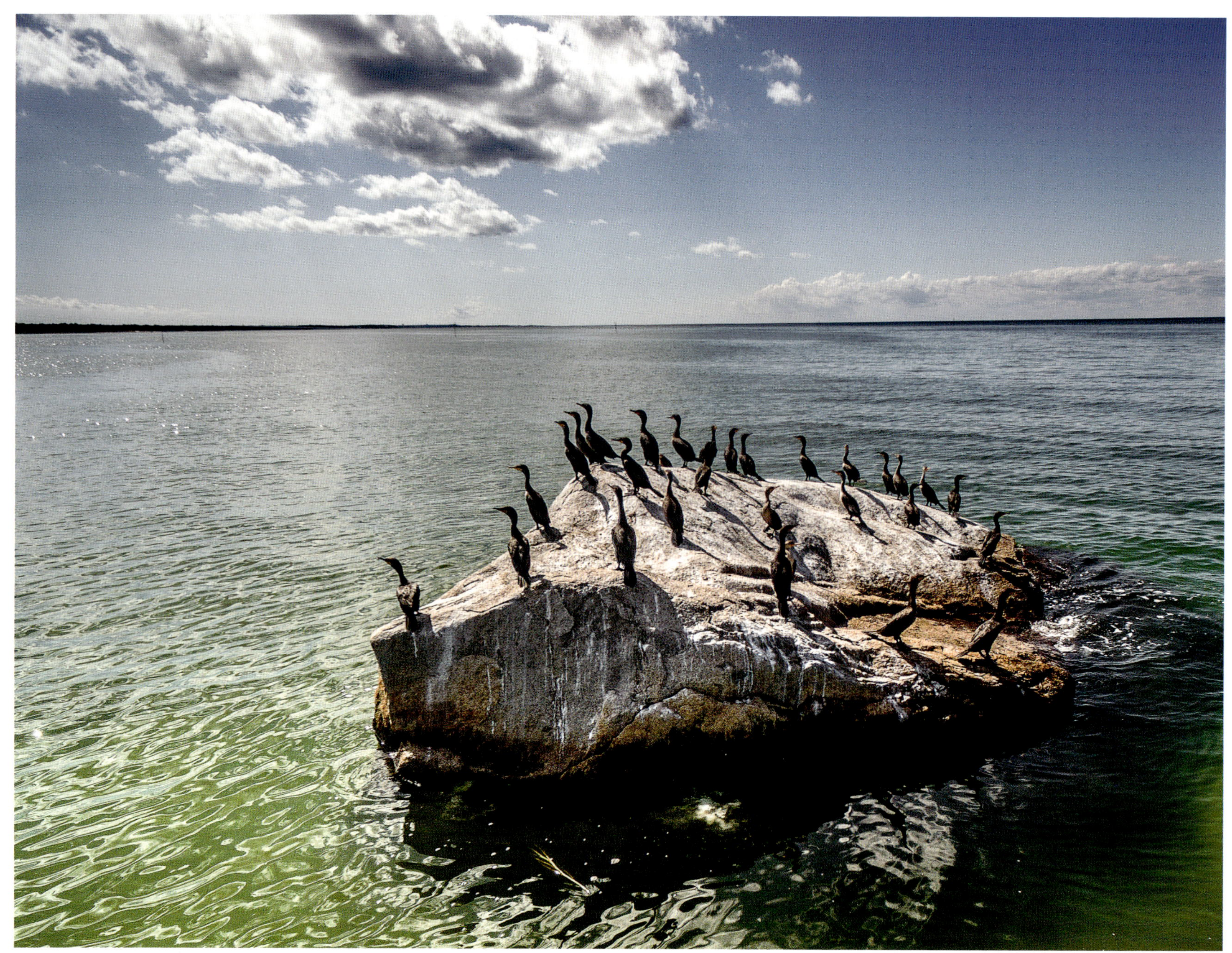

Cormorants resting at the mouth of the Eastham side of Rock Harbor.

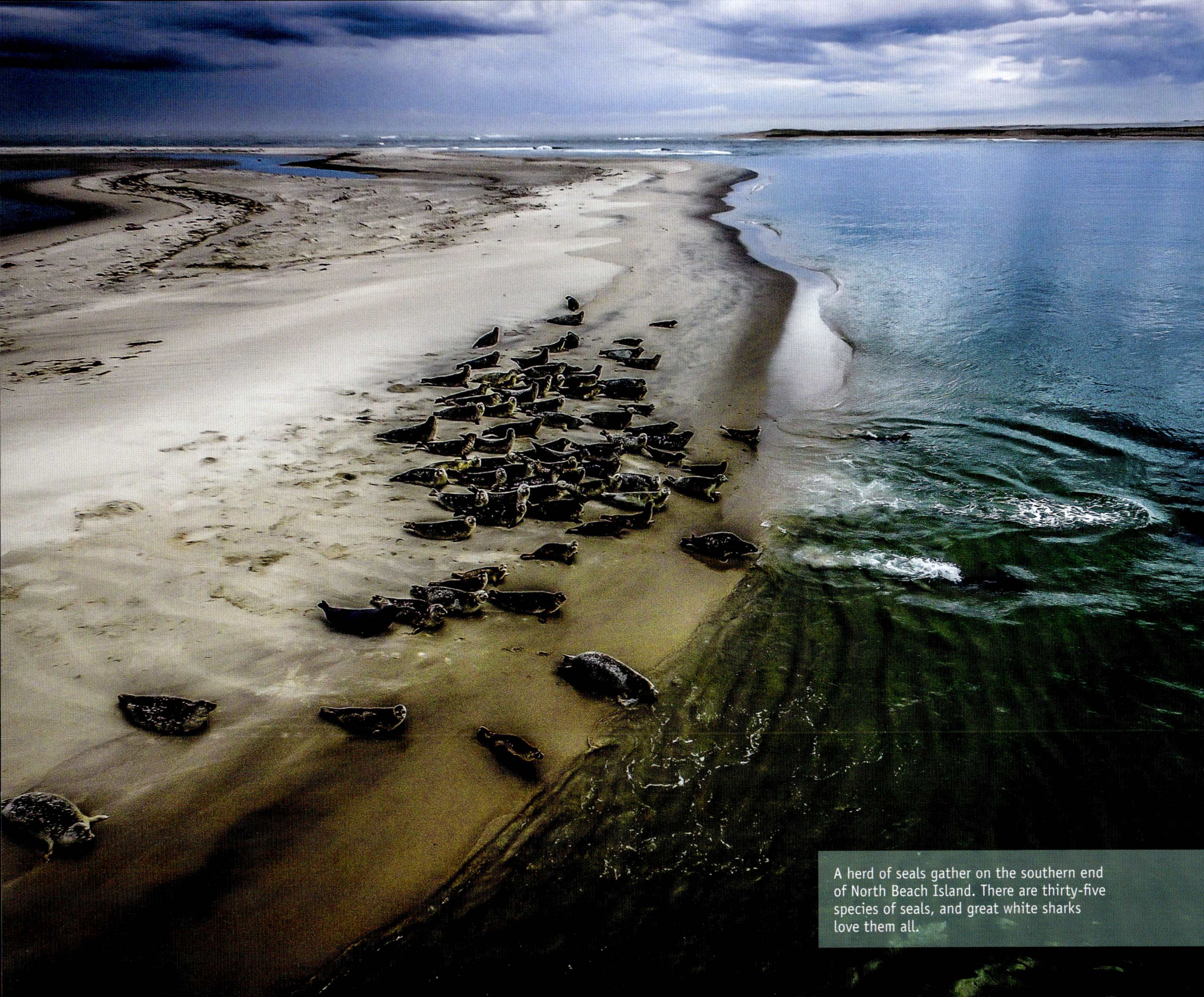

A herd of seals gather on the southern end of North Beach Island. There are thirty-five species of seals, and great white sharks love them all.

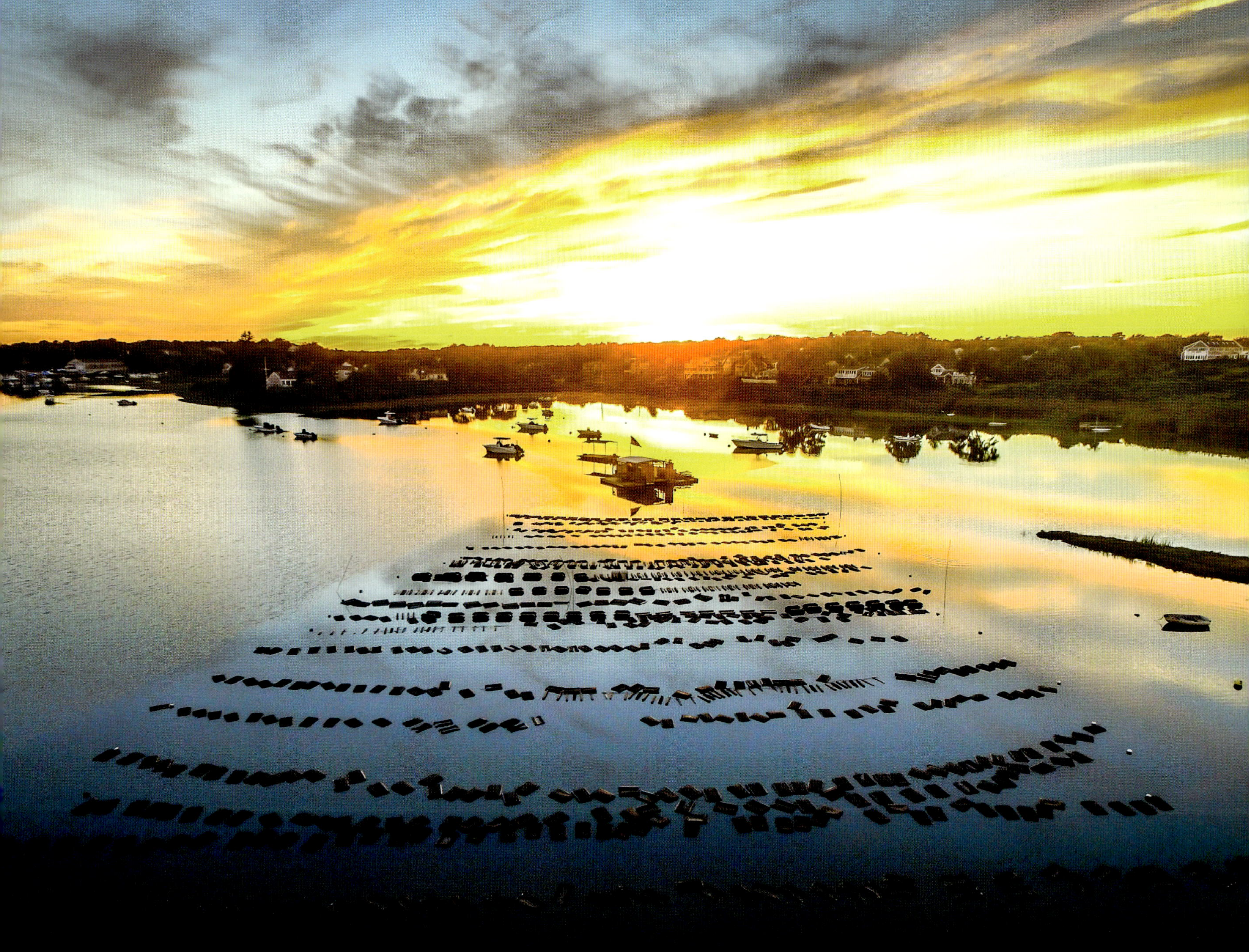

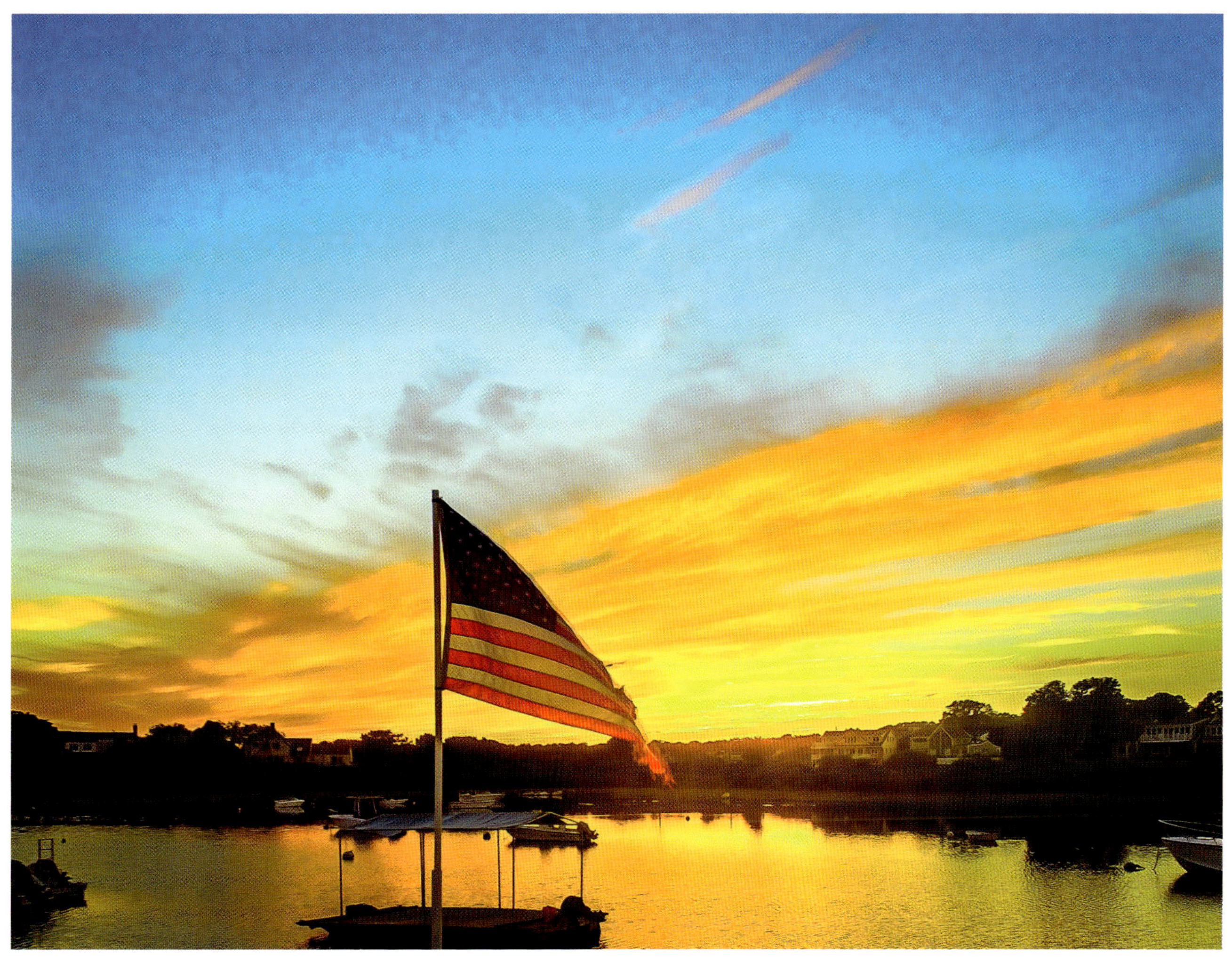

Old Glory at sunset.

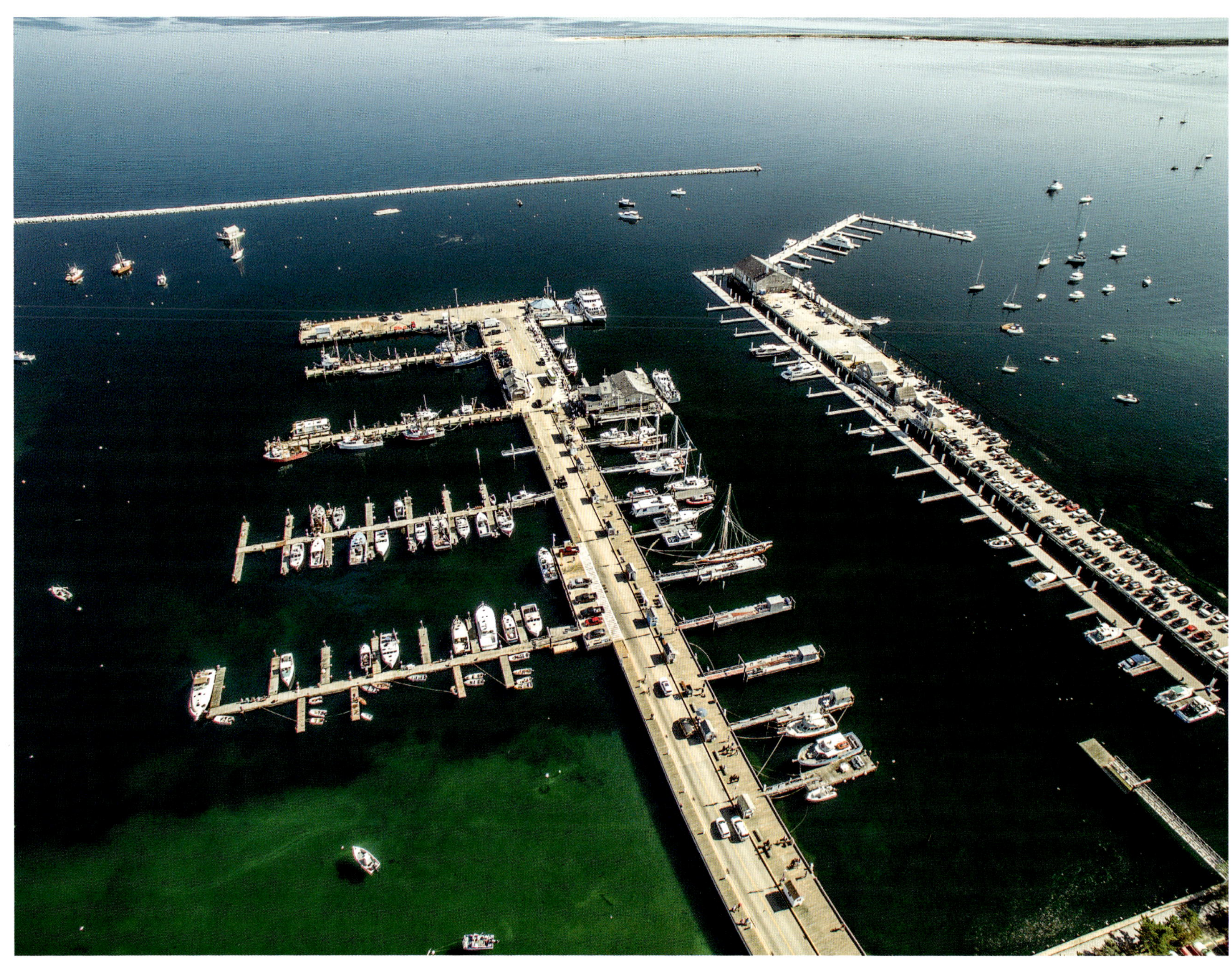

The town pier in Provincetown plays host to thousands of tourists every day even in late September.

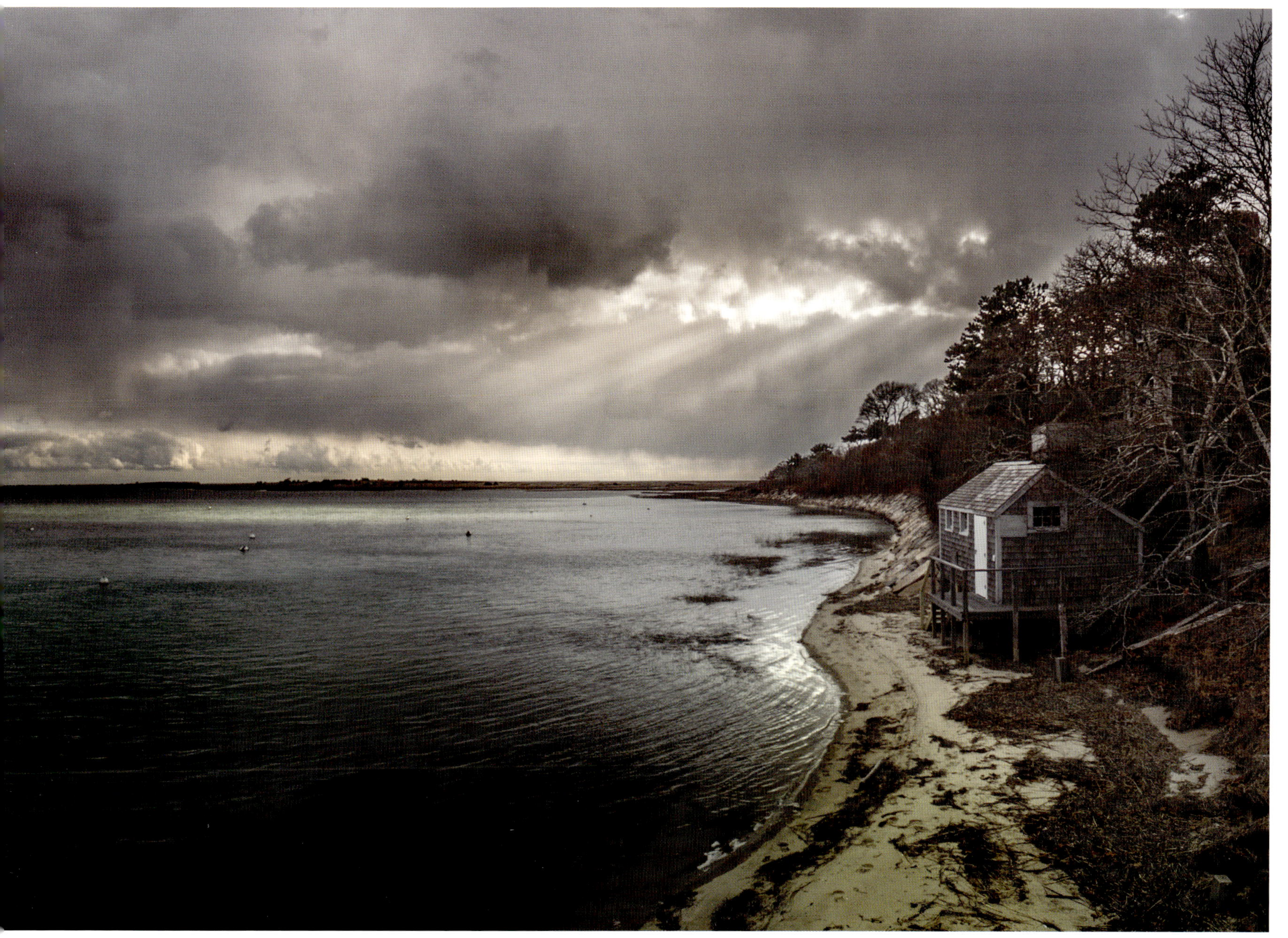

"Shine" - Crepuscular rays, commonly referred to as God's rays, shoot through the cloud cover of a fast-moving front on an exceptionally windy day.

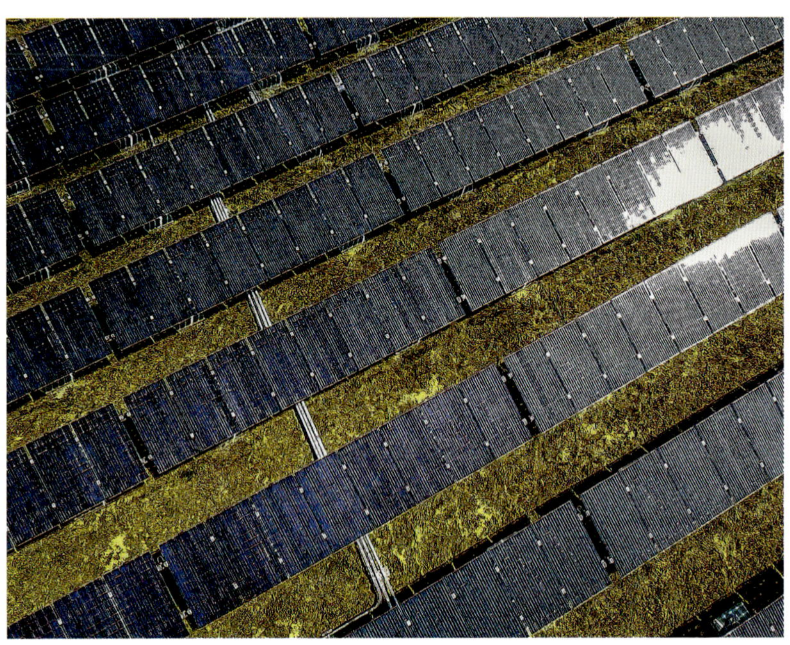

One of the many solar farms on the Cape, which make up five to ten percent of Massachusetts's total solar-panel output.

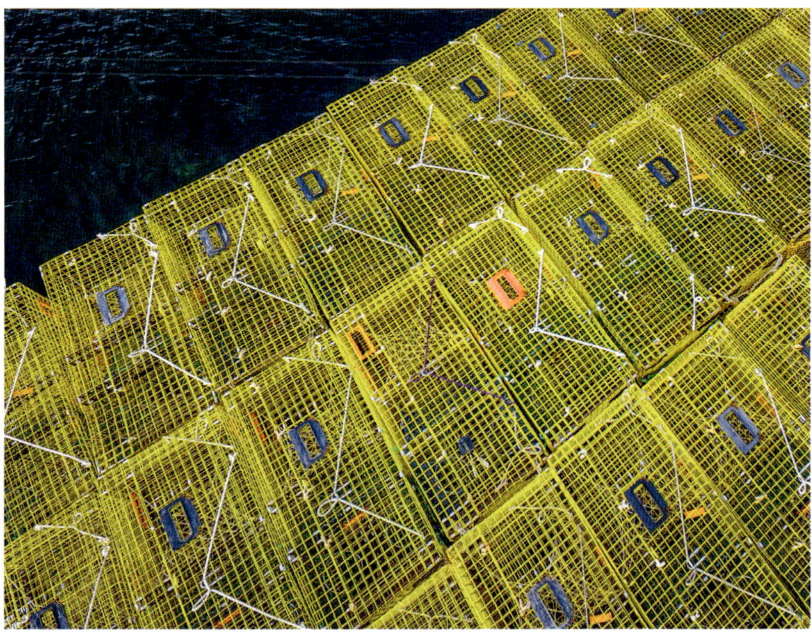

An overburdened barge flexes under the weight of lobster pots stacked ten high.

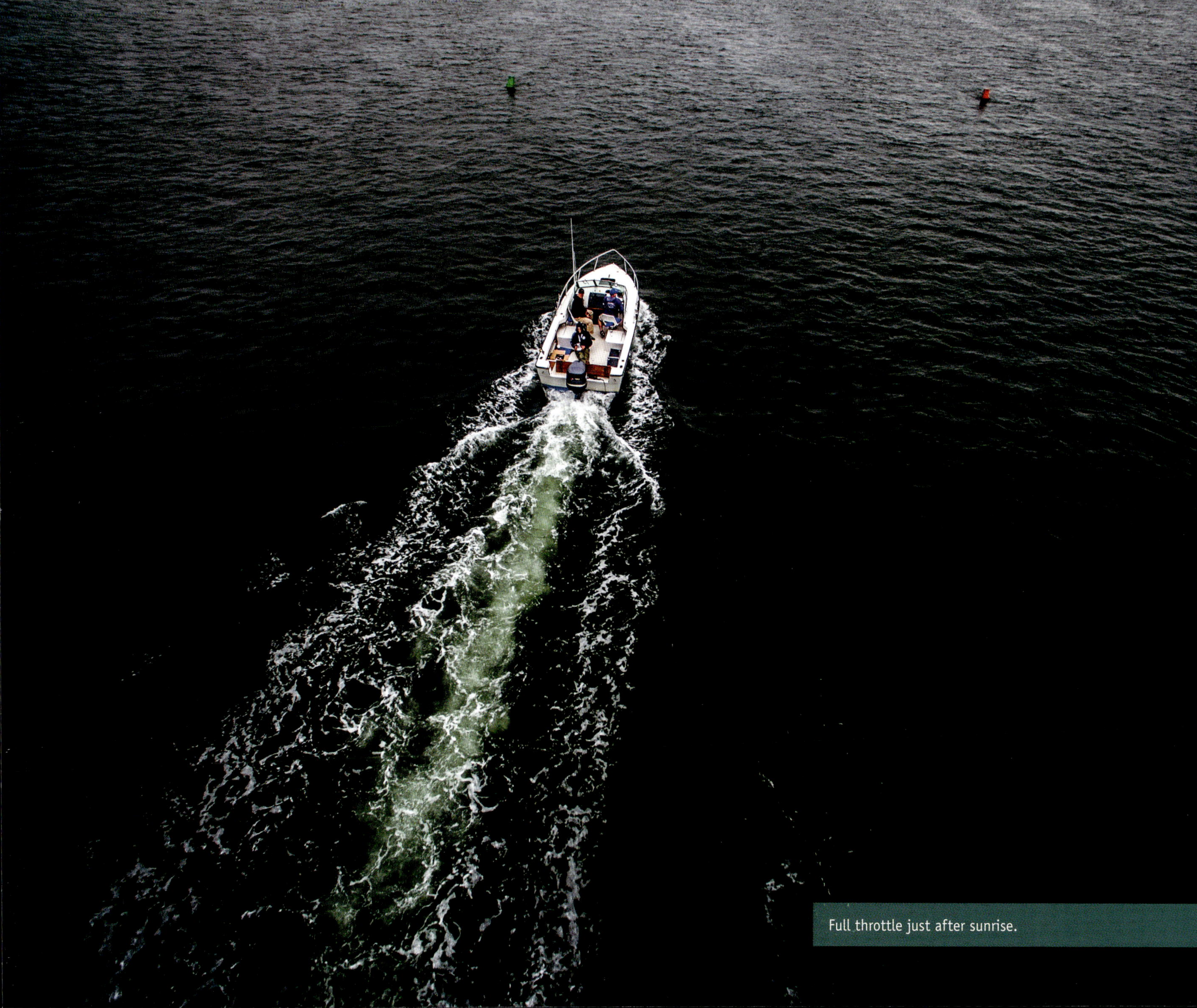
Full throttle just after sunrise.

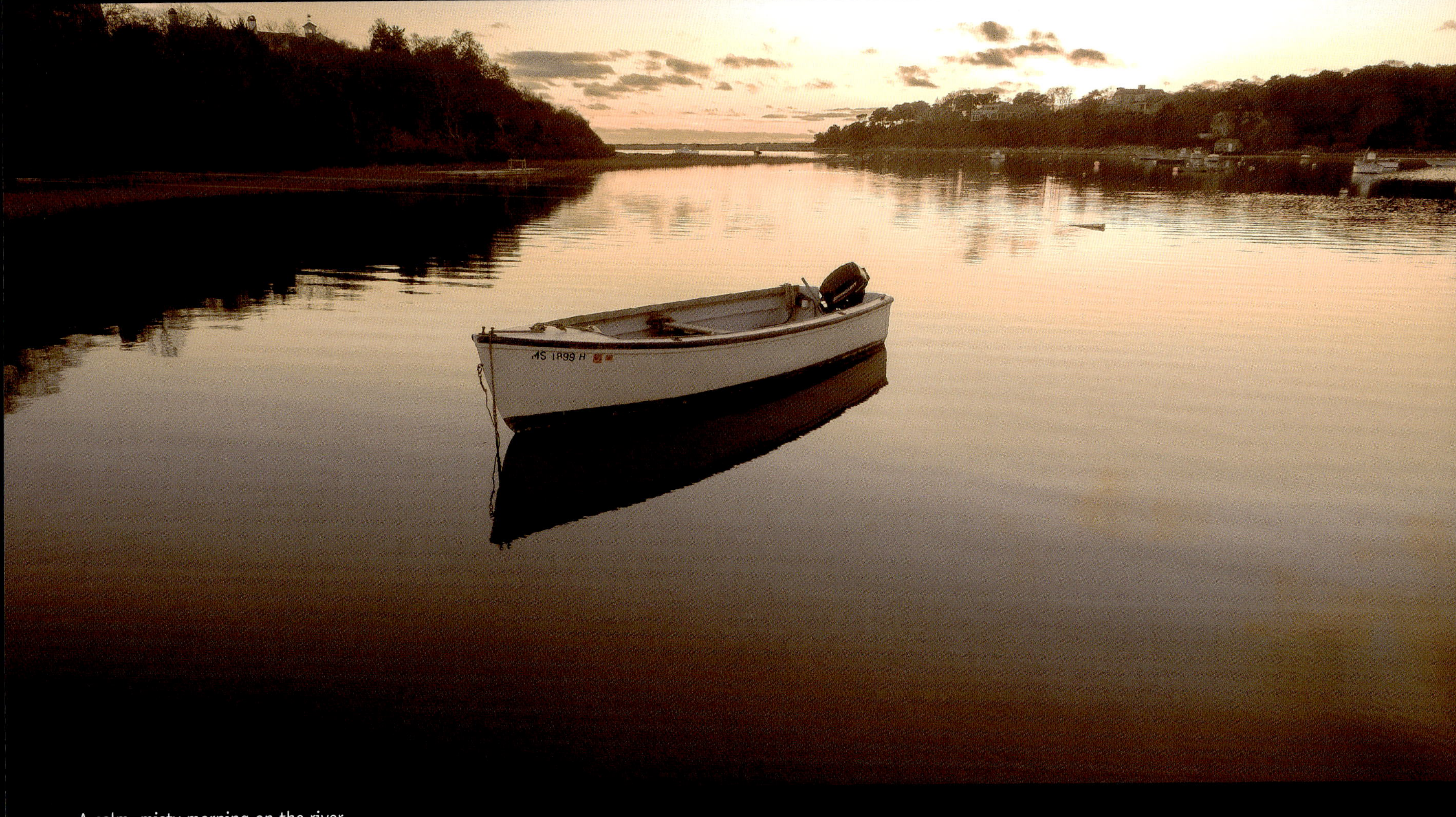

A calm, misty morning on the river.

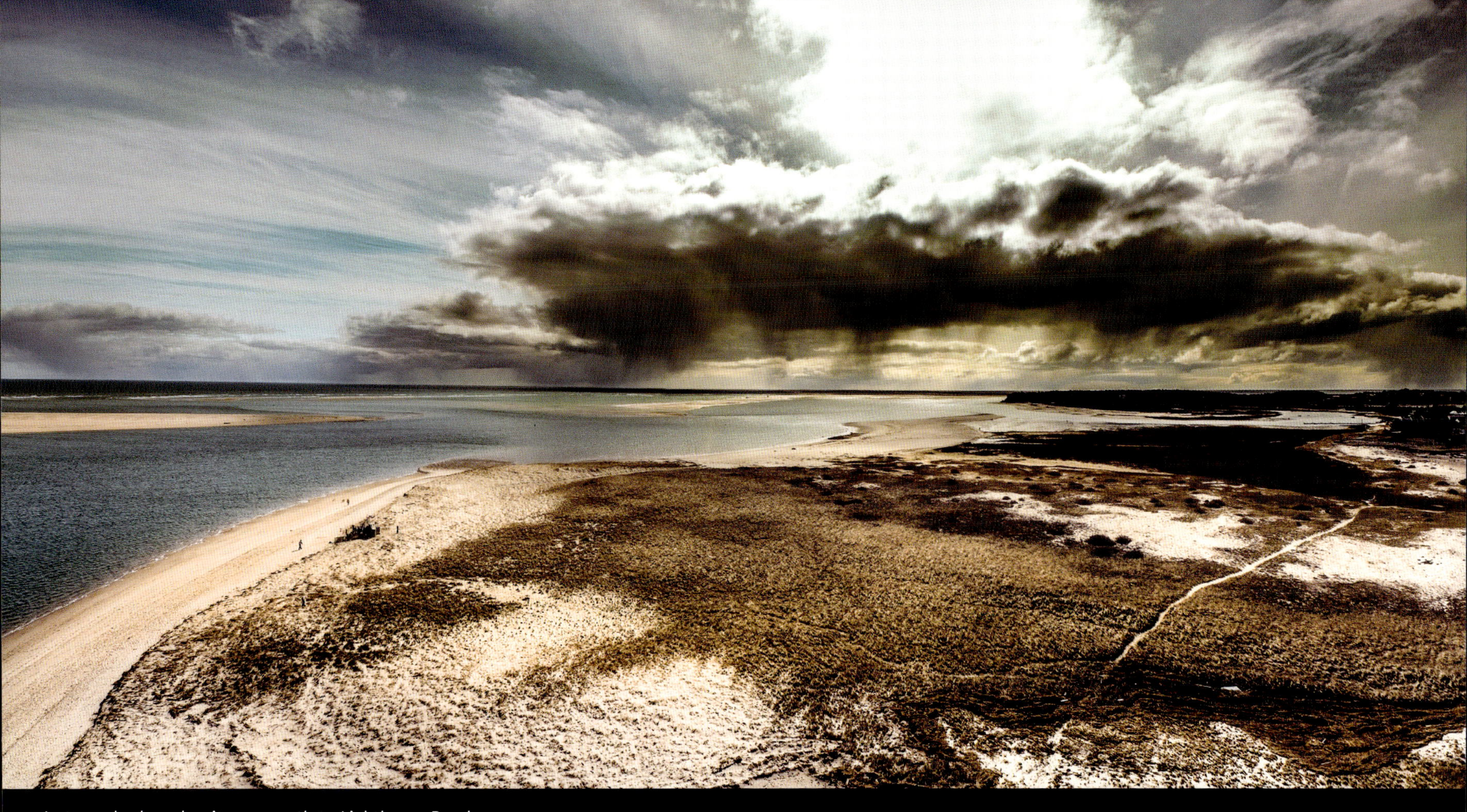

A storm slowly makes its way north to Lighthouse Beach.

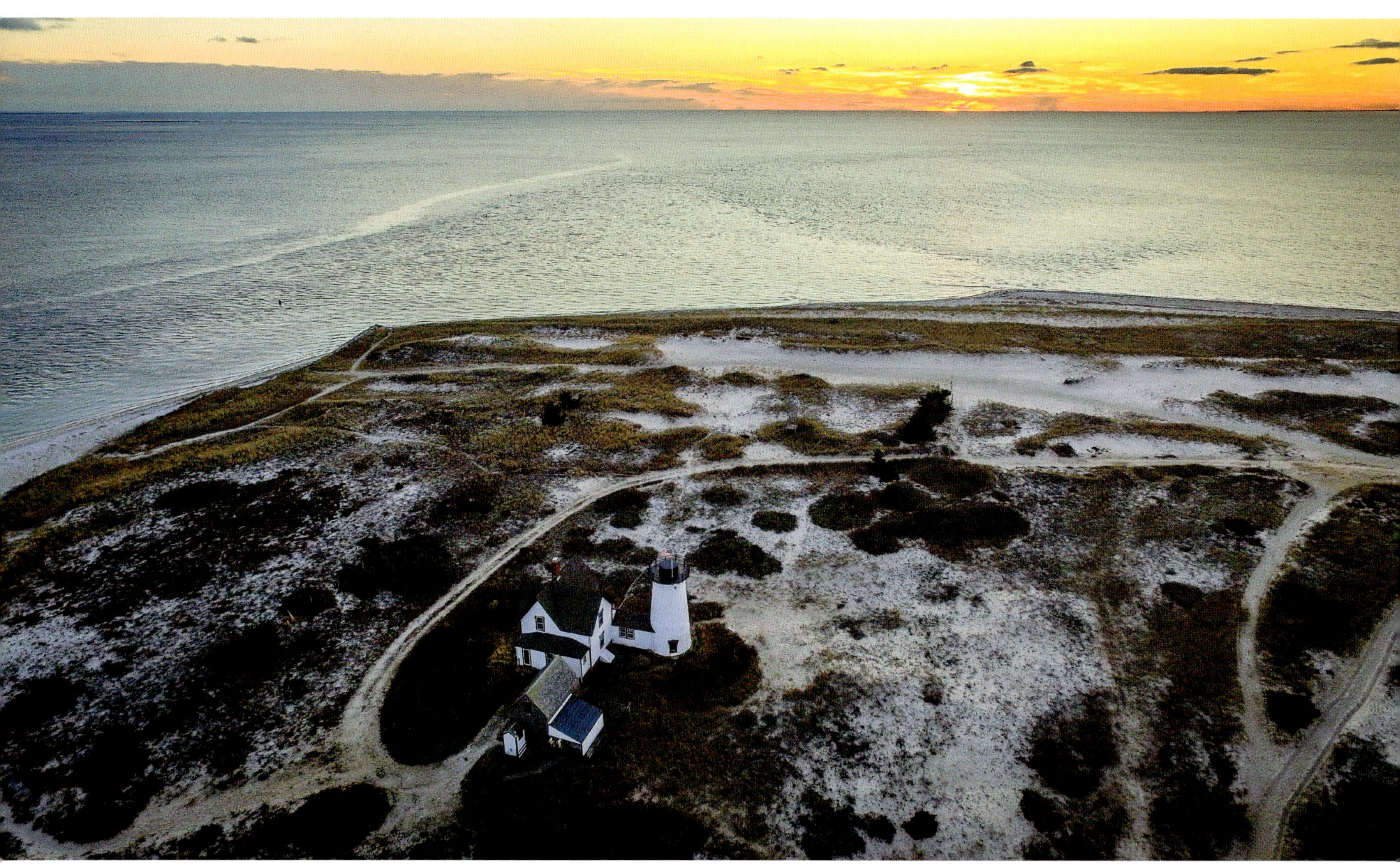

January.

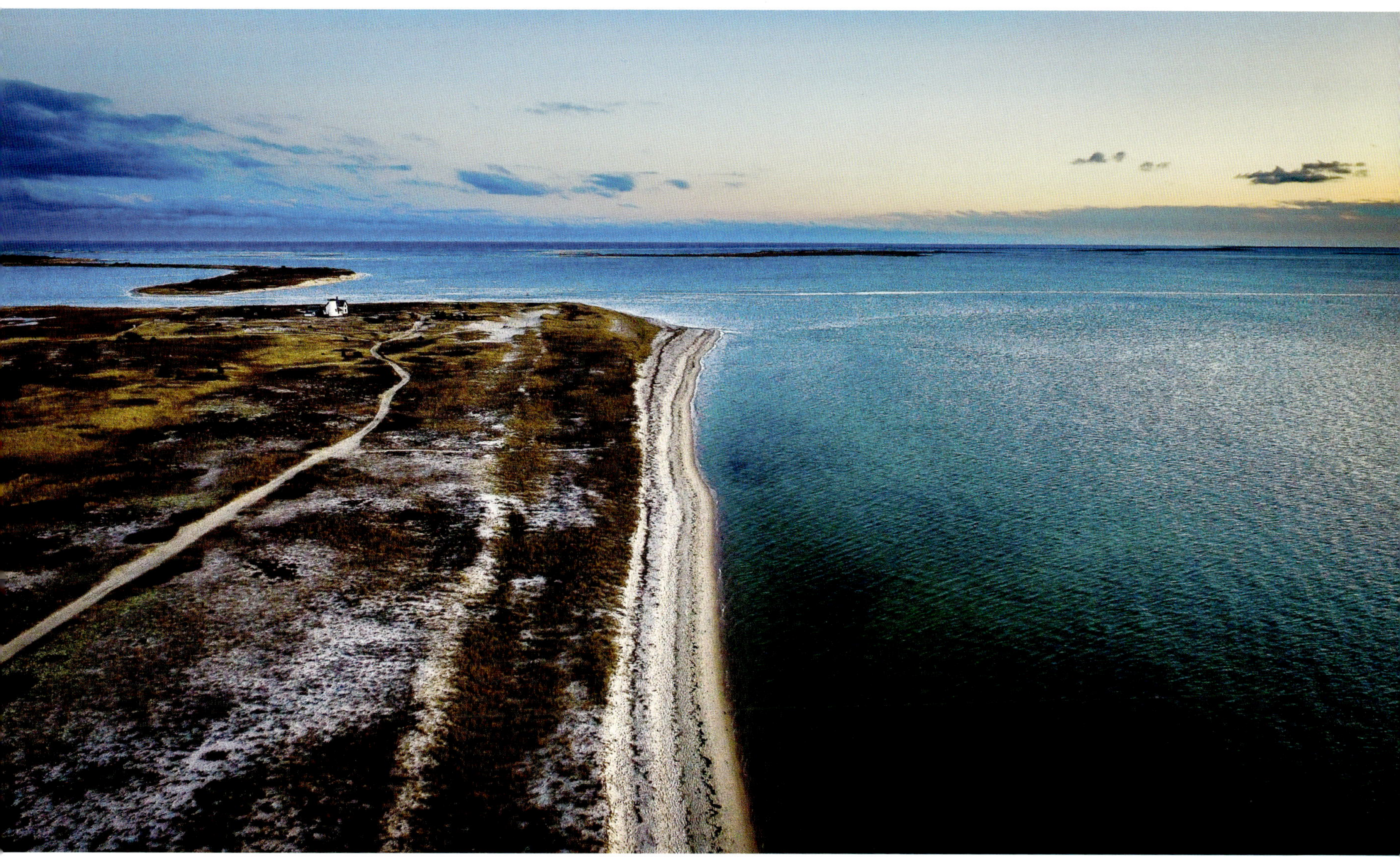

April.

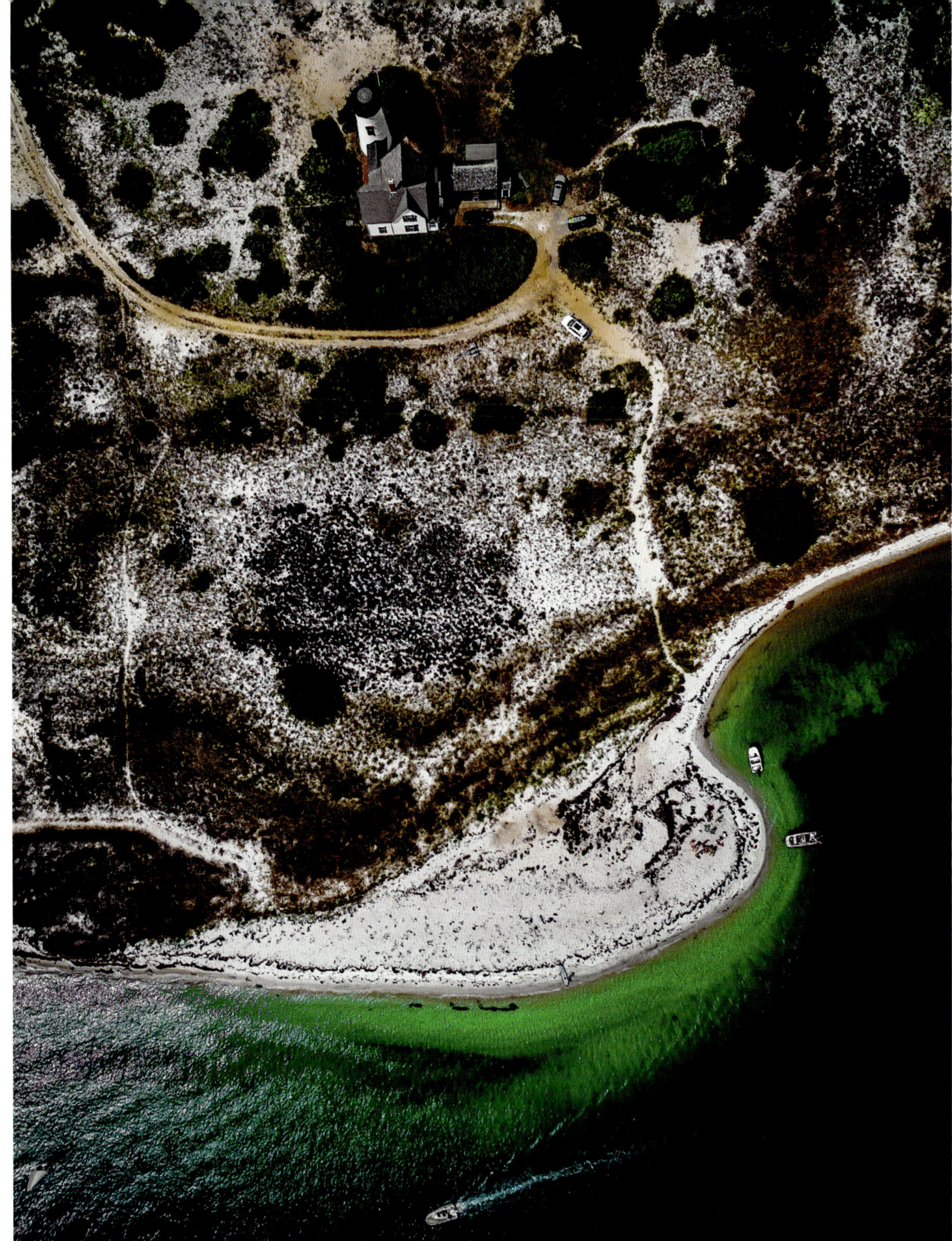

July.

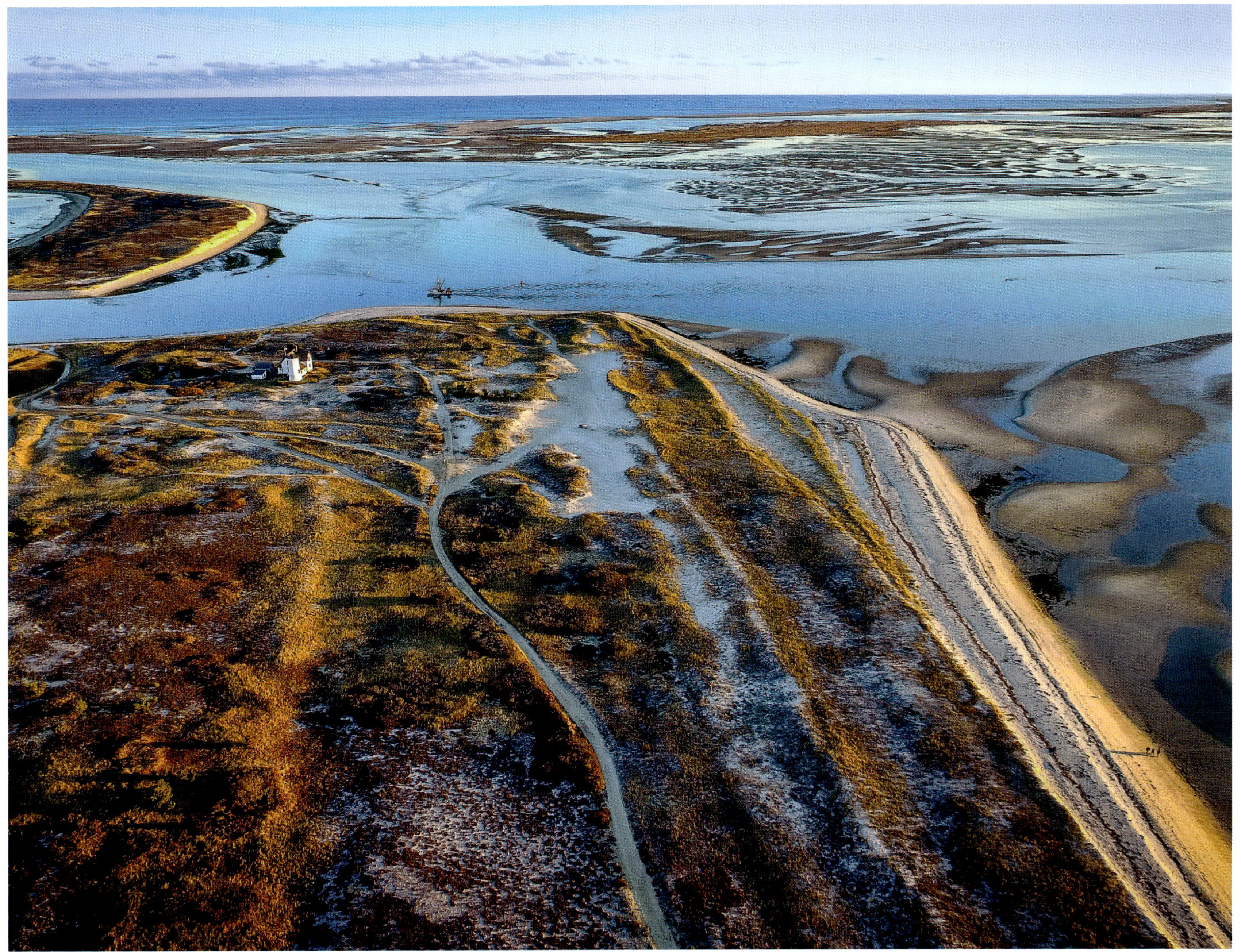

November.

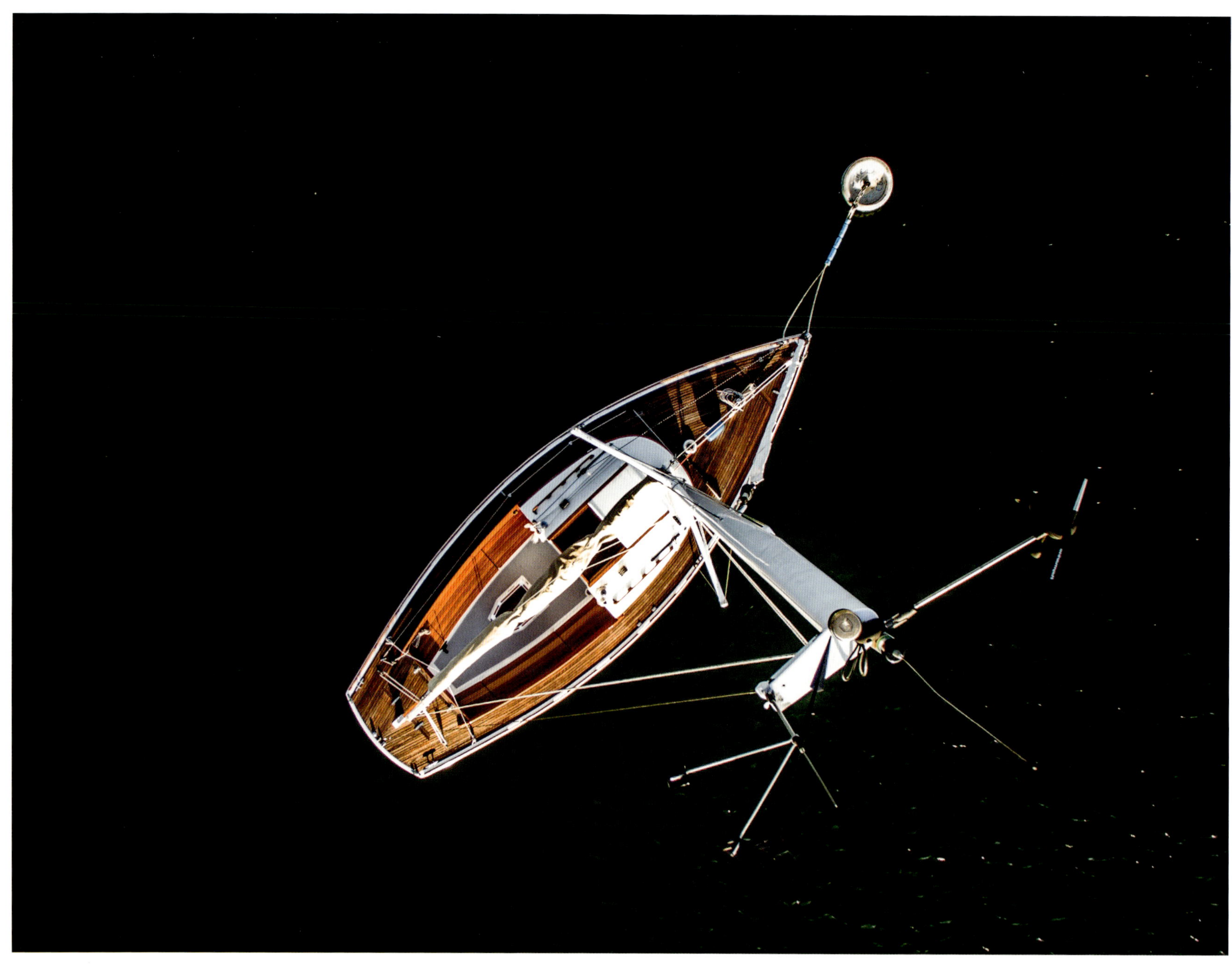

The Stars and Stripes catching the morning light on a windless day.

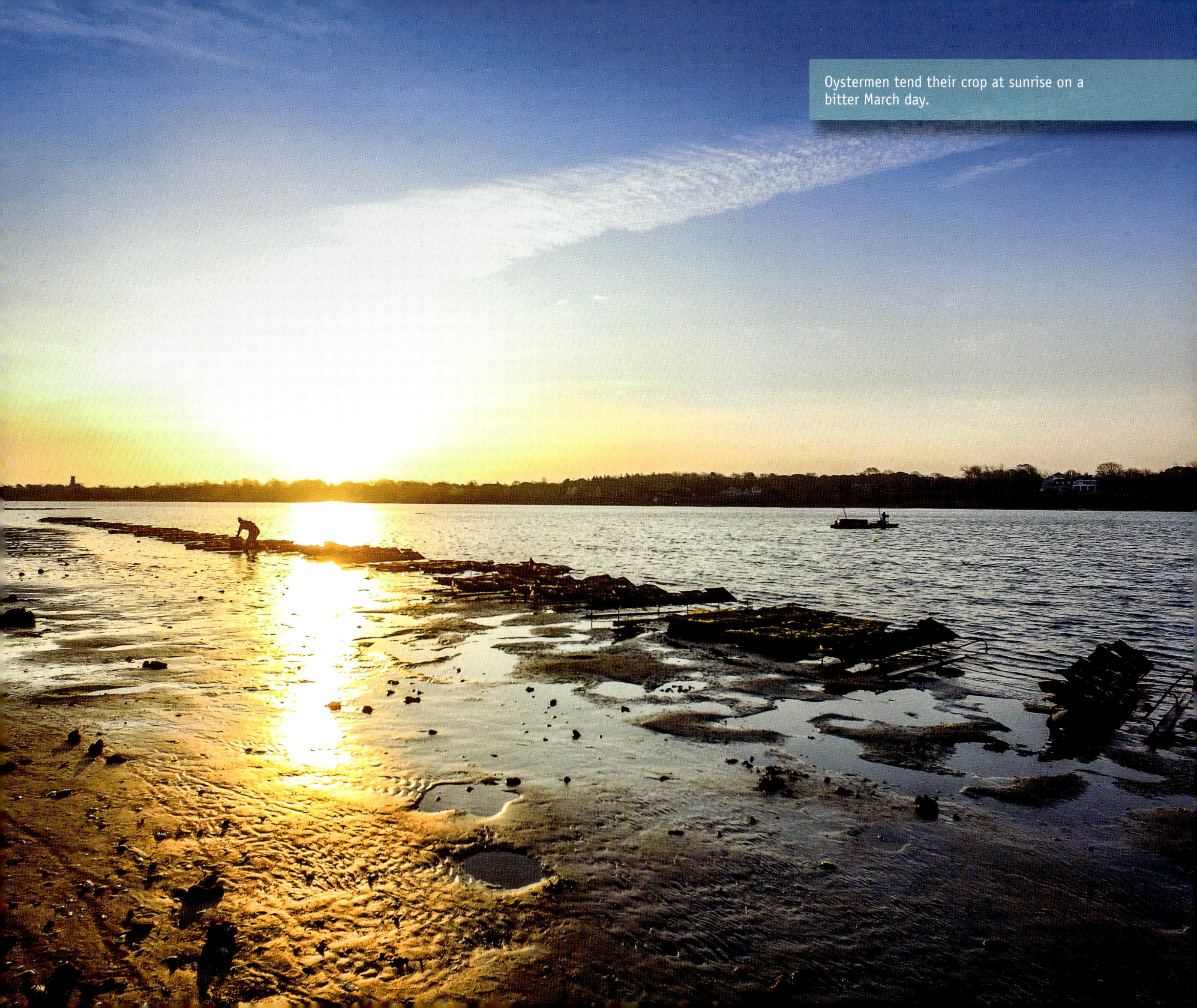

Oystermen tend their crop at sunrise on a bitter March day.

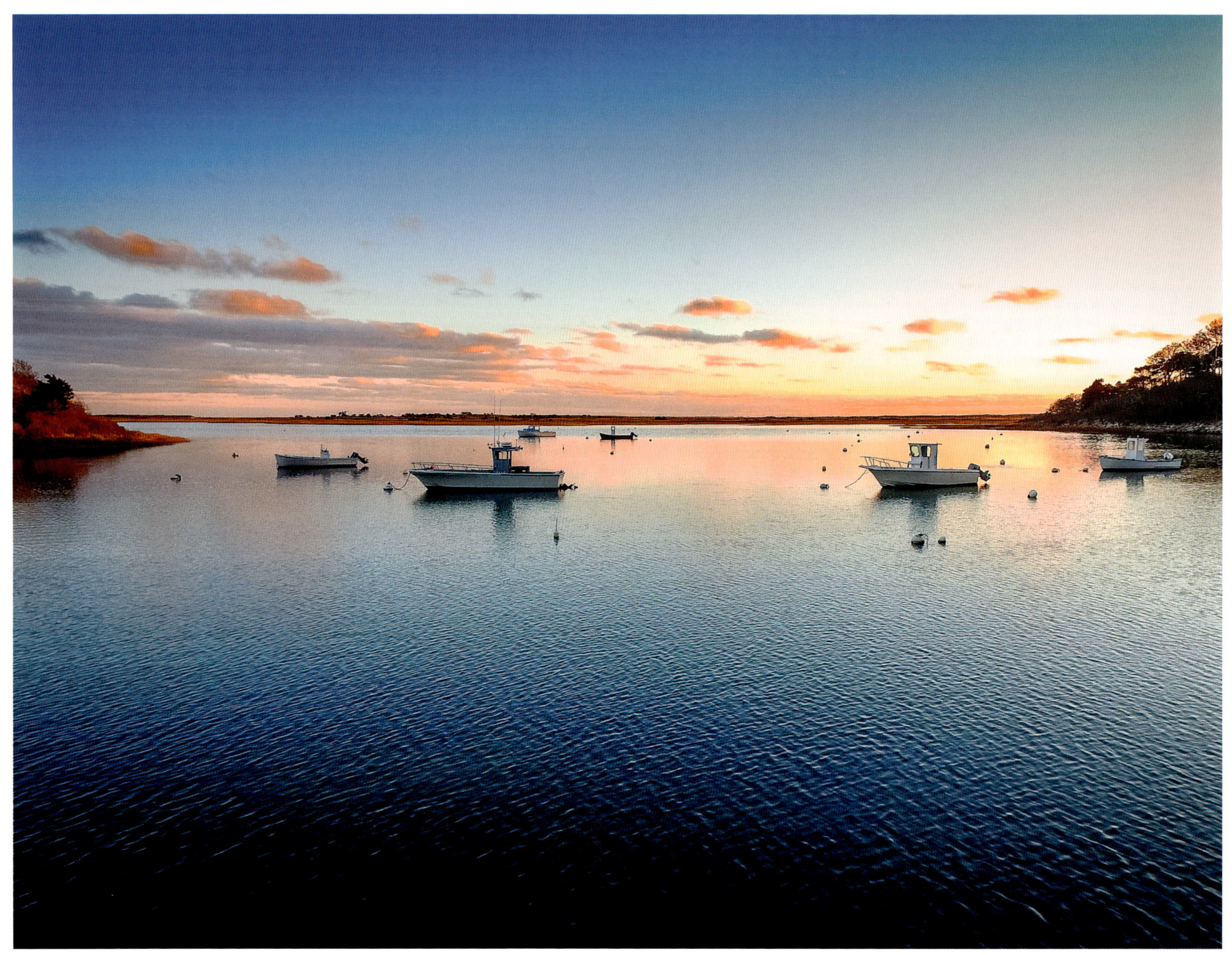

The cool serenity of the last light of an August day.

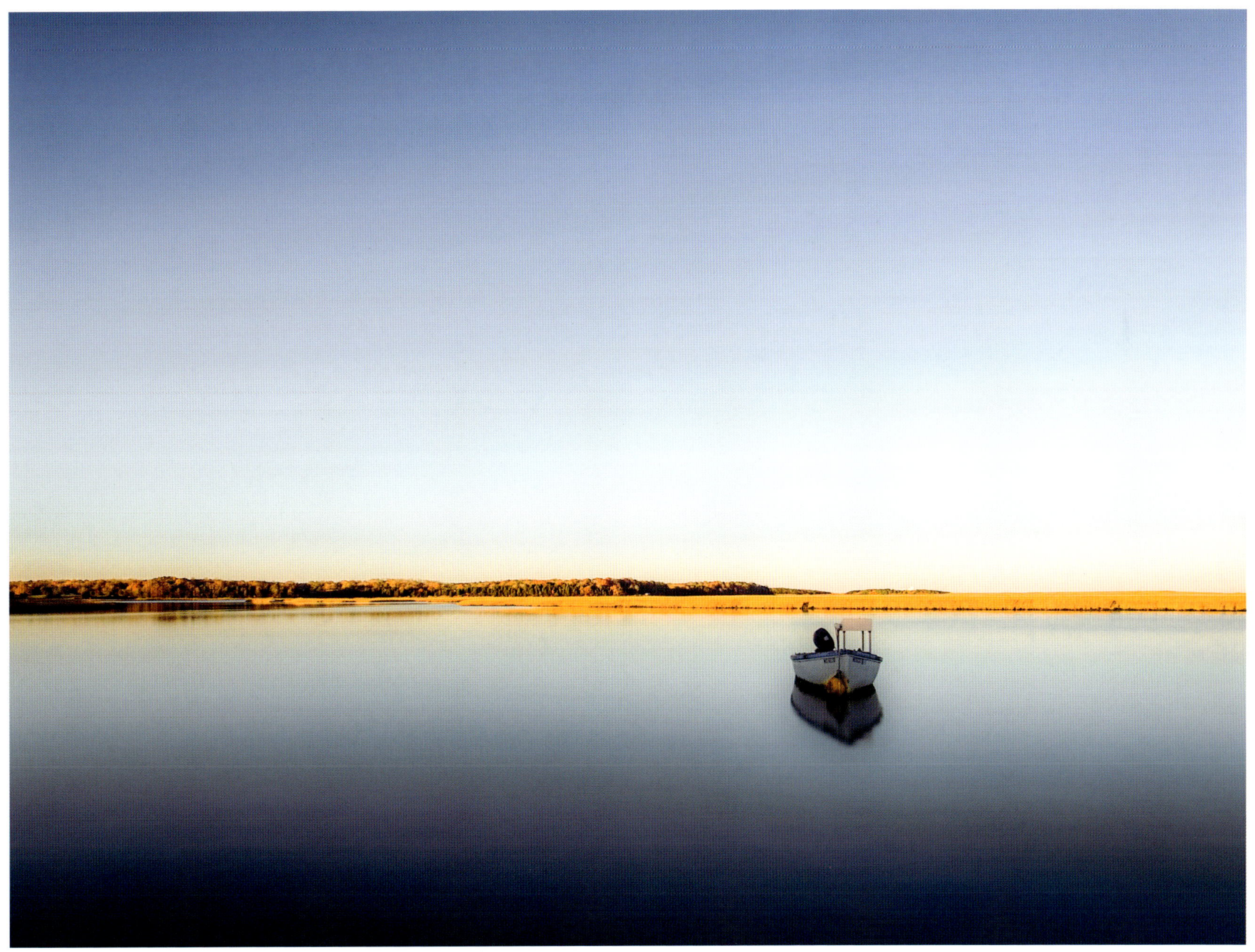

A supermoon occurs when a new or full moon coincides with the closest distance the moon comes to Earth during its monthly orbit. On November 14, 2016, a supermoon rose over the horizon for the first time since 1948, ushering in higher-than-normal tides that swallowed the many marshes that would normally be above water.

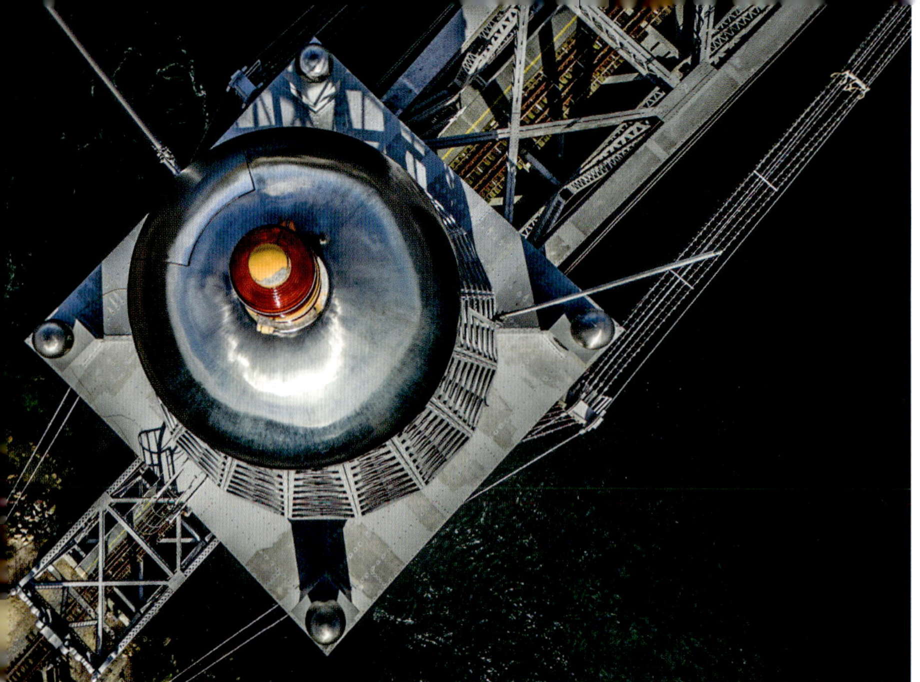

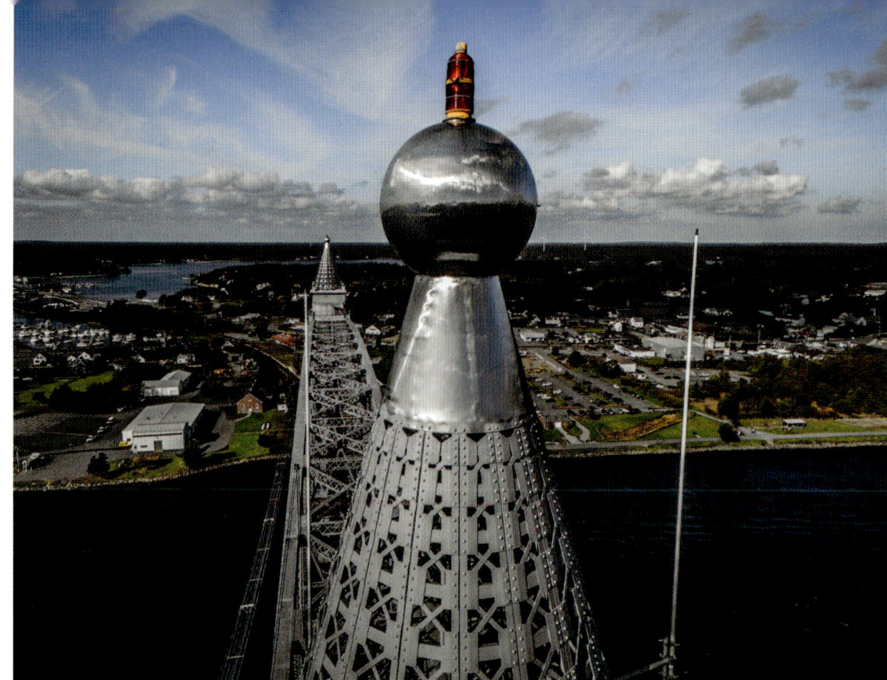

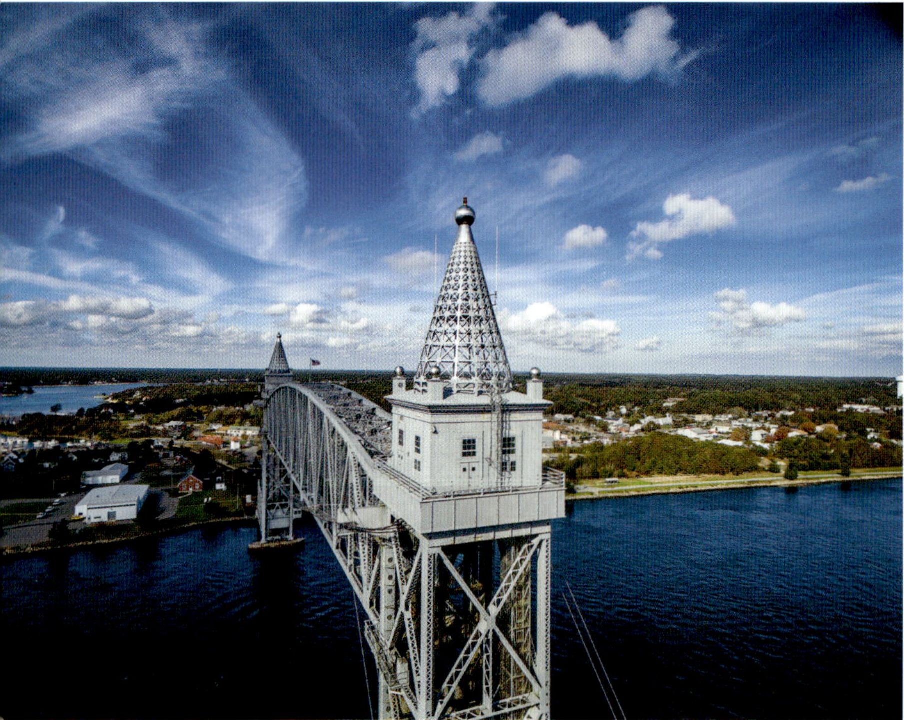

When it was built in 1933, the Cape Cod Canal Railroad Bridge was the longest vertical-lift bridge in the world. The structure underwent a massive $30 million renovation in 2002 and was reopened in 2003.

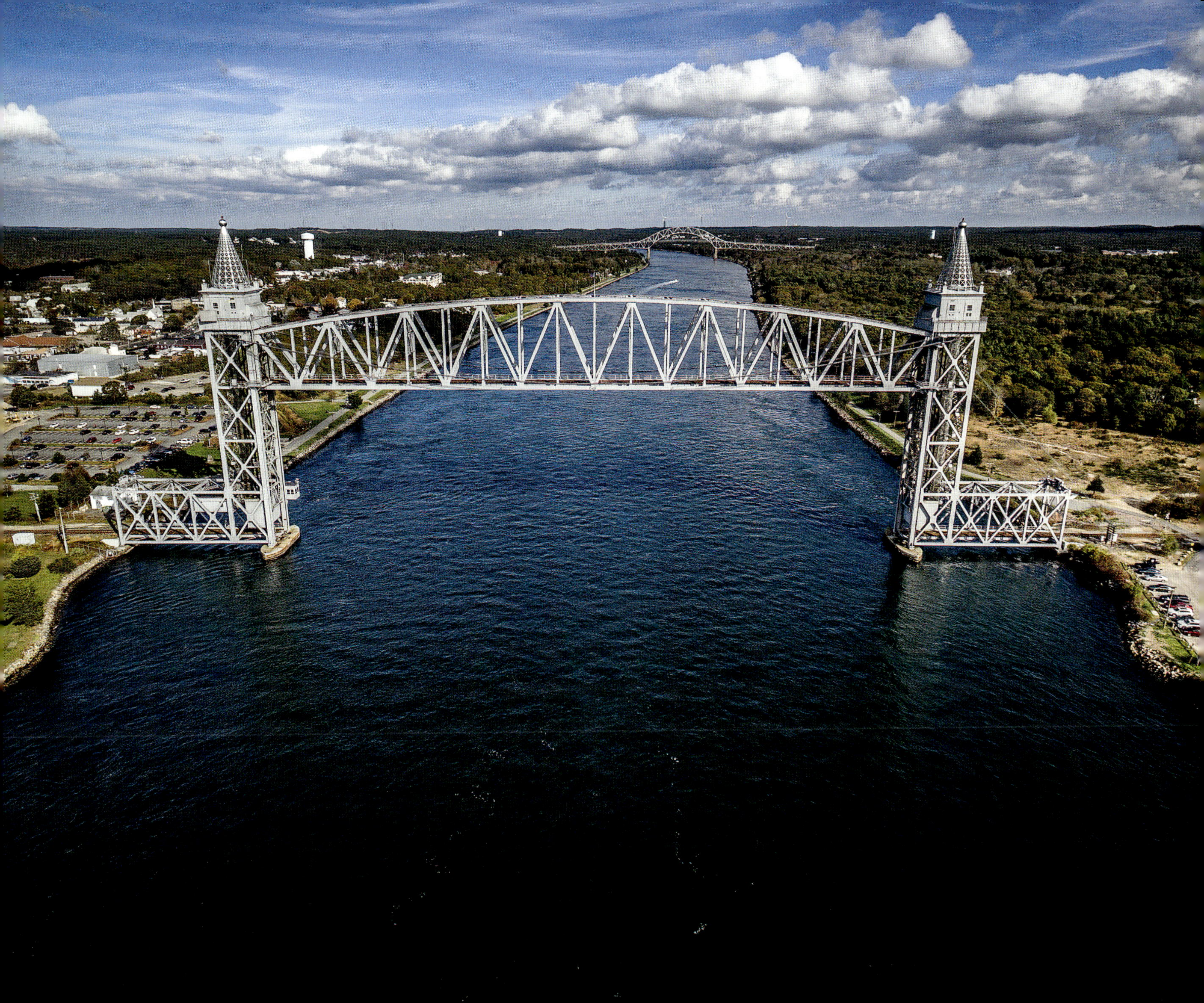

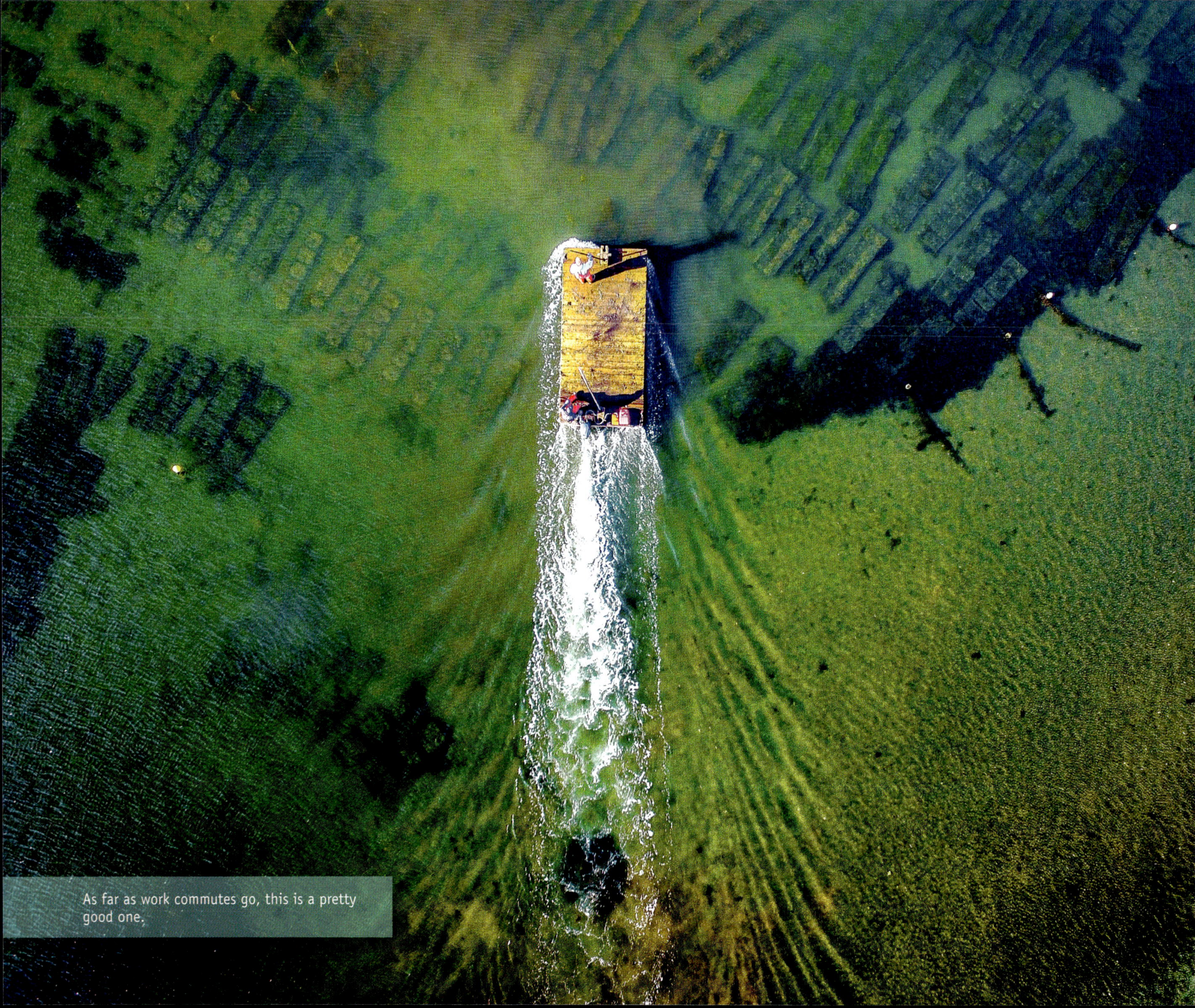

As far as work commutes go, this is a pretty good one.

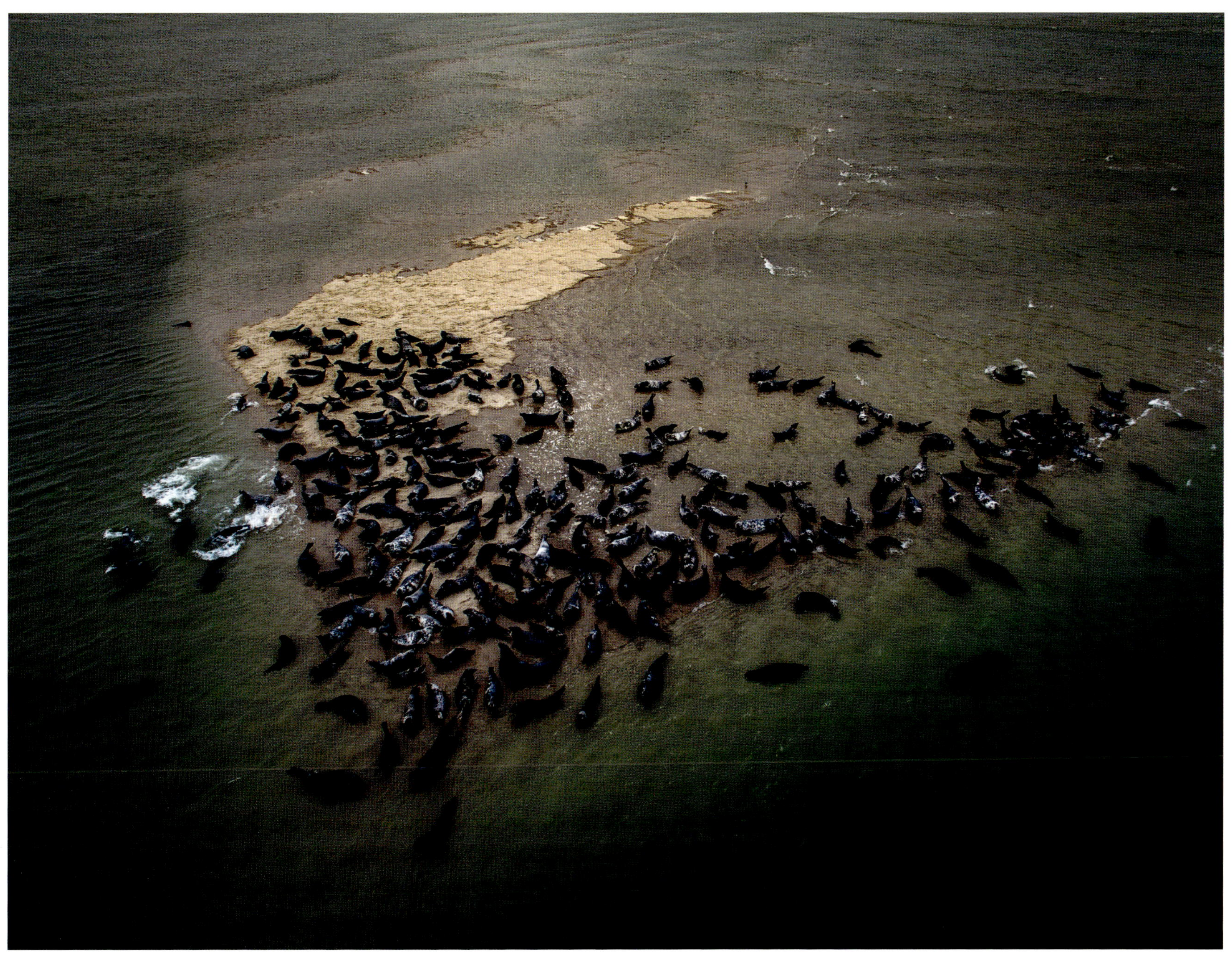

A herd of seals doing what they do best.

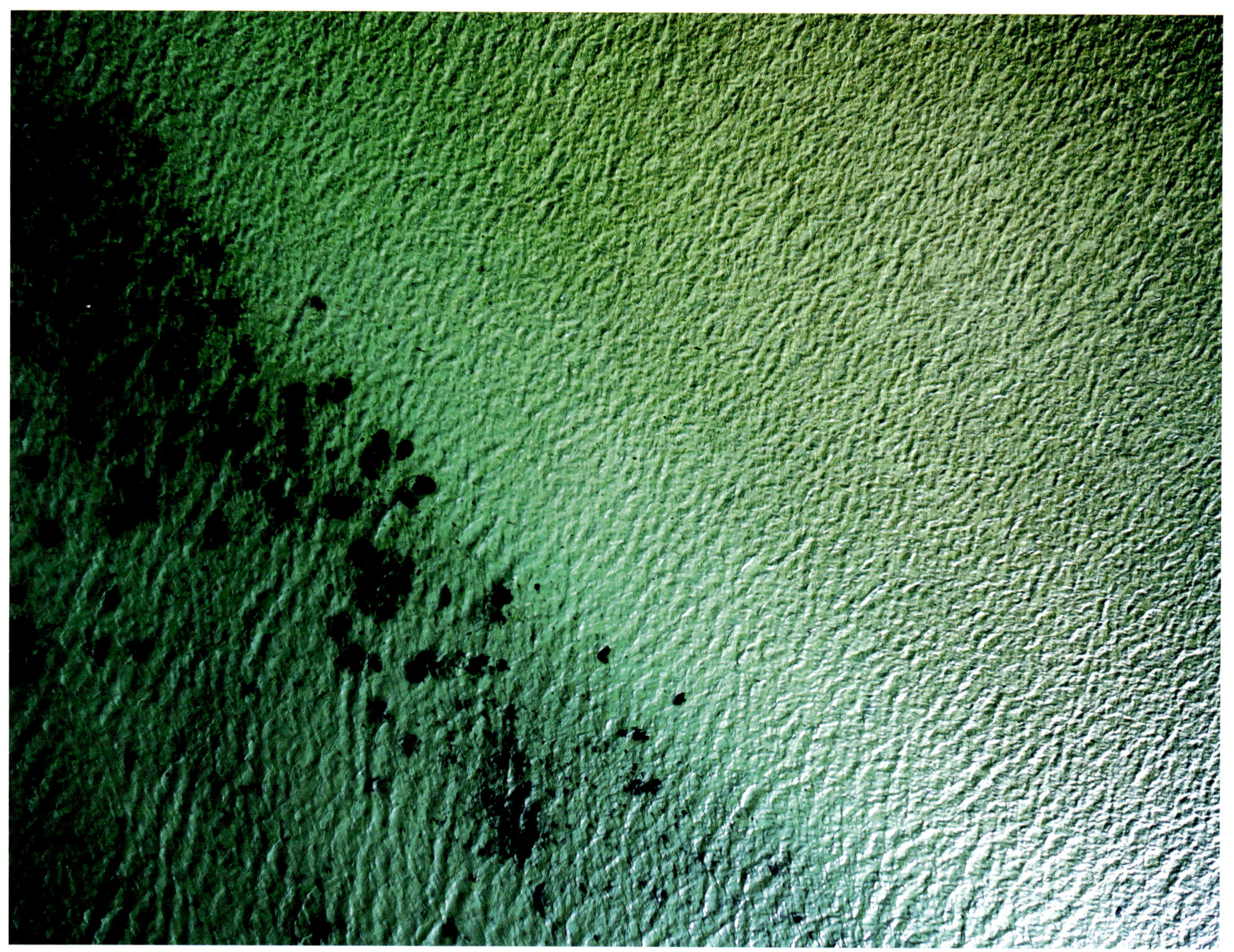

“The Shallows” - Seagrass under a low tide; variations in water depth create gradients of green.

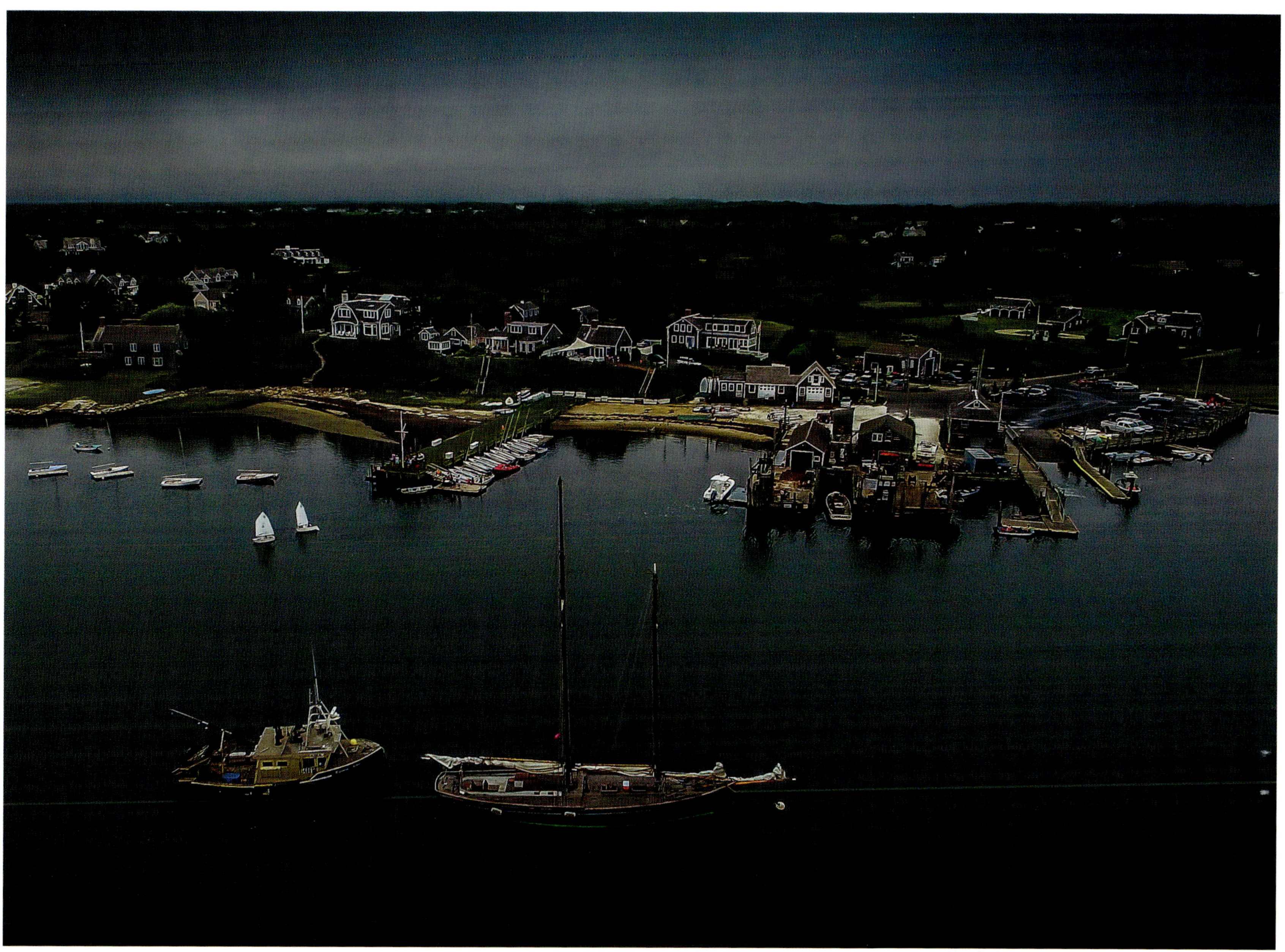

A foggy day at Stage Harbor.

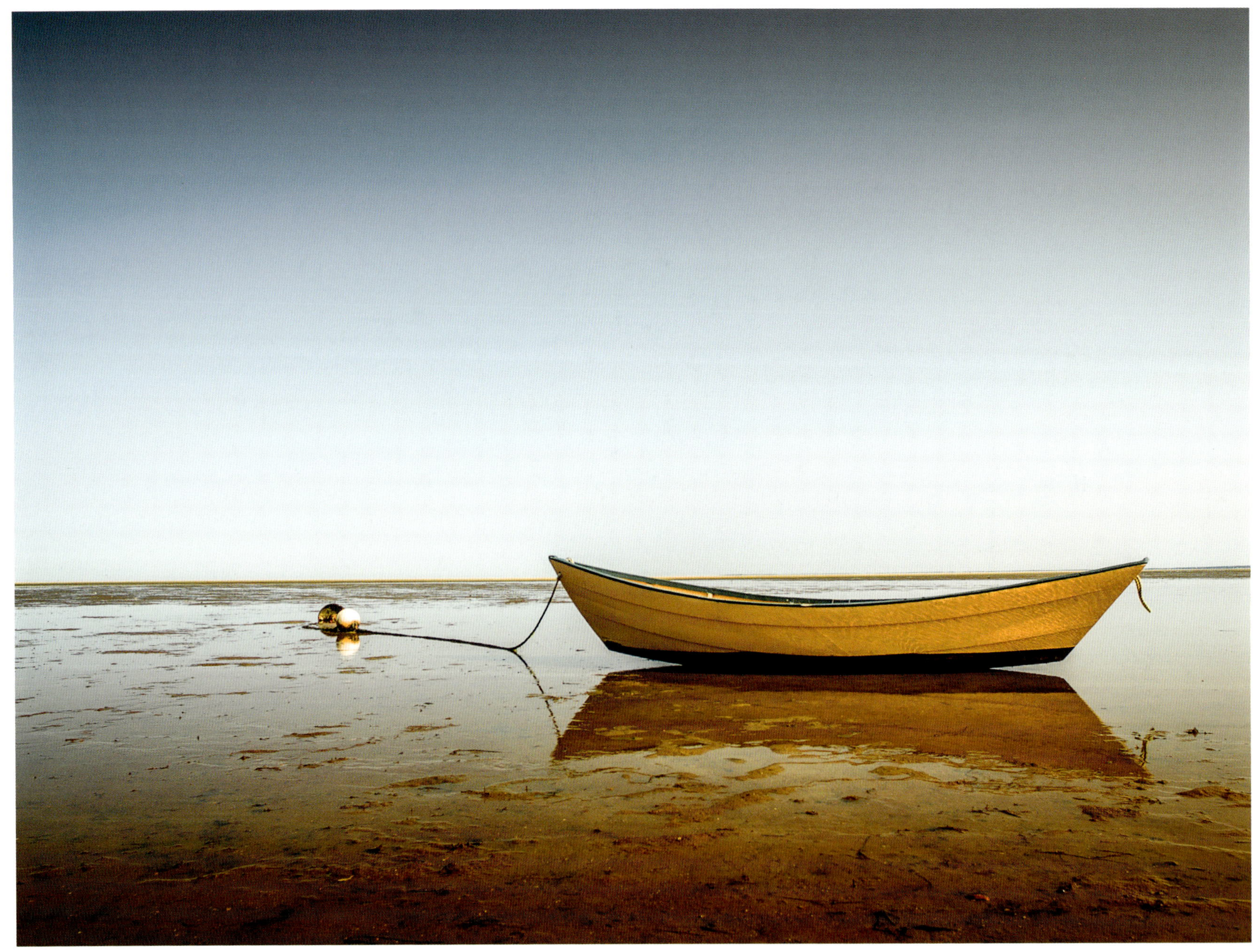

The famous yellow dory is a favorite subject of many Cape Cod photographers. The low tide left just enough water to deliver a reflection in this shot taken just a few feet off the ground.

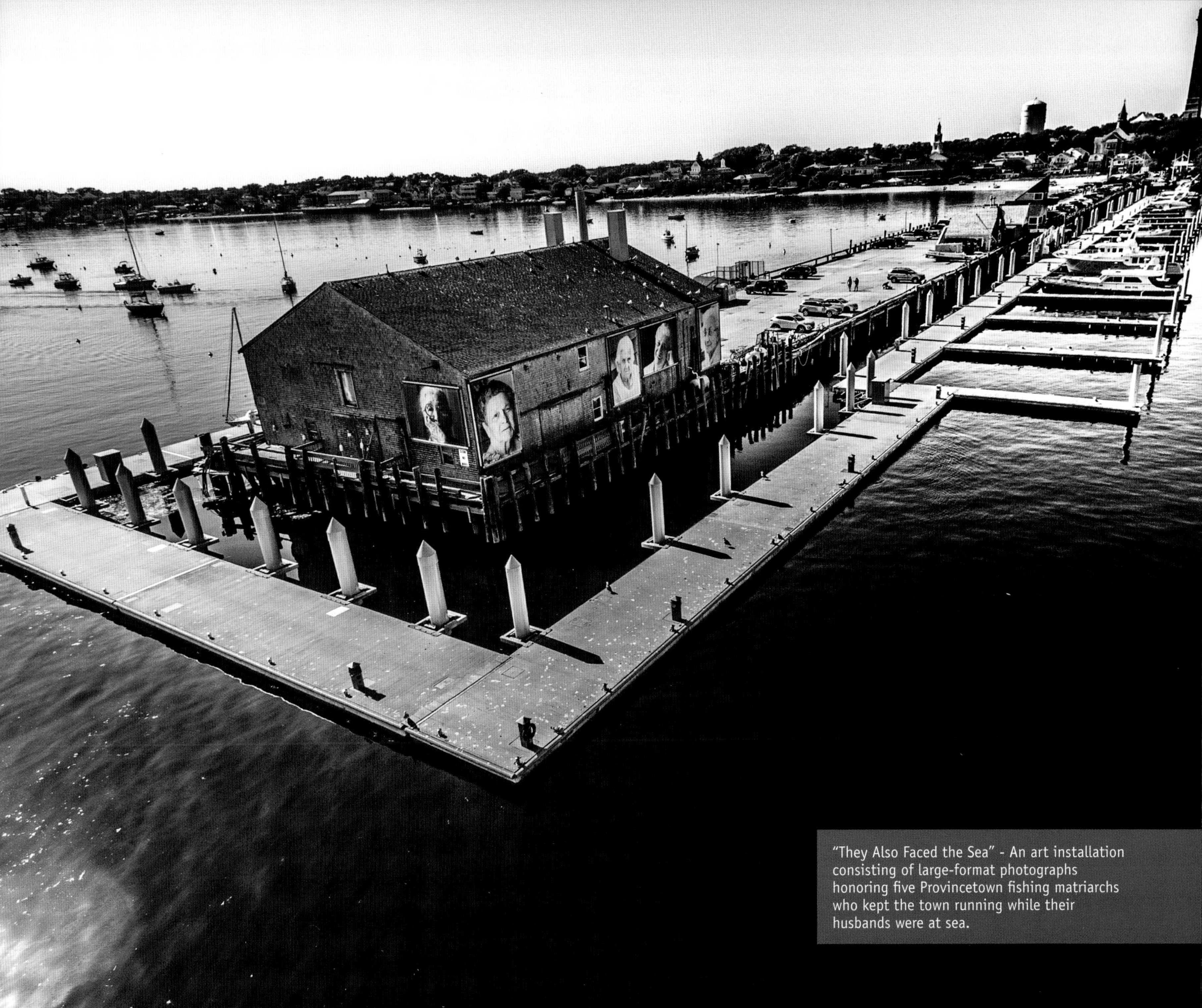

"They Also Faced the Sea" - An art installation consisting of large-format photographs honoring five Provincetown fishing matriarchs who kept the town running while their husbands were at sea.

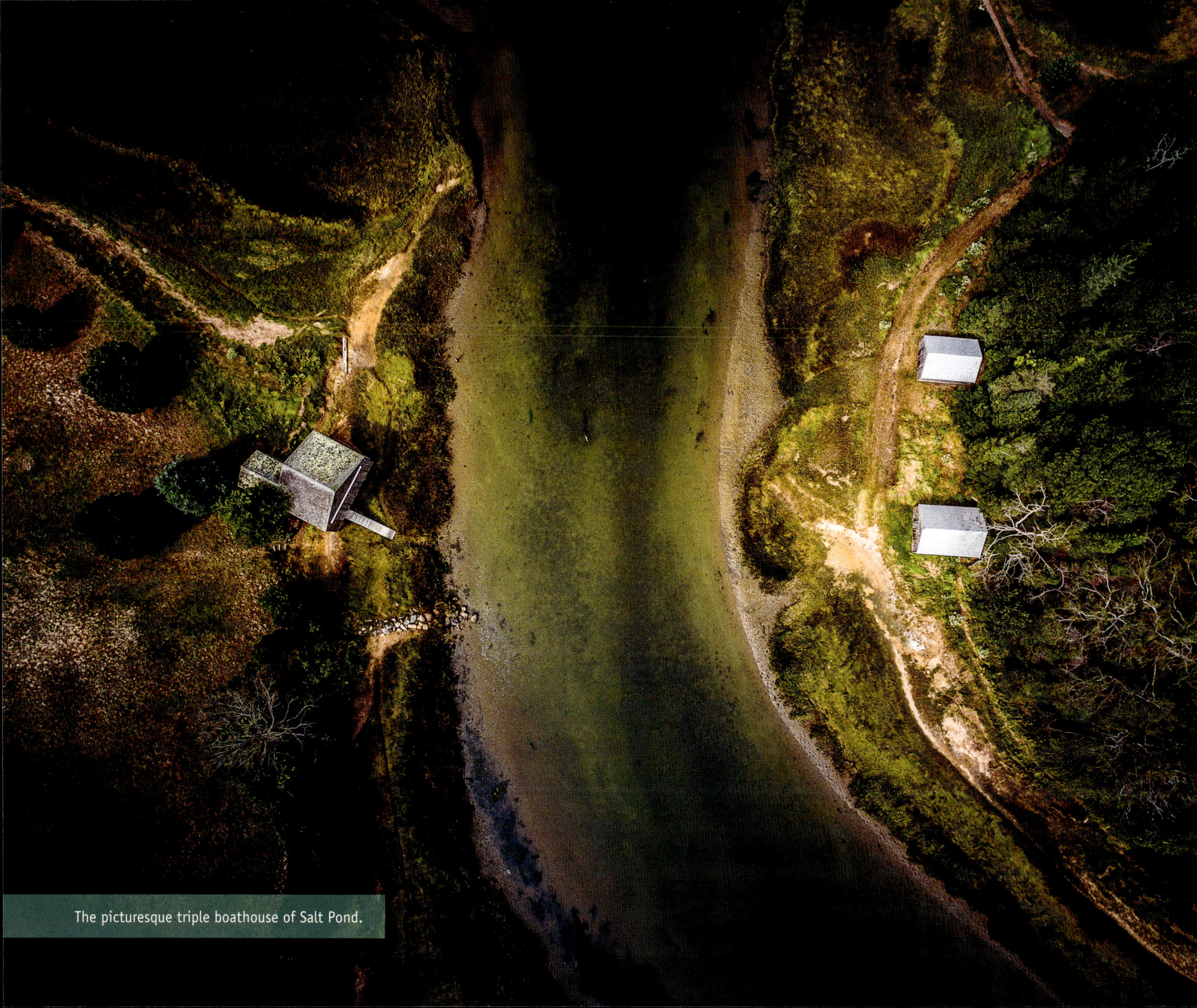

The picturesque triple boathouse of Salt Pond.

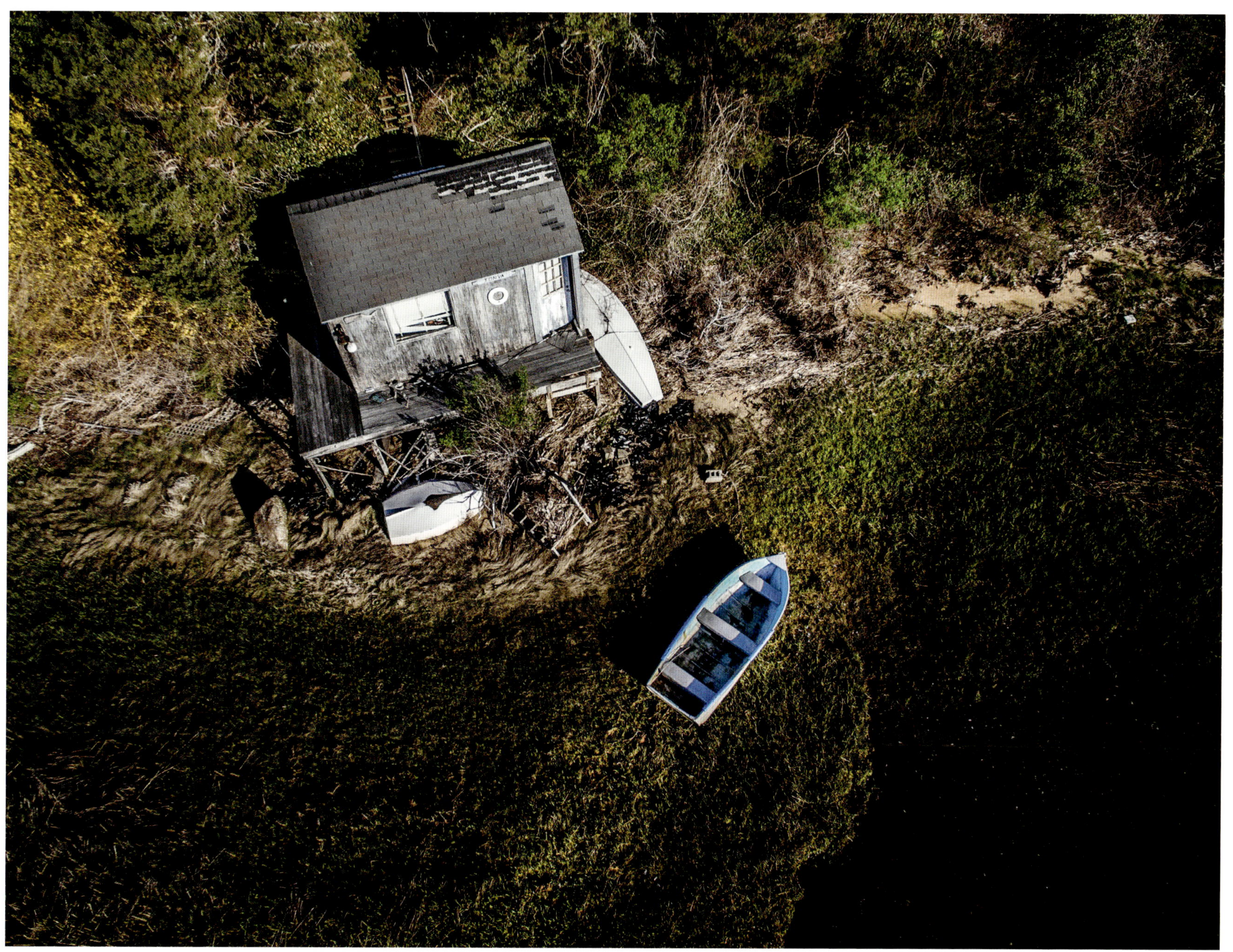

You can find *Tonya* nestled in the northwest end of Ryder's Cove.

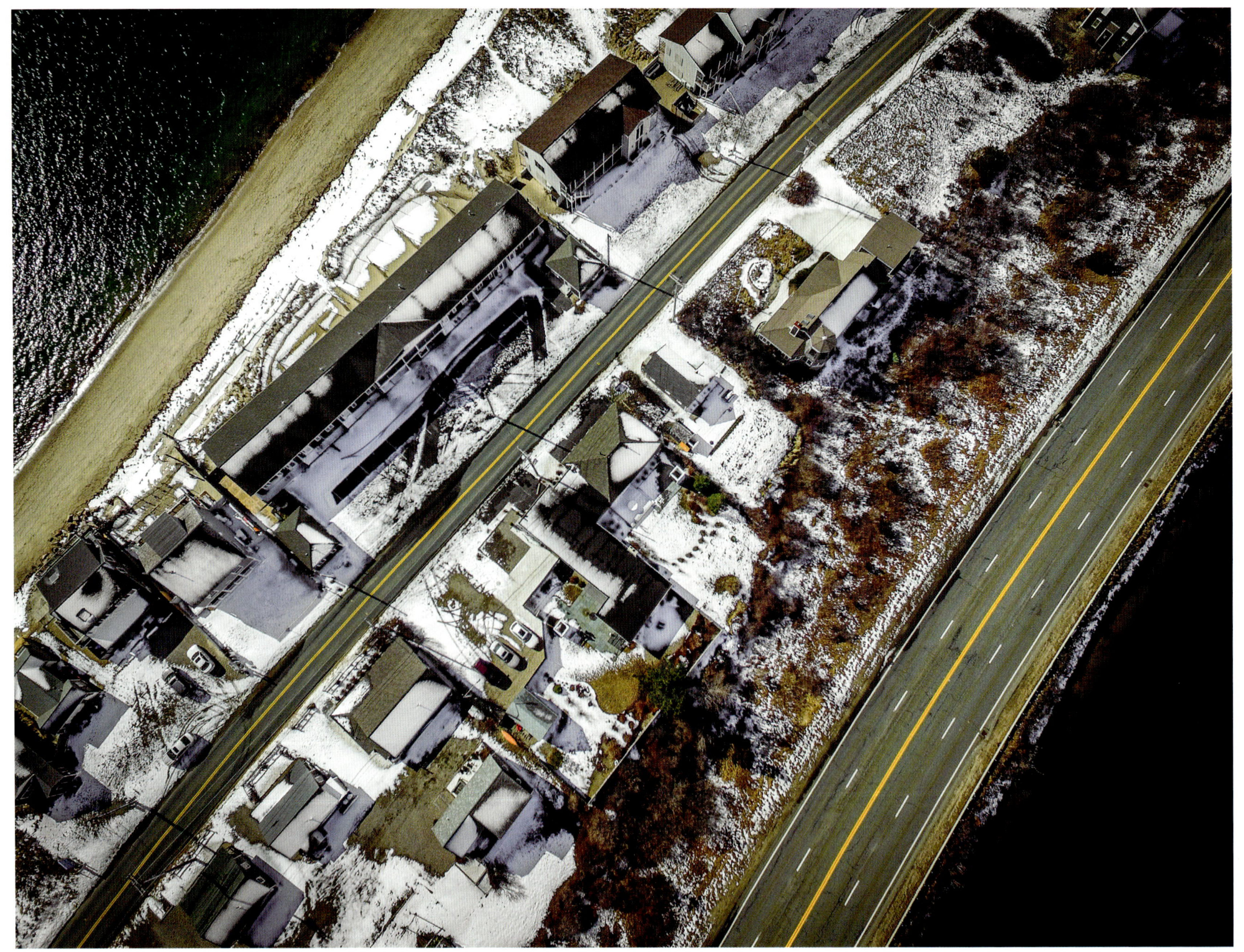

The snow-covered narrow strip of land between the Atlantic and East Harbor with Rt. 28 and Shore Road winding their way to P-town.

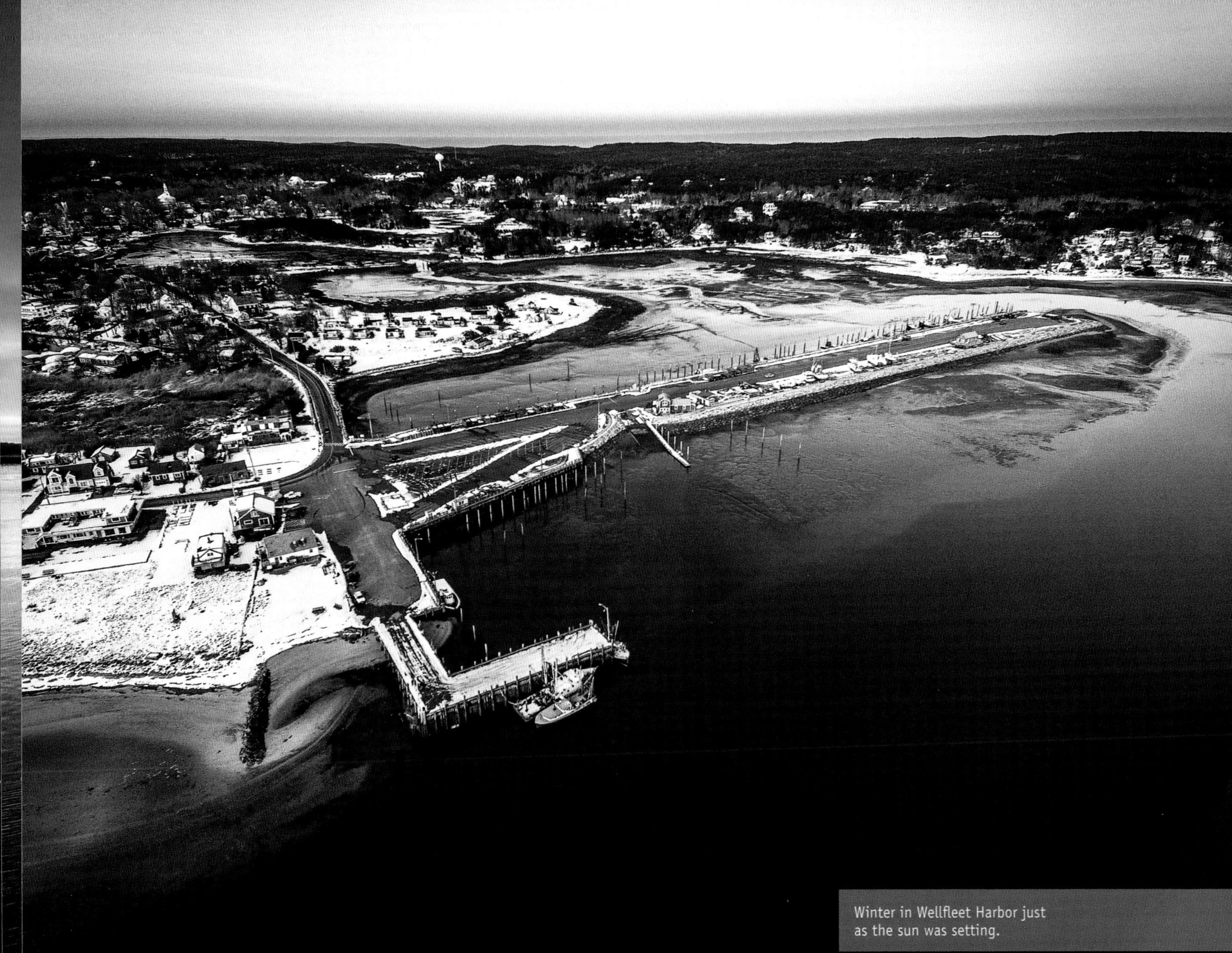

Winter in Wellfleet Harbor just as the sun was setting.

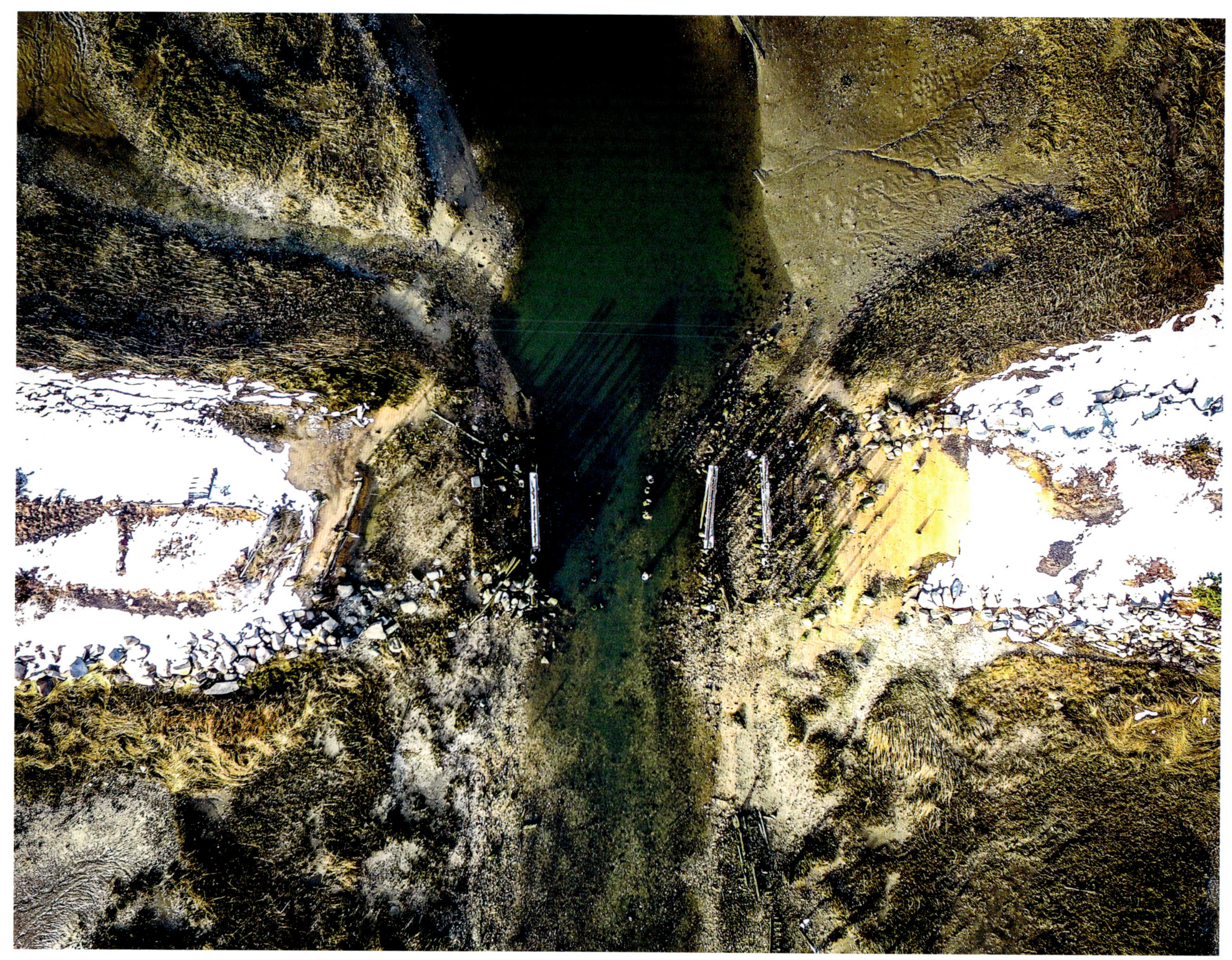

Remnants of Old Colony Railroad Bridge in Wellfleet.

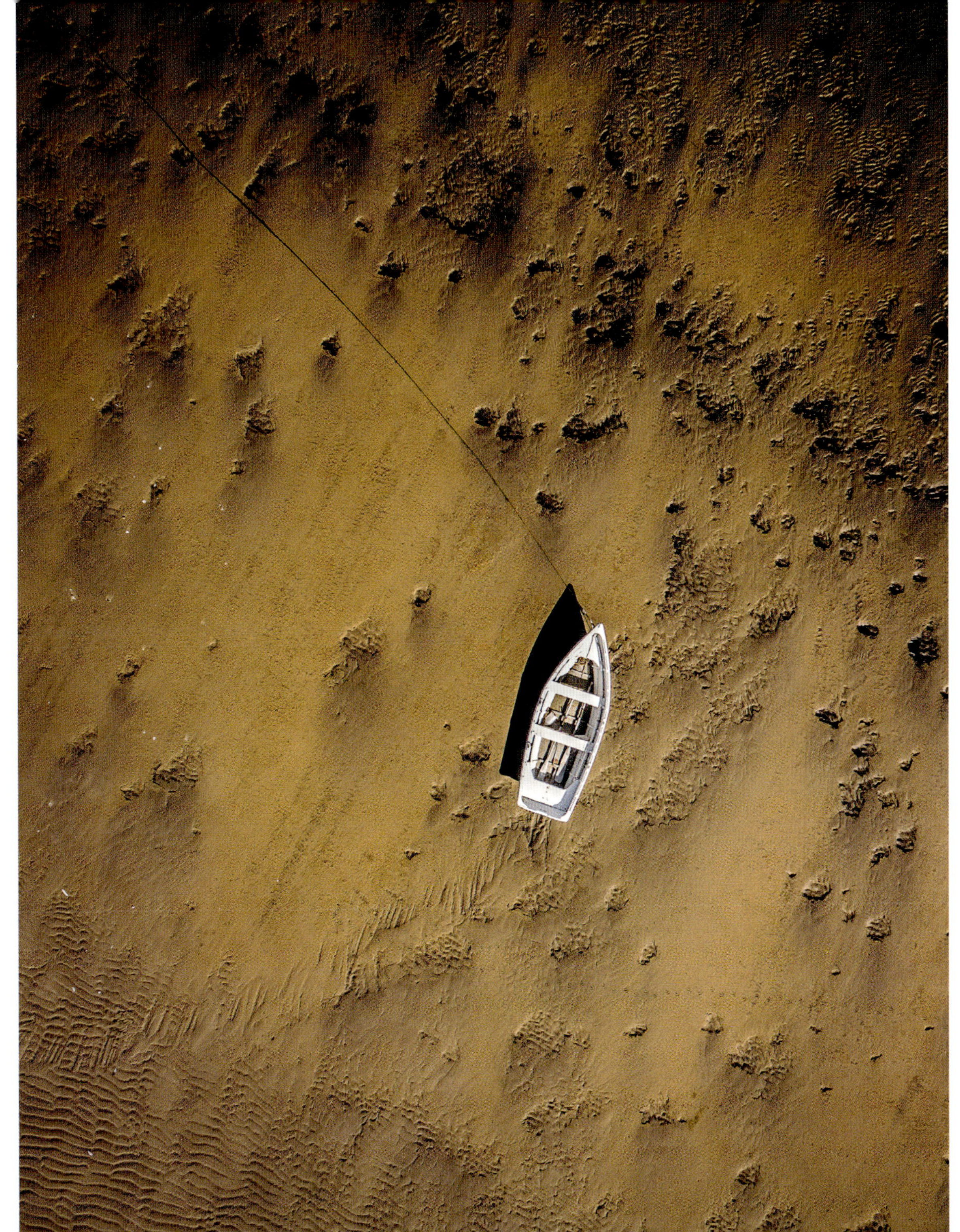

Tides can go out more than a mile in some places on the bay side of Cape Cod, leaving thousands of boats like this one grounded for hours at a time.

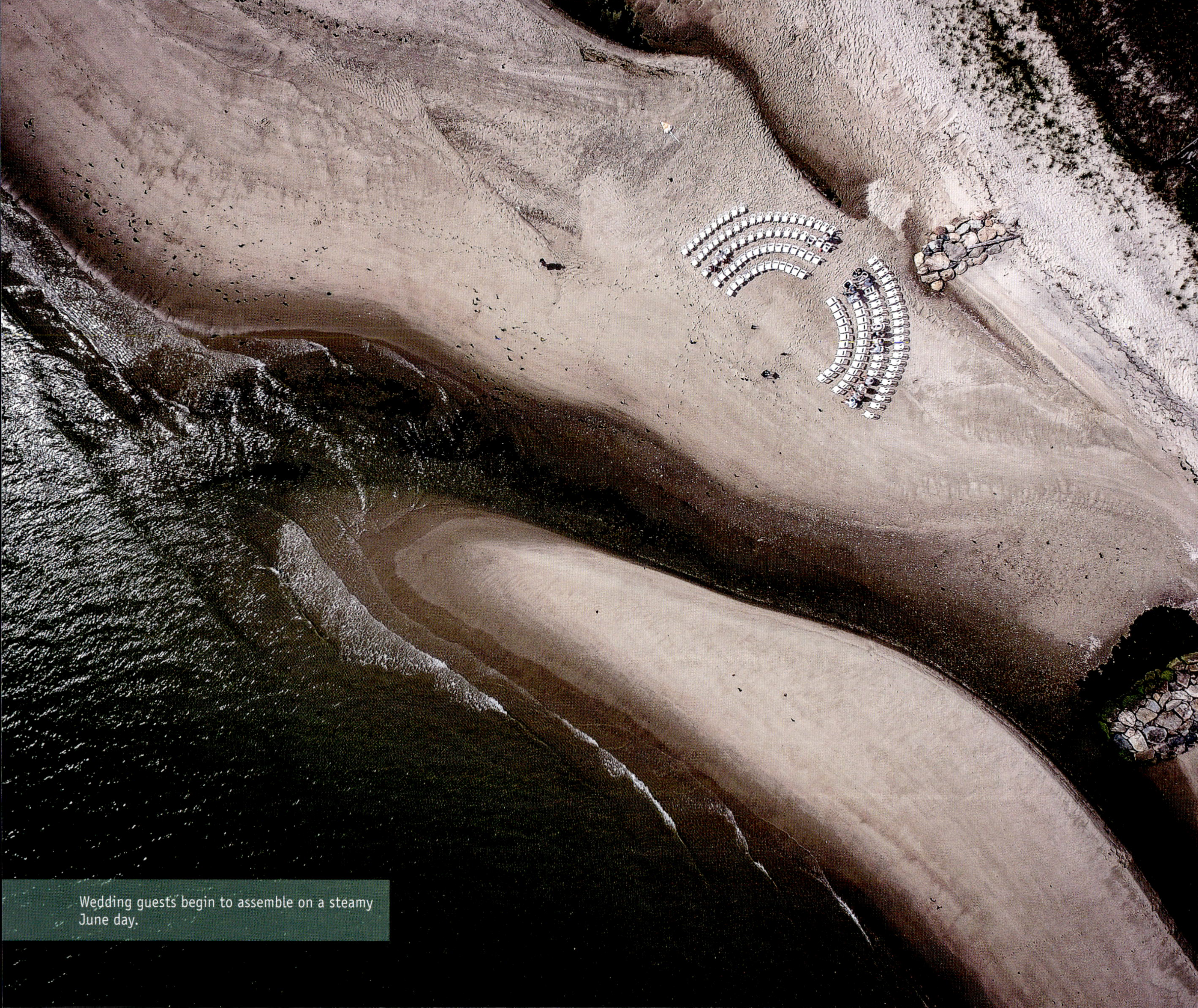

Wedding guests begin to assemble on a steamy June day.

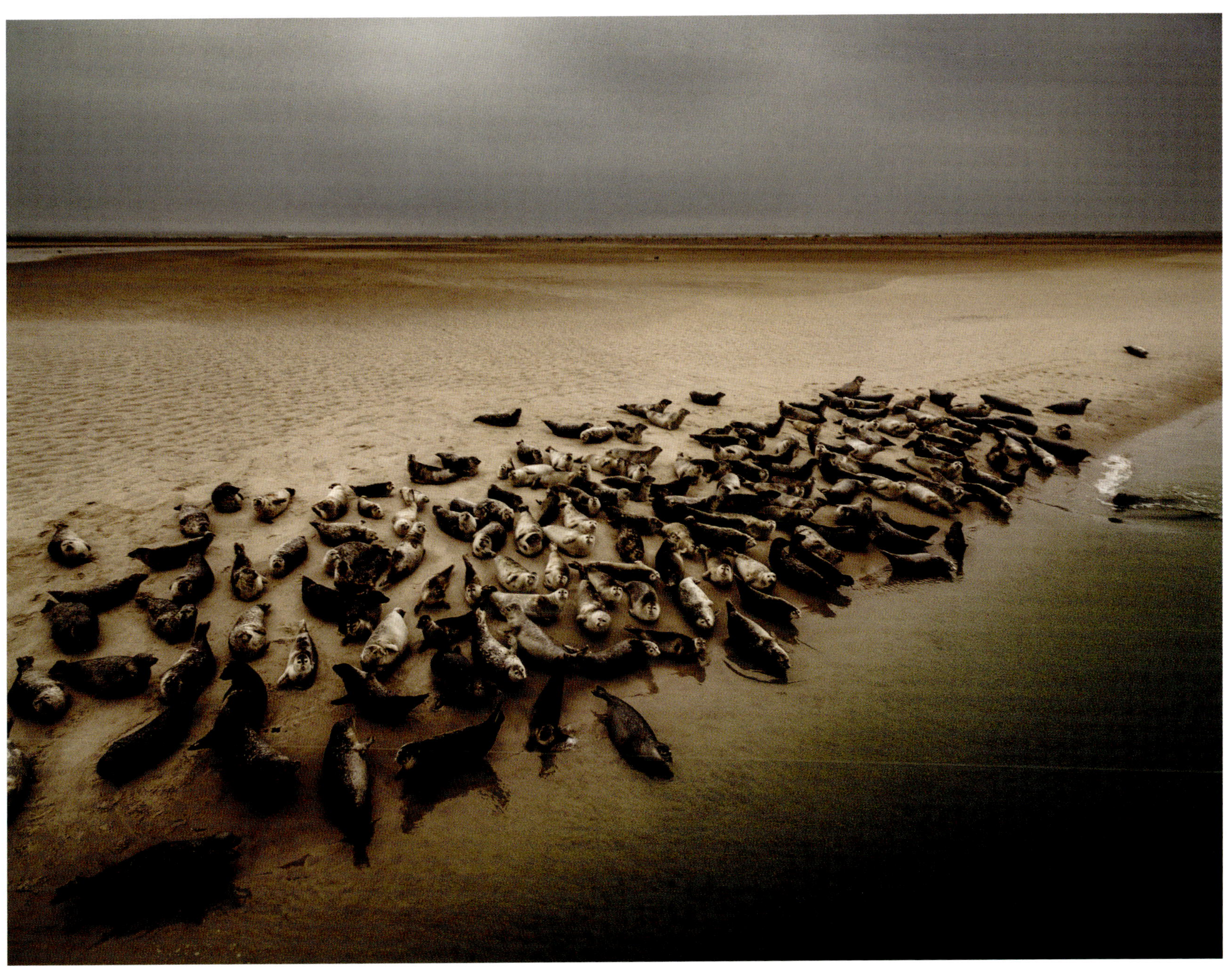

A morning shot of seals as they awake from their slumber and get ready for another busy day of pillaging the local ecosystem.

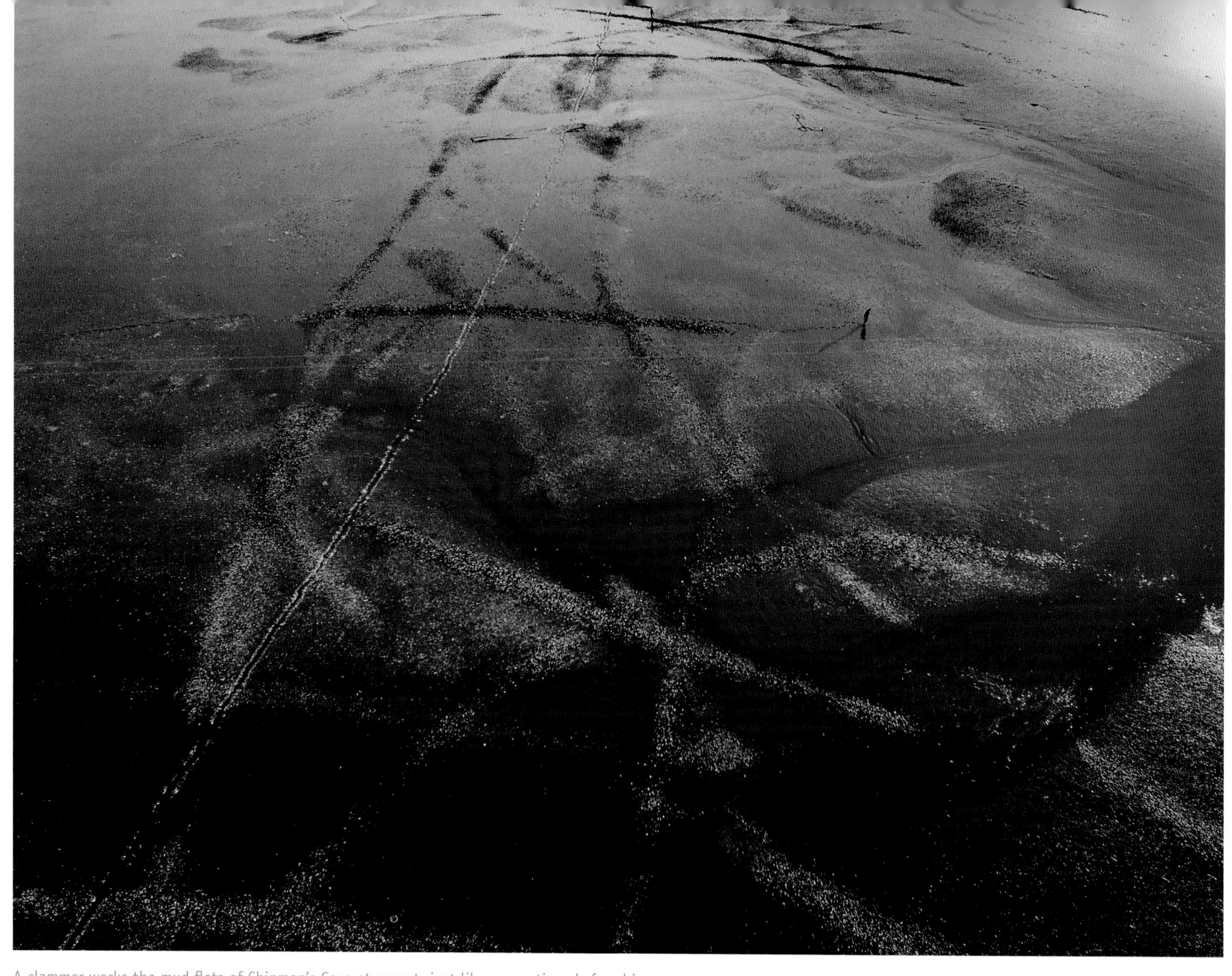

A clammer works the mud flats of Chipman's Cove at sunset, just like generations before him.

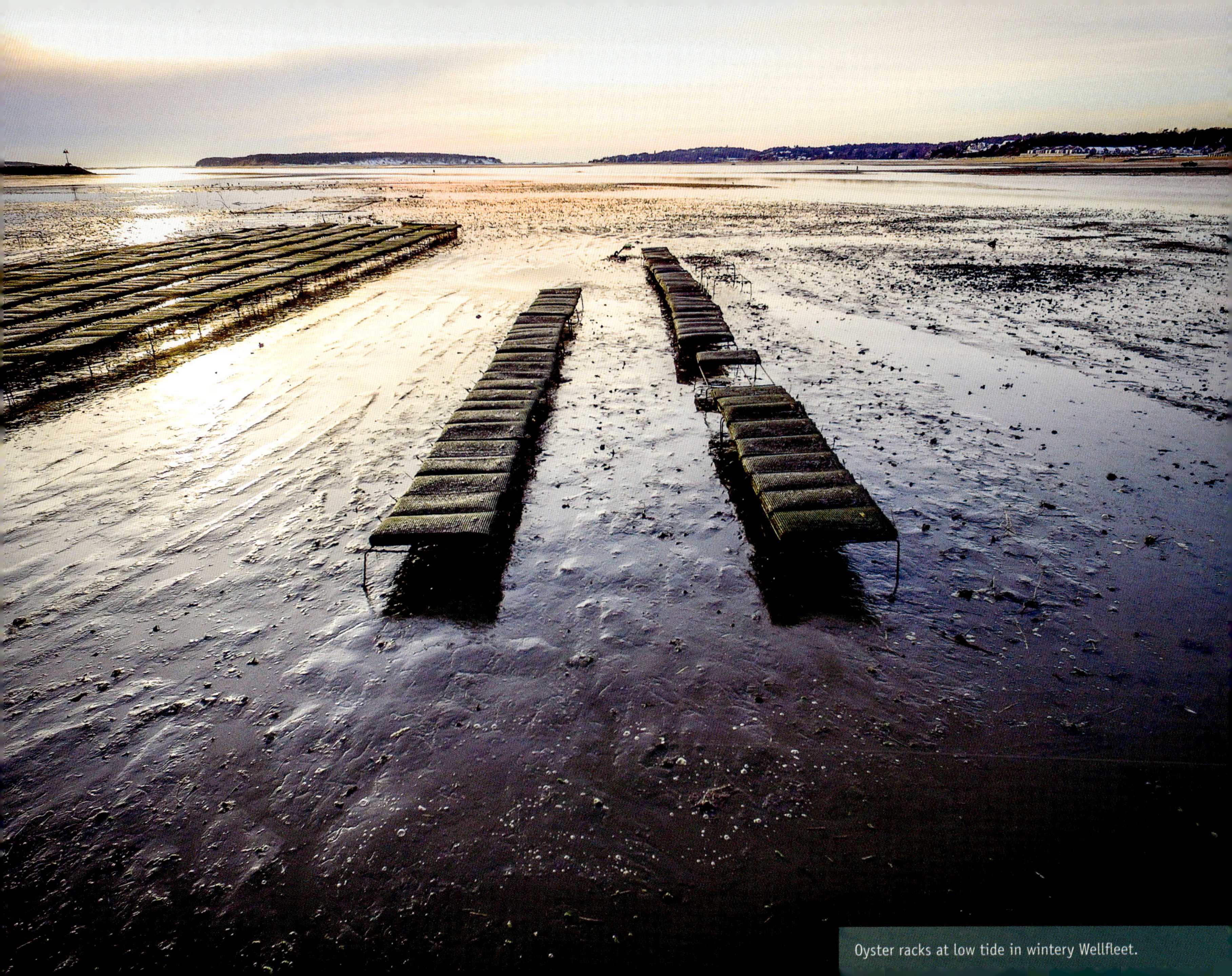

Oyster racks at low tide in wintery Wellfleet.

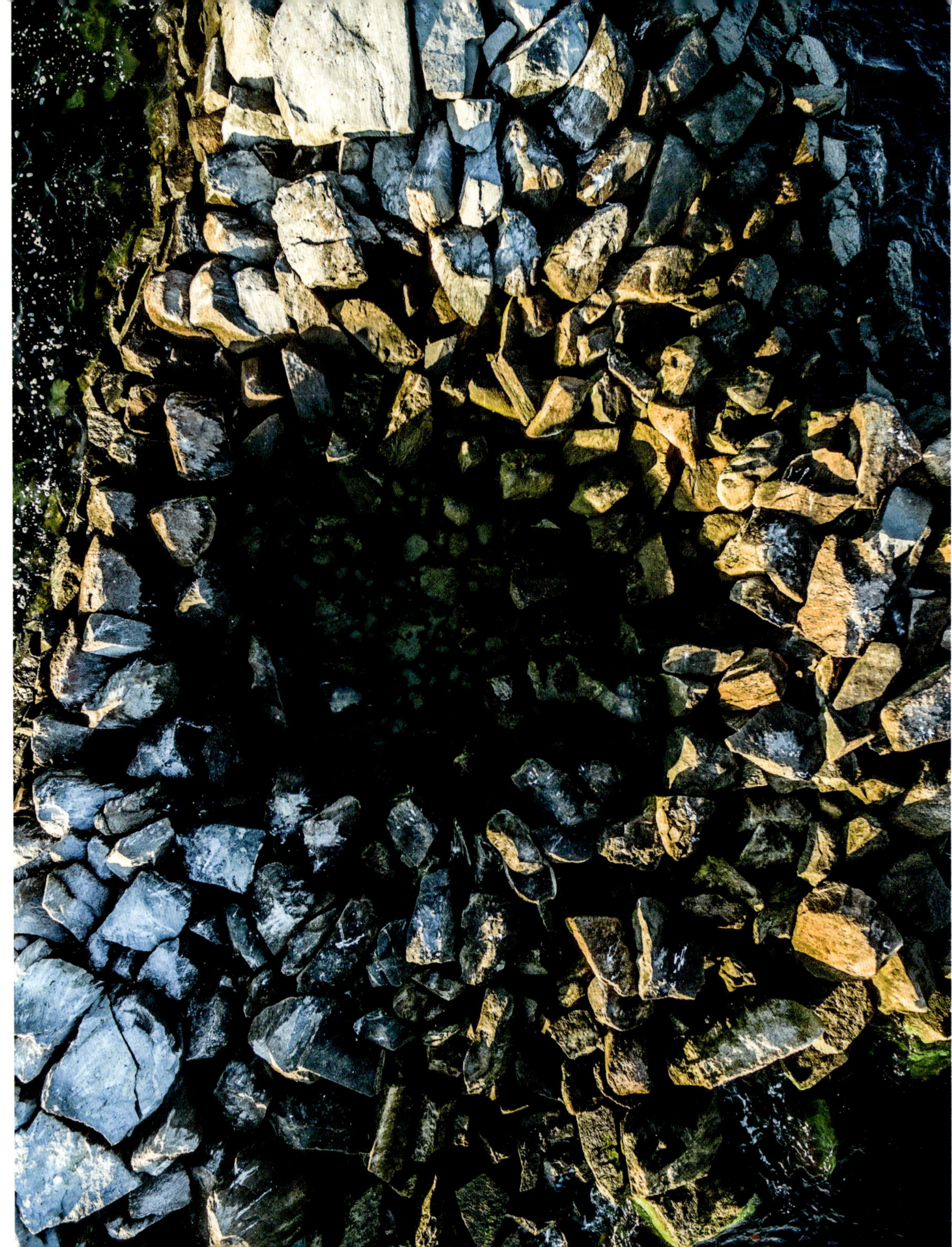

Affectionately known as Bird Shit Island, this breakwater lies almost a mile offshore of West Dennis Beach.

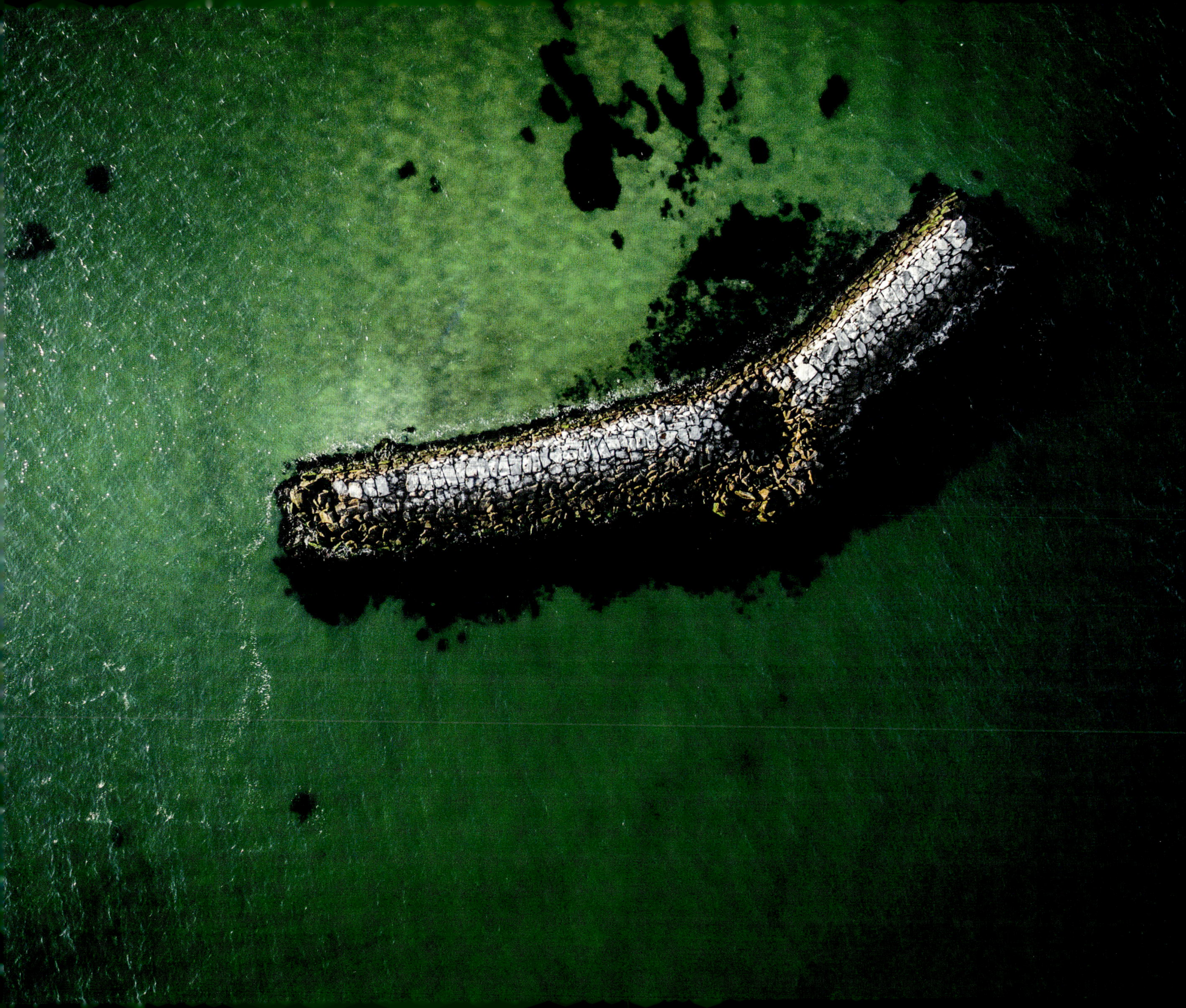

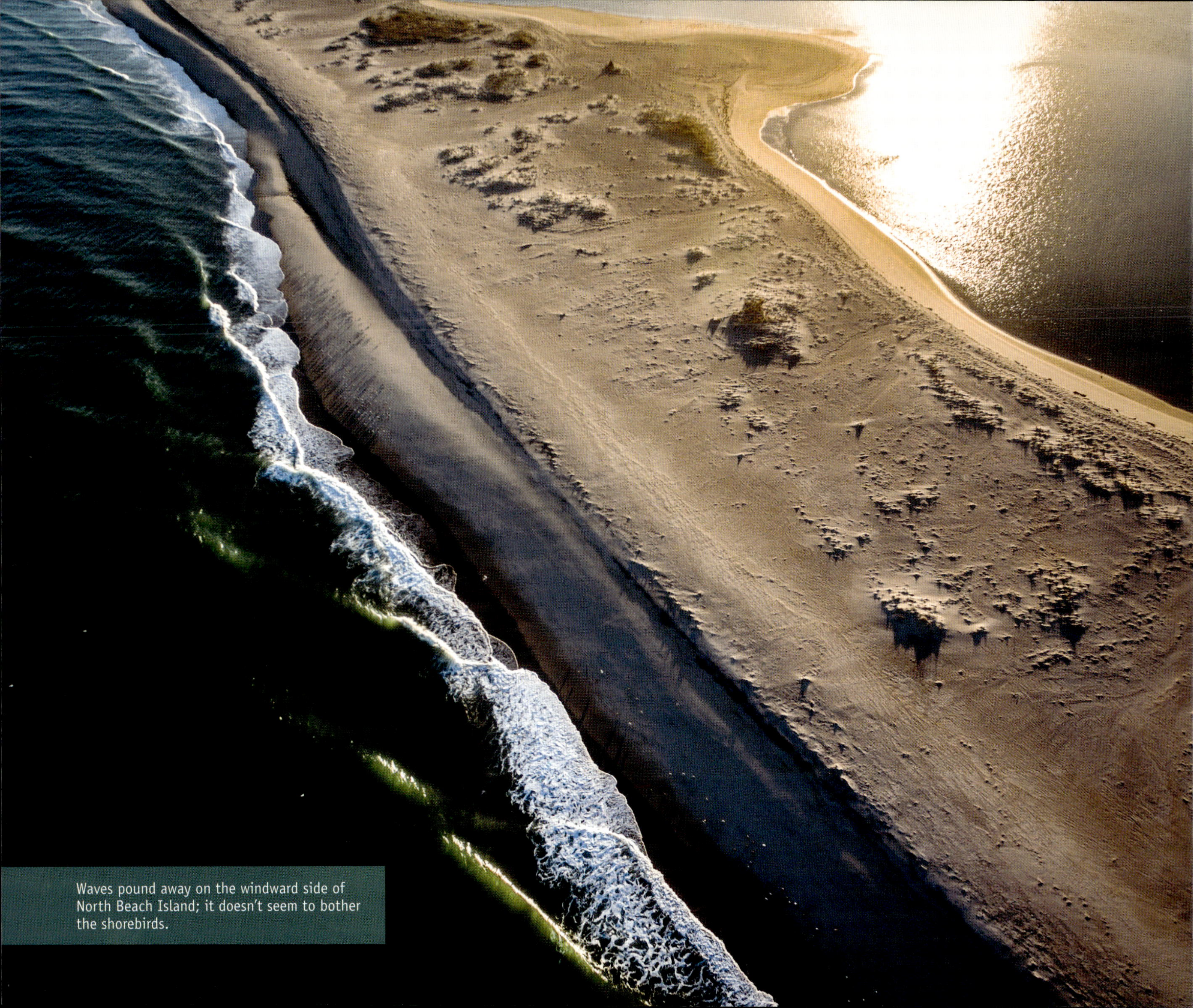
Waves pound away on the windward side of North Beach Island; it doesn't seem to bother the shorebirds.

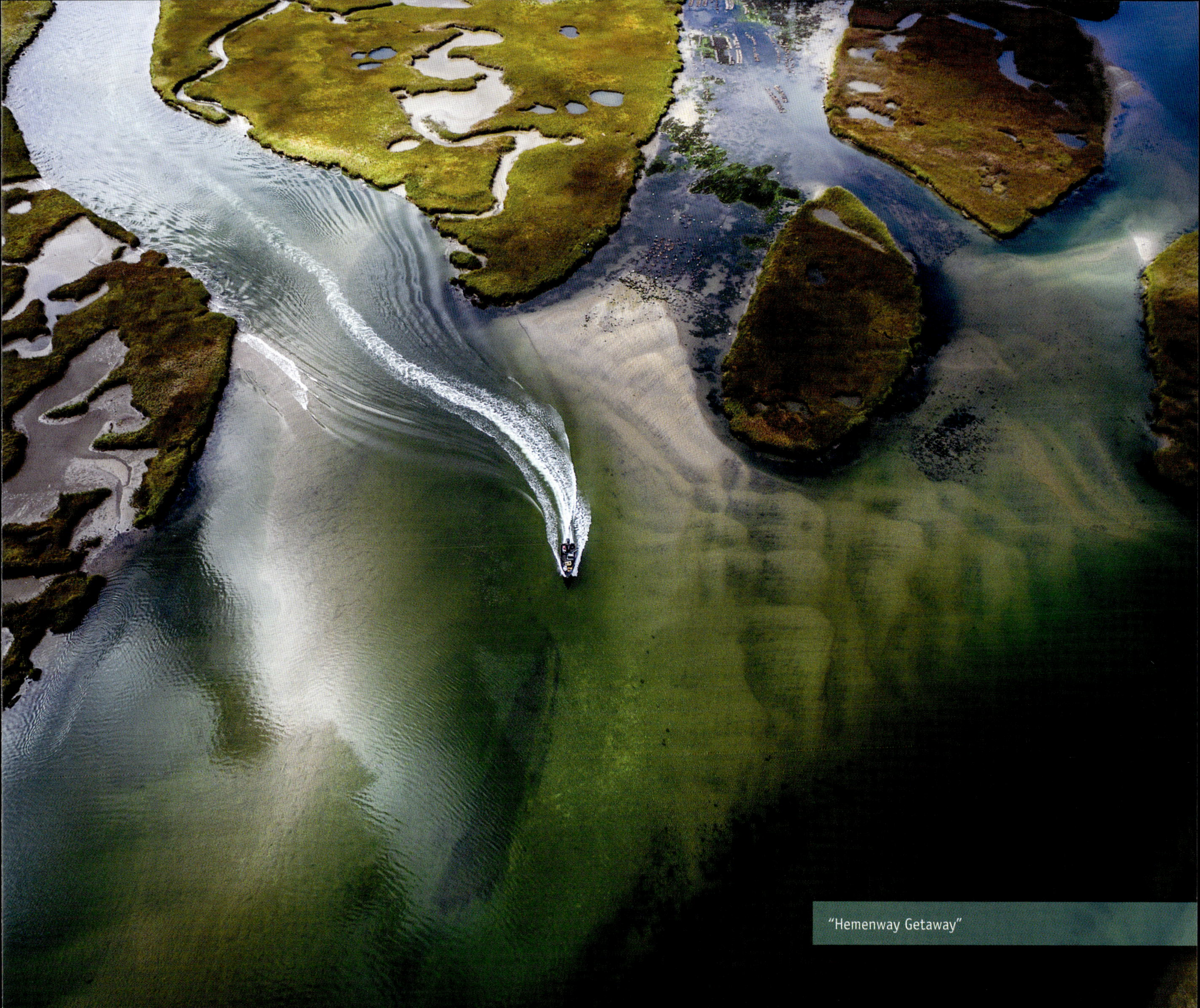

"Hemenway Getaway"

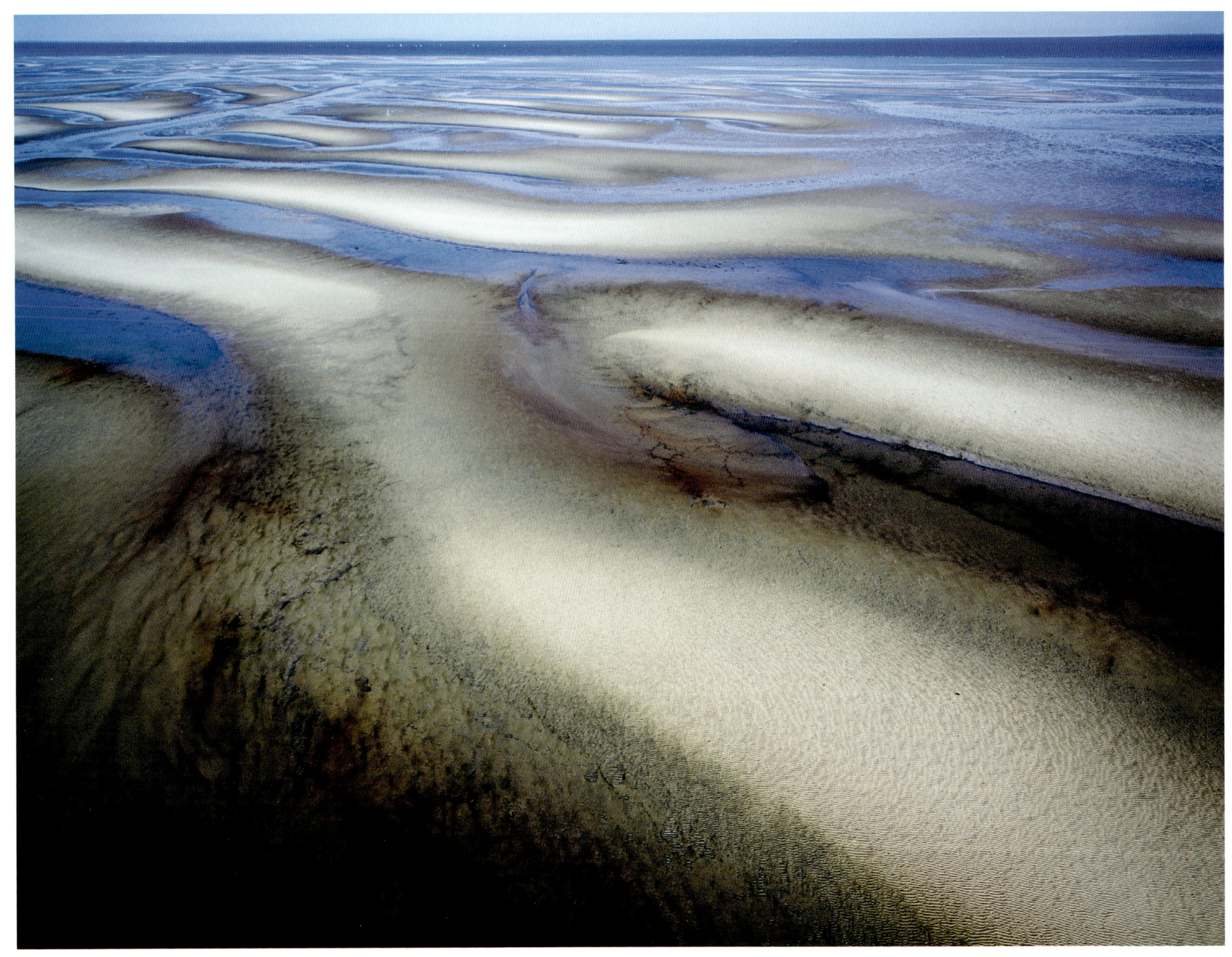

Sandbars and rivulets extend for miles into Cape Cod Bay.

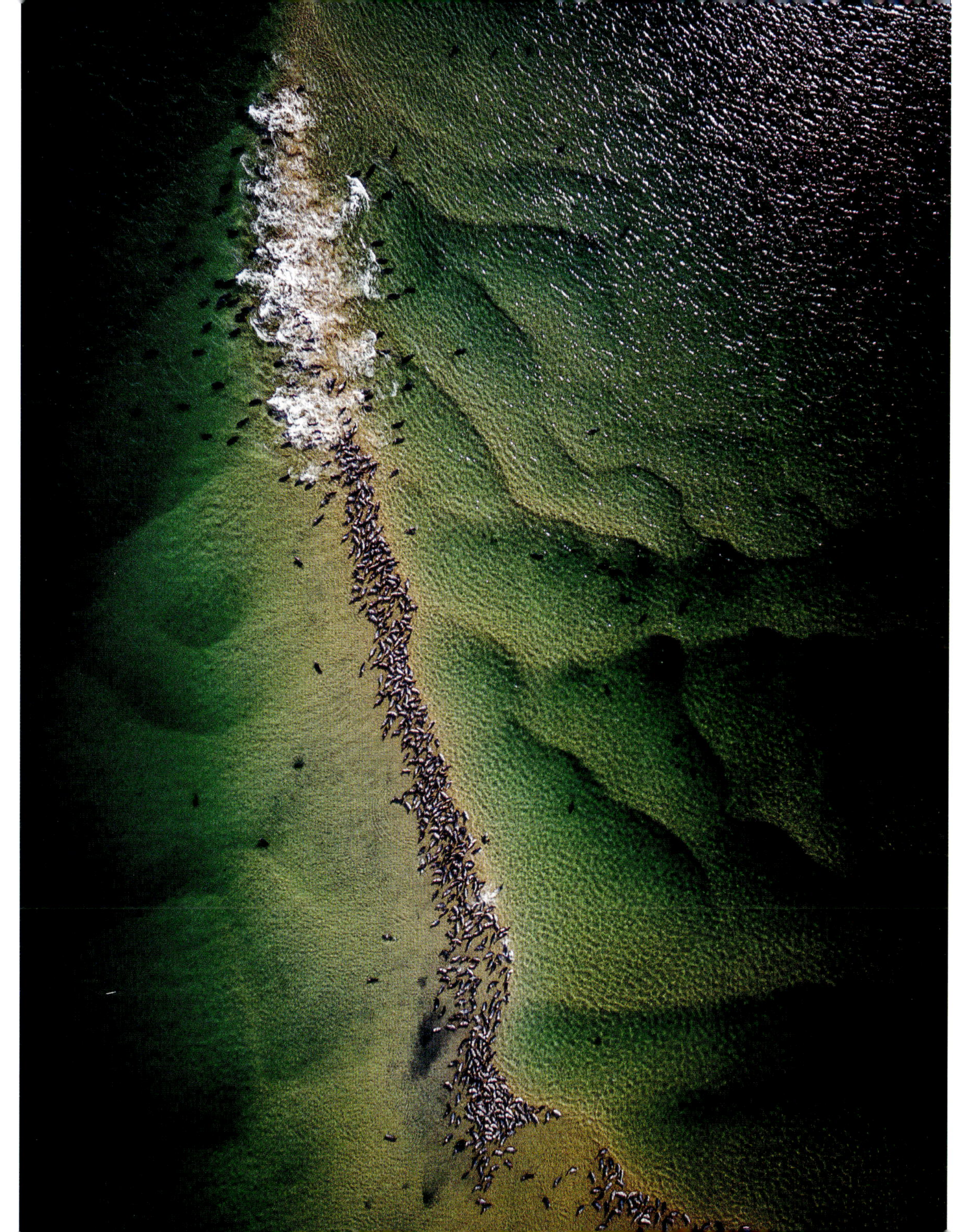

“White Snapdragon” - Seals break from a sandbar into open water, resembling a white snapdragon from above.

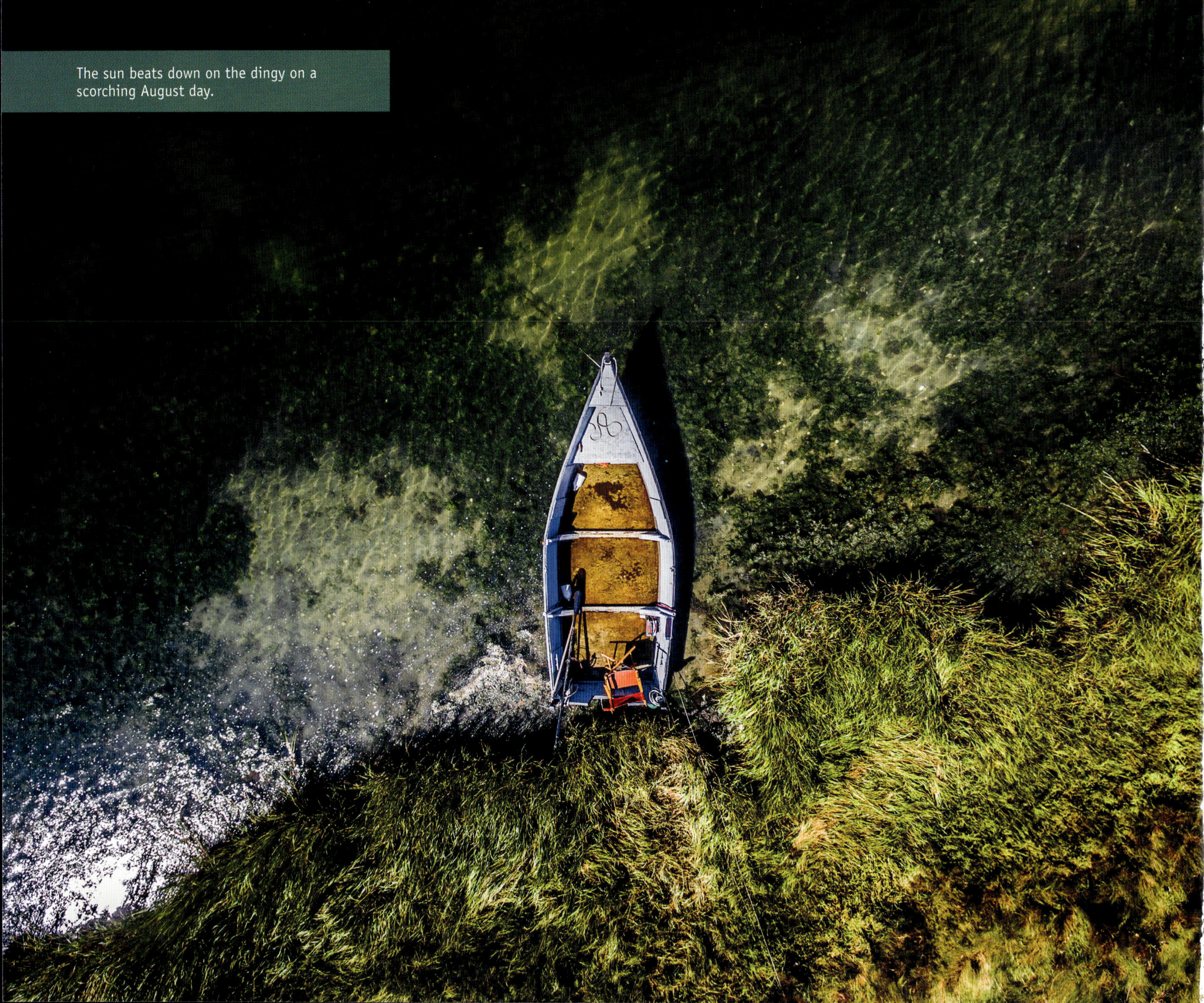

The sun beats down on the dingy on a scorching August day.

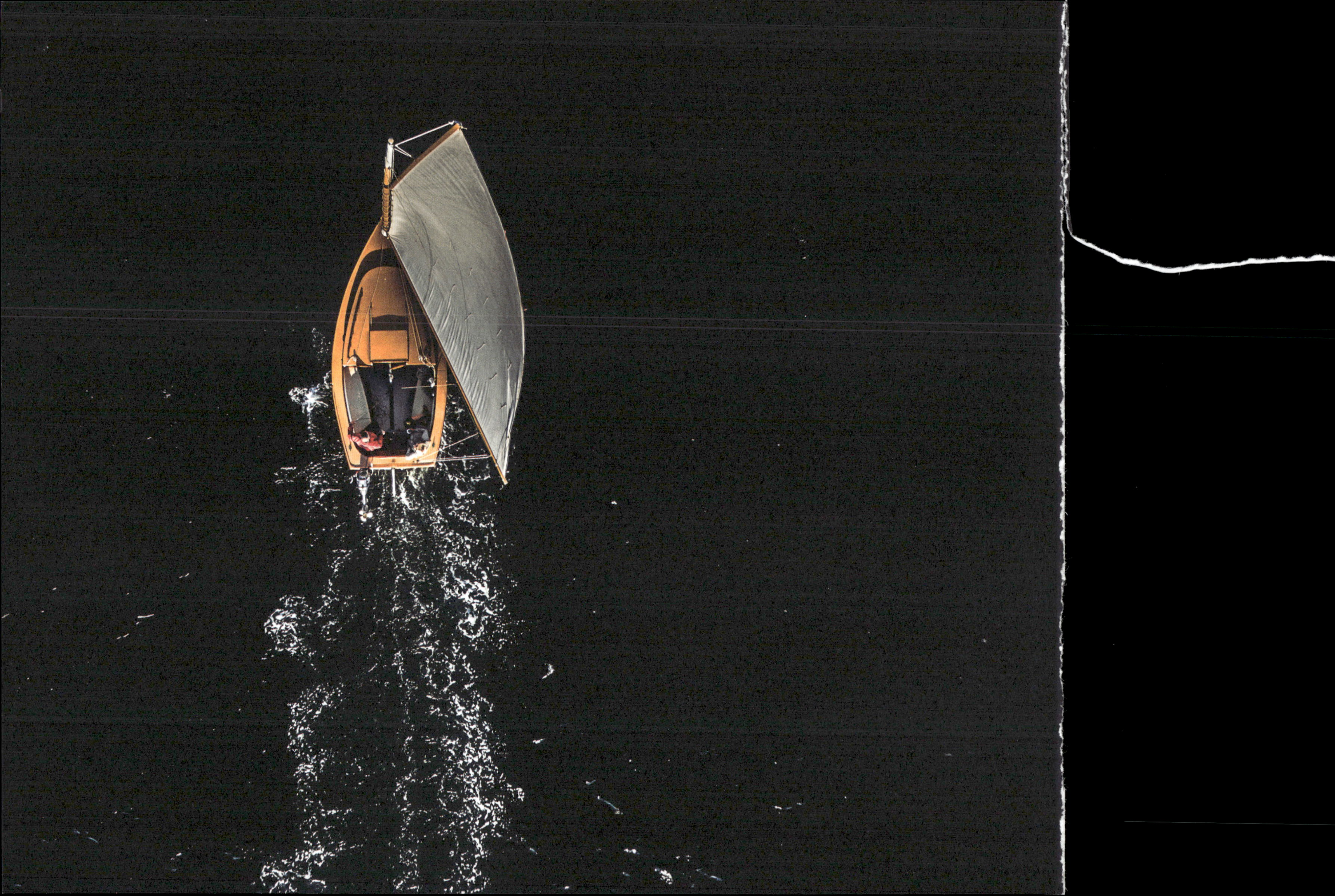